TRADITIONAL FOOD IN SHROPSHIRE

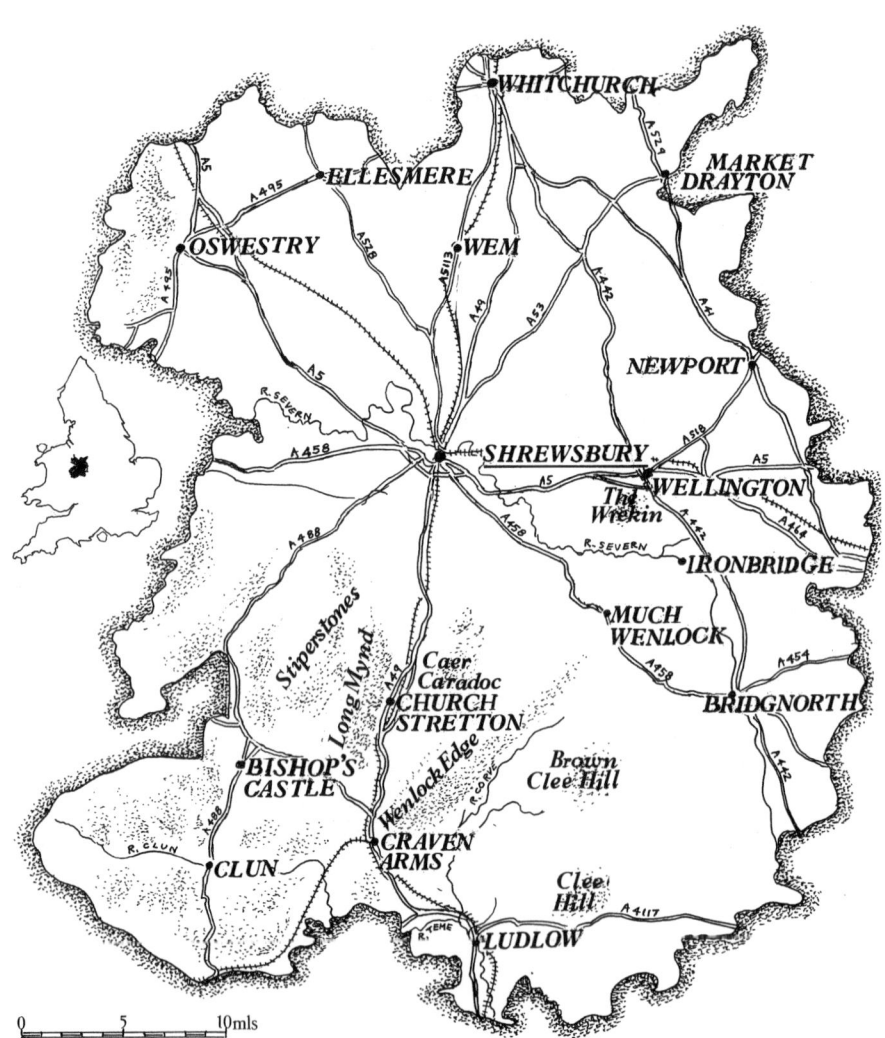

Frontispiece The Historic County of Shropshire

TRADITIONAL FOOD IN SHROPSHIRE

Peter Brears

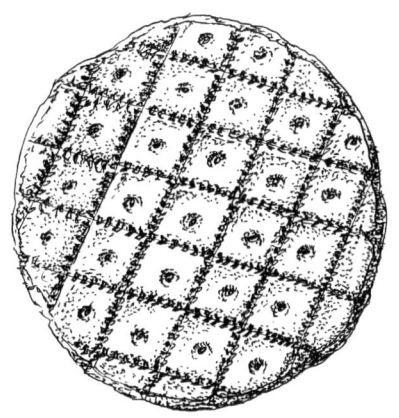

Excellent Press
Ludlow
2009

First published in 2009 by
Excellent Press
9 Lower Raven Lane
Ludlow
Shropshire
SY8 1BL

© Peter Brears 2009

No part of this publication may be reproduced, stored in a retrieval system, or transmitted in any form or by any means, electronic, mechanical, photocopying, recording or otherwise, without the prior permission of the copyright holder.

British Library Cataloguing in Publication Data
A catalogue entry of this book is available from the British Library.

ISBN 1 900318 39 3
ISBN 978 1 900318 39 6

Typeset by Columns Design Limited, Reading, RG4 7DH.
Printed in Great Britain by TJ International Ltd, Padstow, Cornwall.

CONTENTS

Acknowledgements	vii
A Note on the Recipes	ix
Introduction	1

CHAPTER 1
Of Kitchens Great and Small　　9

CHAPTER 2
Everyday Fare　　43

CHAPTER 3
Something for Tea　　83

CHAPTER 4
Festive Foods　　111

CHAPTER 5
From the Cradle to the Grave　　149

CHAPTER 6
Having a Do　　155

CHAPTER 7
In Halls and Manor Houses　　165

Bibliography	197
Notes	201
General Index	207
Recipe Index	211

ACKNOWLEDGEMENTS

I would like to thank David Burnett of Excellent Press, Ludlow, for first suggesting this study of traditional food in Shropshire, and for seeing it through the various stages of its publication. Gathering the information would have been impossible without the help of a number of organisations and individuals. The most important of these is Shropshire Archives in Shrewsbury, with its unrivalled collection of local books and archives made readily available through its constantly helpful staff. The staff at the Ironbridge Gorge Museum Trust, the Leeds Library and the Yorkshire Archaeological Society Library have also given access to the Shropshire material in their collections. Anyone working in this county must also thank its scholars of both past and present generations, the works of Georgina F. Jackson, Eric Mercer, Barrie Trinder, Jeffrey and Nancy Cox and Madge Moran being of national, rather than just local significance.

In addition I would like to thank a number of individuals who have provided me with considerable help, these including John Gall and Rosie Allan of Hollinside, Peter G. Howell and Julia L. Ionides of Ludlow, David de Haan, John Kenyon, Helen Haynes, Liz Young, Alison Healey and most particularly to Susan Houghton, for her great assistance in enabling me to bring its manuscript into final completion.

Further thanks are due to Shropshire Archives, for permission to reproduce a number of extracts from manuscripts in its collections, as listed in the Bibliography.

Peter Brears
Leeds
2009

A NOTE ON THE RECIPES

Since many historical recipes were written as *aides-mémoire* by cooks who assumed that everyone knew what they were doing, they frequently omit such essential details as methods, oven temperatures and timings. For this reason they are here presented in their modernised, rather than manuscript forms. The original quantities and procedures are all followed as closely as possible, but are now expressed in standard Imperial and Metric measures. Spoon measures all represent their level, rather than heaped quantities, while medium-sized eggs are used throughout. Temperatures, meanwhile, are those of standard ovens, and should be reduced accordingly when using a fan assisted oven.

To ensure authentic results, no allowance has been made for healthy options. Traditional foods abound in saturated fats which, since we no longer burn them off, are harmful when consumed in quantities. Readers are left to choose whatever replacements they prefer, perhaps using vegetarian instead of beef suet, for example, or lower-fat substitutes for butter. However, even the most basic of dishes benefits from the quality of its ingredients. Since the local diet was heavily reliant on home cured bacon, it is well worth paying a little more for the excellent Shropshire dry cured rashers, which fry to perfect crispness, and supply excellent clear lard when used for basting and barding. For this, the modern brine-injected varieties are best avoided.

INTRODUCTION

If you were to ask people in most parts of England 'What do you know of traditional food in Shropshire?', the initial reply is most likely to be 'Where exactly *is* Shropshire?'. Despite being England's largest inland county, an approximate rectangle measuring some forty by forty-five miles, they are unlikely to have stayed within its borders, or even to have travelled through it, unless en route for holidays in Wales. From watching television programmes or reading Sunday magazines, they would perhaps already know that it represents England and its countryside at its very best, but still be unable to describe where it is actually located. As to its foods they might, after some thought, hit on the Shrewsbury biscuit, – but then admit to knowing nothing more. To some with a knowledge of the county it may appear that it lacks the essential elements of modern life, the fast motorway networks, the high-rise blocks of executive riverside apartments, the vast out-of-town shopping centres, and the rapid pace and personal anonymity of city living. In fact it is the very absence of such features which is Shropshire's greatest strength and asset, and one which should be preserved at all costs.

As someone who has spent the last fifteen years travelling to all parts of England, from Cornwall to Northumberland, Cumbria to Kent, I have stayed in numerous hotels and bed-and-breakfasts, and bought my food in an enormous number of local shops and markets in many cities, small towns and villages. The outlets of the major supermarket and fast food chains were rarely absent, and I know from experience that it is possible to survive for weeks on burgers, kebabs or fried chicken. The discovery of a good family-run baker/confectioner or butchers' shop on the high street made an enormous difference, not only to the quality of the food, but also to the quality of the shopping experience. In most parts of England such shops are increasingly hard to find, except, that is, in the less populated counties, and in Shropshire in particular. It would be hard to find a better shopping centre than Shrewsbury, with its fine historic streets masking huge malls housing every national chain store one could ever want, but still with a healthy community of independent food shops and market traders offering products of the very highest quality and excellent value. I have never seen better anywhere in the country, and always leave laden with all I can carry, – well-hung joints, dry cured bacon, and even the best sandwiches I know. Although smaller in scale, exactly the same quality of fresh food and good service is to be found in every one of the smaller markets towns, Oswestry, Ellesmere, Whitchurch, Wem and Market Drayton to the north, Newport and Wellington to the east, and Bishop's Castle, Church Stretton, Ludlow and Bridgnorth to the south.

Their prosperity has always been based on the fertility of the surrounding countryside, for the county has proved a rich source of grain, garden produce and livestock for centuries. As Celia Fiennes commented around 1695, this was a place of 'great plenty and makes cheap living'.[1] Daniel Defoe was equally enthusiastic; 'Here is the largest Market, the greatest Plenty of good Provision, and the cheapest, that is to be met with in all the Western Part of *England*. The *Severn* supplies them here with excellent salmon; but it is also brought in great Plenty from the Dee ... and there is no doubt but the Cheapness of Provision, joined to the Pleasantness and Healthiness of the Place, draws a great many Families hither, who love to live within the Compass of their Estates.'[2]

Particularly in the flatter parts of the county the fields produced good crops of wheat, barley and oats, along with 'muncorn', a mixture of wheat and rye. These ripened first on the warmer eastern side, several weeks before those on the colder, higher lands on the Welsh border-land to the west.[3] Field crops of root vegetables were also grown here, a direct development of the advanced gardening practices of the Elizabethan period when carrots, turnips and parsnips began to be cultivated on a larger scale. Swedes and potatoes arrived considerably later, around 1800. Other crops included hops along the Herefordshire border, cherries in Shrewsbury, and both apples and damsons, as well as the cranberries and wimberries (bilberries) which grew plentifully in the wild. More exotic fruits remained in private gardens however, Fiennes being impressed by the very fine gardens of Whitchurch 'full of all fruits and greens ... exceeding neate with oring and lemmon trees, Mirtle, striped and gilded hollytrees, box and ffileroy finely cut, and fine

INTRODUCTION

flowers.' In Shrewsbury she found gardens 'with gravell walks set full of all sorts of greens, orange and Lemmon trees, ... and a green house full of all sorts of Curyosityes of flowers and greens ... .'[4]

It was a good area for livestock too. Sheep were particularly suitable for the hill country, the old Shropshire breed being almost as large as the Southdown, but with black-mottled faces and legs and less flesh.[5] In the early nineteenth century Montgomeryshire or Smoky-faced and Welsh Black sheep were bred along the border, with a few Alderney at Rowton. By crossing with both Southdowns and New Leicesters, the Shropshire Downland sheep became so greatly improved that they won both the first prize at the Royal Show of 1857, and a considerable reputation for the quality of their mutton and lamb.[6]

Fig 1   All the county's livestock was improved by local breeders in the late 18th and 19th centuries. Here we see one of the 5th Lord Berwick's Hereford bulls at Attingham, Mr George Adney's Shropshire ram at Harley, near Much Wenlock and Sir Charles Boughton's Shropshire pig at Downton Hall, Ludlow.

For cattle, the old-established Long-horns were still being bred in Shropshire in the early-mid nineteenth century, but the improved Shorthorns or Durhams, with their plentiful milk and tallow, were increasingly popular as were the Herefords, also producers of rich milk. Great pride was taken in their breeding, Lord Berwick employing William Davis of Chelsea, one of the most prolific animal painters of the day, to complete thirteen portraits of his best Herefords. At a more practical level, all the herds raised within the county benefited from its rich grazing, readily converting it into excellent beef and milk.

The old Shropshire pig, like other regional varieties, was already nearly extinct by the 1830s, succumbing to improved breeds, which in turn gave way to the almost universal Large Whites.[7] The possession of a pig was one of the most important achievements of the county's cottagers, for its carcase and piglets enabled them to obtain a major source of meat and cash, without which they faced extreme poverty and near starvation.

The county was rich in preserved game, each estate employing gamekeepers to ensure a good bag for sport and for the table. As Hulbert recorded, in the season 'messengers are to be seen in every direction, carrying presents of game to the friends and tradesmen of the Lord of the Manor. This attention and other kindnesses on the part of the nobility and gentry generates and maintains a grateful and kind feeling in return.'[8] As for fish, the Severn and its tributaries produced salmon, trout, eels, carp, pike, and most of the usual coarse varieties. They were traditionally fished by line or by coracle, the coracle fishermen carrying their craft upstream from around Ironbridge, and fishing as they paddled down again.[9]

Some of Shropshire's produce was processed on an industrial scale, its barley being converted in large maltings, for example, preparatory to brewing. It was in dairying however, that the county really excelled. In hundreds of farms, the cream was skimmed off the milk for butter-making. After churning, it was washed and worked to remove the buttermilk, salted for preservation, and made up into 'gauns' or large blocks, those to be sold in Shrewsbury weighing 12lb., and those at Bridgnorth 16lb.[10] Smaller quantities for domestic use were either wrapped in the long green leaves of the specially-grown Sicilian Beet, or made up as individual pats neatly stamped with a distinctive butter-print.[11] All of these were carried off to the weekly markets and the great fairs in the towns, where they found a ready sale to local people and to visiting merchants. To

INTRODUCTION

those who do not know the region, it can come as quite a surprise to find that Shropshire has always been one of England's greatest cheese-making counties.

Writing in 1577, Barnaby Googe stated that 'In England the best Cheese is the Chesshyre and the Shropshyre.'[12] Over the following centuries the county's name sadly lost its association with cheese, even though it continued to produce hundreds of tons each year. Sold as 'Cheshire cheese' it was actually made in numerous Shropshire farmhouses, particularly on the fertile grassy plains to the north of the county. The following account by R. de Gallienne describes his visit to a farm at Market Drayton in the 1890s, but could have been written at any time over the previous two or three hundred years. 'Though we were in Shropshire, it was Cheshire cheese that was being made in the great metal vat [where] a comely daughter had turned up her sleeves from her round arms and was rolling into a canvas the thick, soft custard-like crust [of curds] which the milk, acted upon by rennet, had already thrown up to the surface.

'As we mounted the stairs to the cheese-room, [where] were something like a hundred cheeses of various dates awaiting the visit of the buyers upon their rounds, [she] allowed us to taste one or two, plunging one of those fascinating scoops into their fat yellow sides. It is *the* way to eat cheese. After tasting the Shropshire meadows once more in the form of home-made bread and home-made butter, we went to try the herb beer of a dear old lady who lived down the lane.'[13] Clearly he found this bucolic idyll truly charming, apparently failing to appreciate the sheer volume of hard physical labour involved in cheesemaking. Mary Webb's informed attitude was quite different, for she had seen the process as carried out in the hill farms of the south-west, where the land sometimes bred men full of that Old Testament vengeance and Calvinistic Non-conformity which saw waste as a mortal sin. Here her Eli (who closely resembled Joseph in Emily Brontë's *Wuthering Heights*) found that his young daughter Lily had left twelve pints of milk out in the sun, so that it had turned sour, but it could not be thrown away 'Waste not, want not! It mun be done summat with. Afore you go to bed tonight, you mun set it for milk cheese. You mun scald the things, stretch the muslin, lade the milk, press it. Afore that fetch the sticks, coals and water, and boil it to scald with.' 'There's no muslin', said Lily. 'Your good old father's thought of that', said Eli, 'A father knoweth his own child. There's muslin on your back; when we get in you'll rip [your new blouse] and make the cheese in that.'[14]

As in medieval England, many farms also made virtually fatless hard cheeses from the milk left after the cream had been skimmed off for butter-making. Known as skim-dick or Legh cheese, it was often retained for feeding the farm workers, who apparently acquired a taste for it. 'This is rael cheese, it hanna' a bit o' butter in it.'[15] The full-milk cheeses were sold at the local markets, Georgian Shrewsbury's being held on Pride Hill, where the inhabitants let rooms in which farmers could store and weigh their butter (6d per tub) and cheese (6d per hundredweight) ready for its sale to the visiting merchants. In 1822 the Circus Butter and Cheese Market was opened near the Welsh Bridge, but this was replaced by the new one in Howard Street in 1835. Behind its massive Doric portico, the Butter Market had a vast aisled hall of 5,400 sq. ft., and a similarly sized basement beneath with wide doors to receive wagons loaded with butter and cheese.[16] Here, as in the great cloth-halls of the textile towns, merchants could inspect the produce, make their purchases, and arrange for them to be despatched on the adjacent canal, by road, or, within a few years, by the railway. In addition, massive quantities of cheese were sold at cheese fairs held in towns such as Shrewsbury, Market Drayton and Whitchurch. As photographs of the latter show, hundreds of cheeses were set out in large squares on a protective bed of straw, with narrow passages left between to provide access for both vendors and purchasers. The impressive scale of these fairs clearly illustrates the importance of Shropshire in serving the national appetite for dairy produce, a role which it still fulfils today.

Having read these descriptions of the wide range and great plenty of food grown and processed in the county, we should expect that its traditional foods should be far superior to those of less fortunate areas. It is logical to expect that everyone ate well, enjoying cheap meat, fish, vegetables, fruit and dairy produce, baking wonderful cakes full of eggs, butter and cream etc. In fact, the local culinary tradition is remarkable not for its richness, but for its poverty. Those who actually produced the food had to sell almost all of it to pay their rents and living expenses, only retaining sufficient to just survive from one year on to the next. It had always been like this in rural England, from medieval times through to the twentieth century. Over this long period generations of housewives had discovered every possible way in which the cheapest of foods could be made into a variety of satisfying, economical dishes. Many were based on offal, cheese and minimal quantities of meat and

INTRODUCTION

Fig 2   The large scale sale of dairy produce was a major element in the county's economy. In the 19th century much of it was conducted in great market halls such as the Butter Market in Howard Street, Shrewsbury, built in 1835 (left), or that in Market Drayton (right), shown with the Cheese Fair in progress around 1910.

bacon, for which Shropshire has retained an amazingly complete series of recipes. They comprise the essential core of one of the country's most interesting rural culinary traditions, one well worth continuing or even reviving in these times of financial uncertainty. The ingredients are cheap, the techniques simple, the flavours good, and the results both interesting and satisfying. It is true home-cooking, totally divorced from the restaurant-based food of today's celebrity chefs, but none the worse for that. The following chapters describe how such food was prepared for everyday, festive and ceremonial meals in Shropshire's own culinary tradition, using recipes almost entirely drawn from local sources, and including far more than Shrewsbury biscuits.

The final chapters describe Shropshire's other, quite separate culinary world, that of the county families who occupied its halls and manor houses. They too practised a careful economy, keeping accounts of everything brought in, cooked and served, but on a completely different scale. Into their kitchens came the very best of produce from their home farms, walled gardens, hot-houses and coverts, along with every luxurious delicacy which could be obtained from the great London shops and merchants. Their ladies and cooks gathered their repertoire of recipes either from those left by previous generations, or else collected at distant house-parties and the London summer seasons. This was therefore an essentially national, or more accurately, an international tradition, capable of producing the world's finest dishes. Regrettably it is also the food for which there is the least available evidence, for many cooks were either too familiar with their recipes to need to write them down, or were too secretive to pass them on. Even so, those recipes and menus which do survive all show that the art of fine dining always flourished here, along with the following plant described by C. Hulbert's 1837 description of Shropshire;[17]

> There is ONE TREE, which *though not a vegetable* grows abundantly in most districts, and is in full bloom at Christmas, the *midst of winter*, and that tree is HOSPITALITY.

Before planning the dinner-parties, however, it was always best to start in the kitchens, and discover what facilities they had to offer.

CHAPTER 1

OF KITCHENS GREAT AND SMALL

As in every other English county, Shropshire's kitchens varied enormously in their size, equipment and occupants. By comparison with today, when virtually every home has one room dedicated to preparing very similar foods using almost identical utensils for a relatively small family group, the kitchens of the past presented a completely different picture. The extremes of poverty and wealth, combined with those of status and tradition, were immediately obvious to all, whether they came from a tiny cottage or a huge mansion. Each level of society knew, from long experience, how to make the best of its resources to maintain its own particular lifestyle.

At the bottom of the scale came the temporary shelters built for seasonal use, such as the lambing hut which Robert Rideout made for himself in Mary Webb's *Seven for a Secret*.[1] Round in plan, like an Iron-Age hut, it had turf walls pierced by a door and a window, and a roof of furze. Inside, a rough brazier propped up on four large stones held the coal fire which provided both heating and a means of preparing the most basic of hot drinks and meals.

Many permanent homes were little better than this. Formerly known as Clod Halls, these squatters' cottages represented the long-established tradition of converting open common land into enclosed holdings. Anyone who wished to build one gathered his family and friends on the intended site at nightfall, some then cutting the green turf into squares, which others then used to build up the walls. A previously prepared roof was then set on top and thatched with either straw or rushes. To ensure good title to the land, the fire had to be lit inside and the smoke seen to rise before sunrise. Standing at the doorpost, the new occupant now hurled his axe as far as he could, planting a hedge on the line where it fell, to enclose the plot which he could now bring under cultivation. Such cottages were built in many parts of the county, from rural areas such as Condover, to the more industrial townships such as Ketley. This was reported in 1820 to be entirely 'occasioned by a numerous mining population whose wretched huts have been erected from time to time on the waste'. Inside such cottages, whether built of turf, timber-framing or brick, life was lived in a manner virtually unchanged from that of medieval peasants, their single rooms frequently housing not only a numerous human population, but also a pig or two, a donkey, and some poultry.[2]

The style of cookery practised in such kitchen-living rooms could be very basic indeed, perhaps requiring little more than a cheap earthenware cooking pot. Even as late as 1817 some cottagers around Oswestry were obliged to borrow a cooking pot from a neighbour whenever they needed one. When they promised 'I'll take care of your pot, and keep it out of the way of the pig' they confirmed the continuing presence of pigs in kitchens.[3] Others appear to have made use of a single pot for virtually all their cookery, as shown in probate inventories for Wellington where William Evans, the pipemaker, had only 'one old pott' in 1694, and Joseph Eastrup one sheet-metal boiler called a kettle in 1702.[4]

Most other labourers and lesser craft workers lived in two or three room cottages, which might represent about a quarter of the total housing stock in the seventeenth and eighteenth centuries.[5] In 1803 Joseph Plymley was recommending that farmers should provide young couples with single-storey properties comprising a good kitchen, a pantry and a single bedroom, with a further bedroom should they have a family. Such tenants should also have sufficient land to keep a cow, a garden to produce their own vegetables, and a pig-sty to ensure a regular supply of both meat and income.[6] Later in the century improving landlords such as the Duke of Sutherland and Sir Baldwin Leighton enthusiastically replaced most of their unsatisfactory and old-fashioned labourers' cottages with new ones built to far better standards of construction and accommodation. Good examples might have a large front kitchen equipped with a range and a fireside cupboard for dry goods, and a pantry for fresh foods, a back kitchen with an oven and a boiler, and three bedrooms above.[7] In the more industrialised areas, similar improvements had also taken place.

As the factories, quarries and mines expanded, they drew in large workforces into places where there was no surplus housing. Partly to satisfy this need, and partly to ensure a controllable, permanent workforce, the major industrialists began to build shorter, two-storey terrace cottages. From around 1750 their Tea Kettle Row, Carpenters Row, Nailers' Row etc. had kitchens around twelve feet square, some with a second room on the ground floor and bedrooms above. From these developed the rows of two-up-and-two-down houses, which became the standard form of workers' homes throughout the nineteenth and early twentieth centuries.[8]

The furnishings of 'the house', as the kitchen-living rooms of homes of this scale were generally known, were quite basic, but still sufficient to provide a comfortable existence. Those of William Bate, a labourer and thatcher of Lilleshall, comprised a table, a form, a chair and a dresser, with an fire grate and an iron pot for cooking in 1683, for example.[9] The eighteenth century brought few changes, William Briscoe's 'house-place' at Ketley Brook having a table, a settle, two chairs, a grate and two brass kettles in 1745.[10] From this period there might be some improvements, however, for in addition to the utilitarian working/dining table with its locally-made chairs and forms, well-made dressers and long-case clocks began to make their appearance. By the 1840s they were considered essential for anyone setting up a new home; 'Aye, it begins to look like marr'in when the clock an' dresser's bought'.[11] C.H. Hartshorne described the dresser as 'the chief embellishment of a Shropshire labourer's house, and it is commonly accompanied by a clock in an oaken case, a round deal table and a corner cupboard'.[12] Having developed from a heavy wooden bench on which food was dressed before being cooked, the Shropshire dresser had now become one of the most distinctive pieces of English vernacular furniture. Its narrow table-height top now had a row of drawers beneath it, then an open area extending down to a broad shelf called a pot-board just a few inches from the floor. Above rose a plate-rack, with a distinctive cupboard built into each end in which to store small pieces of china etc. The finest were found around Minsterley, between Shrewsbury and Bishop's Castle, where they were probably made from the mid eighteenth century.[13] Great pride was taken in their appearance, being polished every week, not because they needed it, but because it was 'their day'. The shelves, meanwhile, were decked with Broseley plates, lustre jugs and Coalport china. Rows of cups painted with birds might also hang by their handles from hooks screwed into the fronts of the shelves, making it look 'like an enchanted aviary'.[14]

In rather more prosperous middle-class houses the function of the all-purpose kitchen-living room had already been distributed into a number of separate spaces by the sixteenth century. There might be separate larders, butteries and pantries for the storage of meat, drink, and bread and tableware, for example, while the dining function could be divided into a 'house' or 'hall' for the servants, and either a parlour or, by the seventeenth century, a dining room, for the owners' own family and their guests. The increasing degree of segregation was due to great social changes then sweeping the country. Throughout the medieval period there had been a very close, almost family relationship between landowners and their tenants. It was a tradition based on loyalty and service, the tenantry following their manorial lord on military campaigns for example, or acting as household officers and servants, in return for a degree of protection, their keep when on duty, and the acquisition of social status. Over the generations both parties had gained from this arrangement. In addition, it had influenced the plans of halls and manor houses. As the family dined in its parlour, probably served by the sons of its leading tenants as a form of in-house training in social skills, other senior tenants or dependants acting as household officers took their meals at the top table in the hall. Here they supervised the lesser servants and guests, who were seated in diminishing order of rank down tables leading to the entrance doors. Beyond lay the kitchens and service rooms, again controlled by the household officers. There were few internal barriers, for almost everyone knew each other, and could be trusted.

Following the Dissolution of the monasteries, there was a rapid re-distribution of both land, and the income it generated. Many who took advantage of this situation were able to rise from relative obscurity to considerable wealth and power. They wanted to enjoy the luxuries of the old-established nobility and gentry, but without all the costly encumbrance of employing large households of middle-class retainers. When they bought their manors, they dismissed the old staff, and left them to their own resources. Most servants were now paid a minimum wage, came from a lower social and educational background, and so had to be further excluded from the family's presence. In addition, since they could not be trusted as much as their predecessors, the houses had to be re-designed to provide added internal security.

This change is exemplified in two Shropshire houses. Built as late as the 1570s–80s Plaish Hall was still designed for a medieval style of household. At its upper end were impressive parlours/dining rooms for the family, then a great hall open to a pretended hammer-

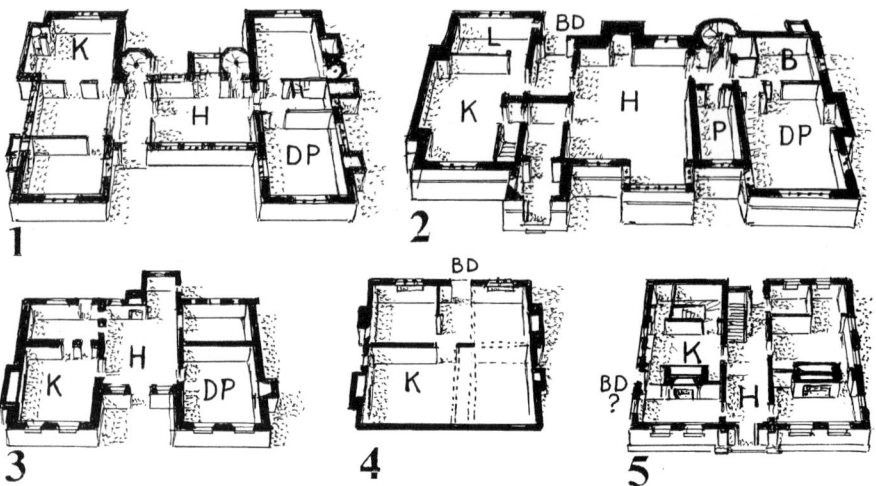

Fig 4 The plans of these Shropshire halls show how they reflected changing lifestyles and fashions as the hall declined from a great reception/dining room to an entrance passage with a staircase.

1. Plaish Hall, 1570s–80s
2. Wilderhope Manor, 1580s
3. Treflack Hall, c. 1600
4. Acton Scott Hall, c. 1600
5. Ash Hall, early 18th century

K – Kitchen   B – Buttery   BD – Back Door   DP – Dining Parlour   H – Hall
L – Larder   P – Pantry

beam roof, and a screens passage giving open access both to the hall, and to the kitchen, buttery and pantry at the lower end. It relied largely on mutual trust to prevent anyone from walking in and helping themselves to the valuable tableware, linen and food stored in the service rooms, or even entering into the family's private accommodation.[15] By way of contrast, Wilderhope Manor was built in the 1580s specifically to meet the needs of a rising Elizabethan 'New Man'. Thomas Smalman was a barrister who needed a local base for his work as Justice in the Council of the Marches at Ludlow Castle. He had no need of the previous owner's retainers, except as providers of rental income, and so designed his new house in a way which separated its public and private areas as securely as possible. Visitors could now only enter through its front door, a wall built across the cross-passage (unforgivably removed in the 1970s) funnelling them into the single-storey hall, but no further. A strong, barred door at its upper end led not only to his parlour/dining room and the chambers above, but also to his pantry and buttery, ensuring that all his valuables were totally safe. Service access to the larder and kitchen at the lower end was by a back door, anyone approaching it being observed through a window at its side. Once inside, one lockable door led into the service rooms, and another into the hall, so that the cooked meals could be carried in whenever required. In all its essential elements this was a thoroughly modern house with separate front and back doors, a reception-cum-servants' hall, private family rooms with their own [butler's] pantry, separate best and back-stairs, and a virtually enclosed kitchen/larder area.

In most large Shropshire houses of the sixteenth century the kitchen fireplaces had wide hearths bridged by either a masonry arch, as at Wilderhope, or by a strong wooden lintel which supported the chimney stack above. Perhaps the best fuel to be burnt here was wood, which burned cleanly when dry, giving a good heat and luminous flame. However, standing timber was always an expensive and carefully managed commodity, so most cottagers would rely on either hedge trimmings or dead branches pulled from trees with long wooden 'ronging hooks'.[16] The larger diameter logs were known as big wood or 'chumps', while the smaller branches and twigs were 'chats'. These burned very quickly and fiercely, providing the proverb 'Love of lads and a fire of chats is soon in and soon out'.[17] When bound into long bundles they became 'kids' or faggots, ideal for heating brick or stone-built ovens.[18] Branches of gorse or broom called 'chags' were also used whenever a rapid burst of heat was required.[19]

In some parts of the county, particularly to the north between Shrewsbury and Ellesmere, there were plentiful supplies of peat, locally known as turf. When cut into narrow blocks in late spring, allowed to dry out and shrink over the summer, and harvested before winter set in, it provided a good, slow-burning fuel, good for boiling and frying, but not much use for roasting or heating masonry ovens. In the late sixteenth century Thomas Churchyard, a Shropshire man, described how;[20]

> Good turffe and peate, on mossie ground is won,
> Wherewith good fires is made for man most meete,
> That burneth cleere, and yeelds a savour sweete
> To those which have no nose for dayntie smell,
> The finer sort, were best at court to dwell

In his *Antiquities & Memoirs of the Parish of Myddle*, Richard Gough gives an excellent description of the transformation of the local turf industry as it developed in the latter years of the seventeenth century;[21]

> For fewell, although many of the greatest woods are cutt downe, yet there is sufficient left for timber and fire-boot for most tenements. There is likewise a Turbary in Haresmeare which belongs to the Lord of the Manor, and was formerly of great benefit to the neighbours; but now they have taken a trade carrying them to Shrewsbury and selling them; soe the Turbary is much wasted and the Turfes are much dearer. Soe that a yarde of peates which was formerly at 8d is now sett at 2s. Note that a yard of peates is 80 square yards – viz: soe many peates as can be digged in and layd to dry upon soe much ground.

Wood and peat were never going to be able to fuel all the fires required by families as the population expanded during the eighteenth and nineteenth centuries. Fortunately the county had ample coalfields, barely used during the medieval period, but ripe for commercial exploitation. During the second half of the sixteenth century the coal mines at Broseley, Madeley and Benthall began to expand, so that by the 1650s it was able to serve not only the local domestic customers, but others along the Severn from Tewkesbury up to Shrewsbury and on into mid Wales. While other English coalfields still extracted their supplies from bell-pits dug at regular intervals down into the coal, those in the Severn Gorge pioneered the long-wall system, which enabled entire seams to be followed with a far greater efficiency.

Where wood and peat were the main fuels, the fires burned best on the flat surface of the hearth, a pair of andirons holding them in from the sides, and sometimes a fender retaining them in front. In contrast, coal had to be burned in a raised hearth with masonry hobs to each side, a cast iron or masonry fireback, and a front and base of parallel iron bars to draw in the required draught, and give out both radiant heat and spent ashes.[22] The earliest form of iron grate was simply a pair of andirons linked by iron firebars and placed between the masonry hobs. The main disadvantage of this arrangement was that it was very difficult to control the size of the fire, but this was soon solved by providing them with an iron plate called a niggard to each side, so that its length could be adjusted as required.[23]

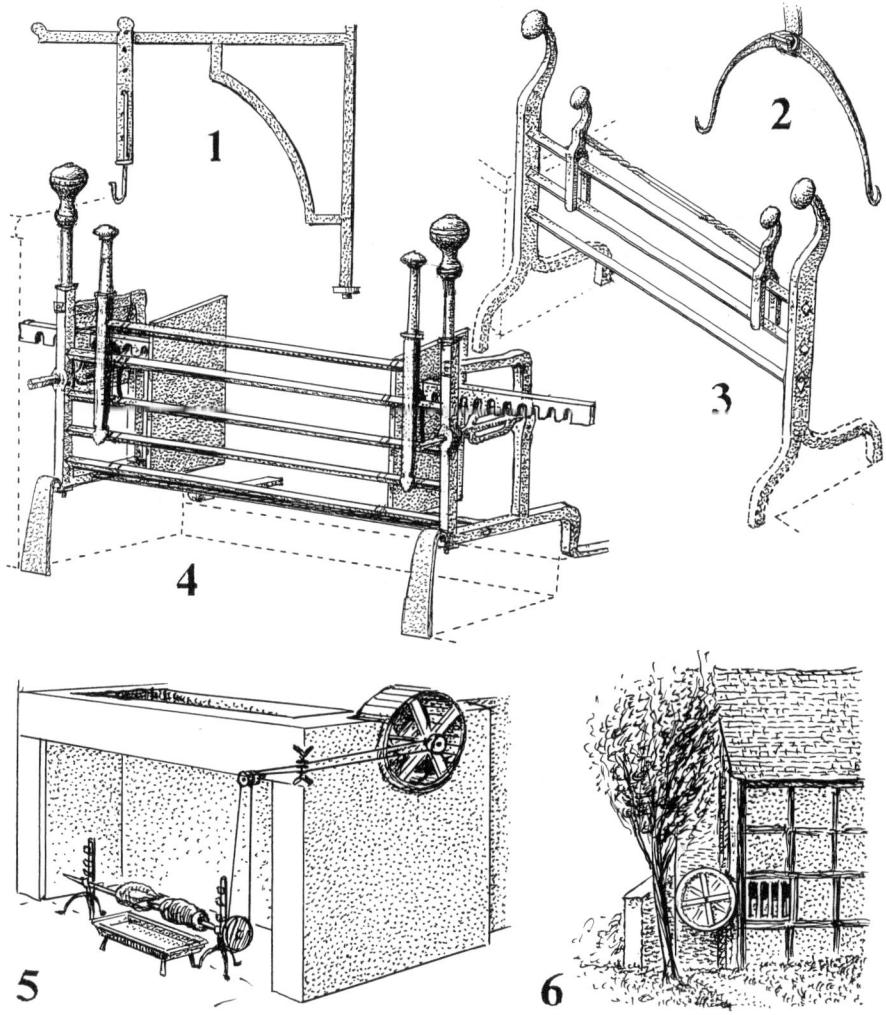

Fig 5 The ironwork within traditional fireplaces included:

1. A chimney crane or sway pole, with an adjustable pot-hanger or hangless, from which hung;
2. A pot gale, geal or goal, with hooks for different sizes of cooking pot.
3. A simple grate, this one probably being installed into a cottage at Lightmore near Coalbrookdale around 1790.
4. A high-quality grate, with niggards winding in and out from each end, and a removable top bar. This mid-late 18th century example may be seen in Ludlow Castle.
5–6. A dog wheel to provide the motive power for spits rotating in front of the fire. These were never particularly common, 6 being photographed at a cottage opposite Hopton Wafers church in 1909.

Within the chimney, above the level of the arch or lintel, it was customary to build in a horizontal wooden bar called a gaypole or balk. This was ideal for hanging up freshly cured bacon joints to dry in wood-smoke; 'That par o' chawls [pig's cheeks] mun be shifted from the chimley balk, they bin getting quite reaisty'.[24] Its main function, however, was to support lengths of chain with a hook at each end called links, long S-shaped bars called pothooks, or ratchet-adjusted, hook-ended pothangers or hanglesses, by which cooking pots could be suspended over the fire. Each might have a centrally-hinged pair of hooks called pot gales, goals or geals on its lower hook, these enabling pots of varying sizes to be safely held in place. In some kitchens a chimney-crane called a sway pole or swaylpole was fitted instead of a gaypole.[25] It performed the same function, but was hinged out from the fireback, so that the pots could be swung forward and out of the smoke whenever they needed to be filled, stirred or emptied.

Up to the early seventeenth century most metal cooking pots were made of copper alloys such as brass, latten or maslin. Kettles, for example, were open-topped, round-bottomed, legless vessels of beaten sheet brass known as battery-ware, strengthened with wrought iron rims and bow handles. Maslin kettles were similar in shape, but were made by casting a bright form of brass called maslin in either loam or sand moulds. Two pierced lugs extended above their rims to grip the ends of their iron bow handles. The most popular of all boiling vessels were known simply as pots, even though they were made of moulded brass or bronze, rather than of pottery. They had bag-shaped bodies, flaring rims to receive lids, hanging loops for suspension over the fire, and three legs for standing in the embers, all these features making them particularly useful in the kitchen. Today we call them 'cauldrons'. In Shropshire the smallest size of pot, one about 7ins/18cm diameter and one gallon in capacity, was known as a marmit, marmalett, or even marmalade, these being the Anglicised forms of the traditional French *marmite*, a cooking pot.[26]

The pots made and used in Shropshire were quite different in design to those of other regions. A particularly interesting group were discovered in a patch of boggy ground at West Felton, five miles south-east of Oswestry, in the late Victorian period. Of some eight, five and a half, and three gallons capacity respectively, they had a straight vertical, and an S-shaped diagonal raised stripe rising above each of their three legs. This may have helped to ensure a

OF KITCHENS GREAT AND SMALL

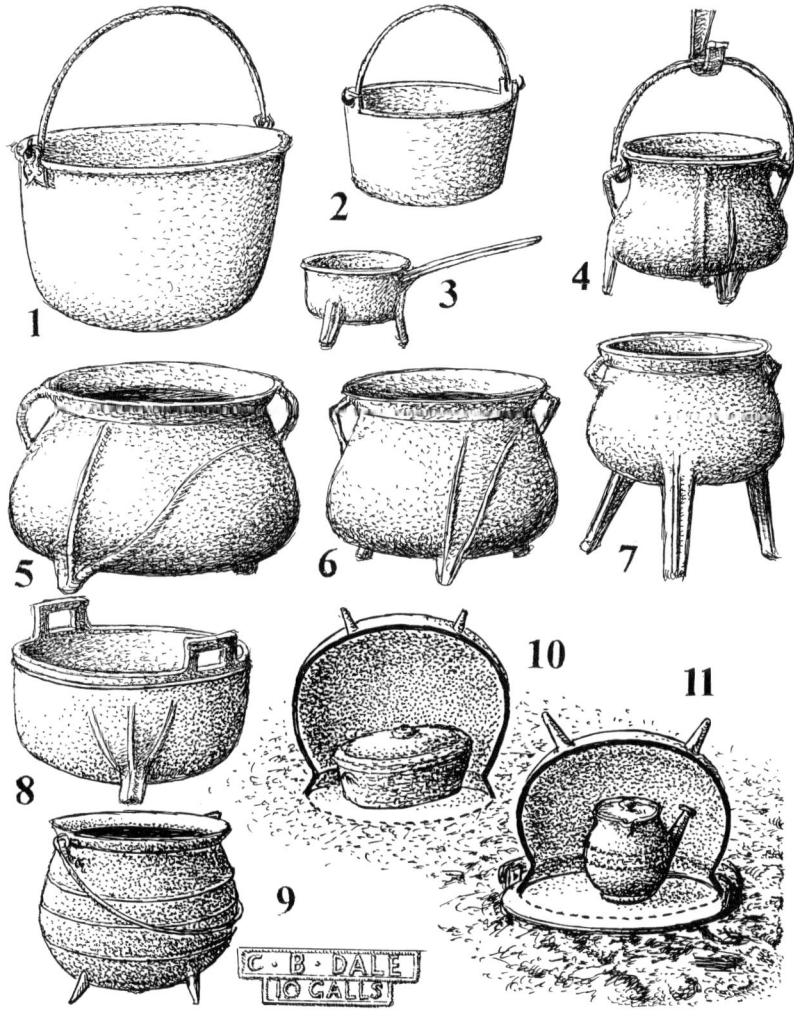

Fig 6 Metal cooking pots were the mainstay of Shropshire traditional cookery. These examples show:

1. A sheet brass iron-rimmed kettle.
2. A cast brass maslin kettle.
3. A cast bronze skillet.
4. A 12th century cast bronze pot found at Llwynymaen, Near Oswestry.

5–7. A group of similar pots lost by Royalists retreating from Oswestry in 1644, and found at Felton Heath.

8. A local variety of cast bronze chafer.
9. A 19th century Coalbrookdale cast iron pot.
10. Baking a pie under a pot on a hot hearth.
11. Baking a pipkin under a pot on a bakestone set on a bed of glowing embers.

good flow of metal during the casting process, but if so, it was not a practice followed elsewhere. Since these pots would be quite expensive, it is difficult to understand why they should have found their way into a bog. The explanation appears to be the Civil War. In late June, 1644, the Royalist forces were drawn up around Oswestry, which was then in Parliamentary hands. Like most troops of the period, they probably 'requisitioned' various goods from unwilling local householders, carrying them off when Sir Thomas Myddleton drove them away from the town and pursued them for five miles towards Shrewsbury on 2nd July. Pots are difficult to carry, especially when running for dear life, and so these three seem to have been abandoned here, sinking into the soft ground, and remaining there for two and a half centuries.[27] A further group of six similar pots was discovered in construction trenches at Lwynymaen near Oswestry in 1982, these too perhaps being lost during the campaign of 1644.[28]

Such pots were primarily designed for boiling and stewing, over the fire, but in Shropshire they also served as baking ovens well into the nineteenth century, especially where no other form of oven was available. Around Oswestry in 1817, where fires still burned on the flat hearthstones, it was customary to sweep them to one side and put a baking dish of food, perhaps potatoes and meat bones under a pastry crust, in its place. A cooking pot was then upturned over it, the heat of the hot hearth being sufficient to cook it through, 'and you can't think how nice a pie it is'. Alternatively a pottery pipkin of food could be stood on an iron girdle placed directly over some of the hot ashes, and then covered with the pot, potatoes and salt herrings being one of the dishes cooked in this way.[29]

As well as being hung over the fire, other cast bronze vessels were designed to stand in the embers, giving a gentler and perhaps more controllable heat, and better access for stirring. The larger, called chafers, had the rounded bottoms and three short legs of cooking pots, but their sides rose vertically to a flat rim, above which rose a pair of integral rectangular handles. Skillets had the same body shape and three legs, but were smaller, and had a horizontal handle extending from their rims, rather like a saucepan.

By the early-mid seventeenth century ironfounders had developed new methods by which they could cast iron cooking vessels. This was of great commercial and social importance, for iron was much cheaper than copper alloys such as brass or bronze. There were many poor people who could not afford the expensive alloy vessels, but would eagerly buy their cast iron alternatives. The iron might not conduct the heat as well as bronze, might be more brittle, and be subject to rust if left damp and ungreased, but it was far better than the only other affordable alternative, pottery. In July 1635 one John Brown had been granted the monopoly of the sole making, selling and transportation of iron pots etc. in England. Since he had immediately raised the price of cast iron goods by 44%, and cast his pots with thick walls, so that they were heavy to lift and took more fire to heat, a complaint was brought against him in the Long Parliament.[30] As a result, the monopoly was broken, leaving the way clear for others to make iron cooking vessels.

The best sources of information for tracing the contents of historic kitchens are probate inventories, since they list and price every portable artefact remaining in a property at the time of its owner's death, only excluding items of very low value, and not worth bothering with. That of Thomas Owen of Condover Court, dated 1599, provides a wealth of evidence of how a Shropshire gentleman's household cooked its food in the late Elizabethan/early Jacobean period.[31] This house, only just completed at the time of his death, is the finest Elizabethan property in the county. It was probably designed by John Thorpe, one of the greatest architects of the period, the actual construction being by William Hancock, master mason. With an elongated H-shaped plan, its central porch led right into its great hall, and left into a buttery, a pantry, and a large kitchen to the rear. This was a very well-supplied room, having two great fireplaces and a pastry oven. Here he still used wood fires, the logs being held within a pair of andirons and a fender listed as an 'iron to lay before the fire'. For roasting, he had two racks. They were turned by two clockwork jacks, showing that he was very up-to-date, the first record of a jack in the *Oxford English Dictionary* being only twelve years earlier. Being mechanical, they saved all the uncomfortable and boring time spent in turning the spit by hand. Others in the county, such as Andrew Sockett of Wellington, used a 'Dogg wheel' instead, this being a small treadmill which used dog-power for the spits.[32] At Hopton Wafers, between Ludlow and Cleobury Mortimer, an old cottage opposite the church had its dog-wheel mounted on the outside of its kitchen chimney, the shaft apparently going through to operate pulleys inside the fireplace.[33] At Condover, there were three dripping pans and a brass ladle, which respectively caught the falling fats and juices, and basted them back over the roasts, to keep them moist.

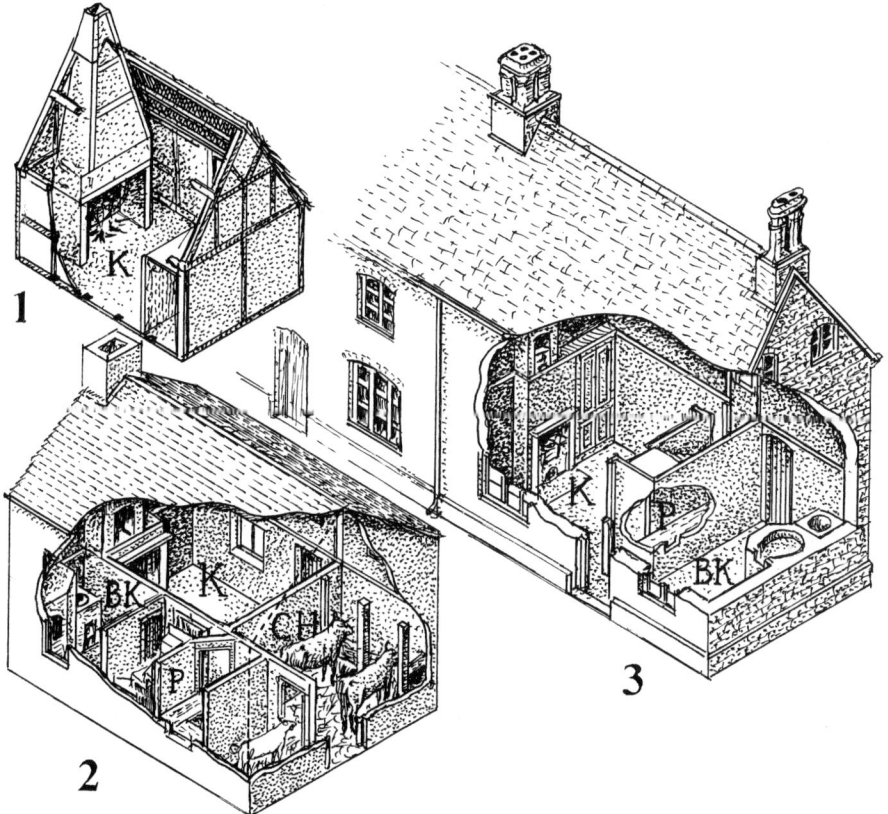

Fig 3 Many 16th or 17th century cottages had just a single living room with a fireplace at one end, the family in the middle, and their livestock at the other, as at The Old Shop, Somerwood, Upton Magna (1). They were still in use in the 19th century, but by then were being replaced by improved versions such as (2), designed by John Davies in 1813, which included a cow-house and calf pen, and (3), built on Sir Baldwin Leighton's estate, which finally got rid of the animals, and provided a very comfortable home.

K – Kitchen   BK – Back Kitchen   CH – Cow House   P – Pantry

terrace houses for their employees in the mid-late eighteenth century. Some in the mining districts followed the traditional single-storey pattern, one row at Lilleshall having twelve 25 × 12ft cottages set end-to-end as a single 350ft block. Despite having separate kitchen-living rooms and sometimes a store, such houses might prove damp and dirty, especially if the piggeries and ashpit toilets were too close. The Coalbrookdale ironmasters preferred to build

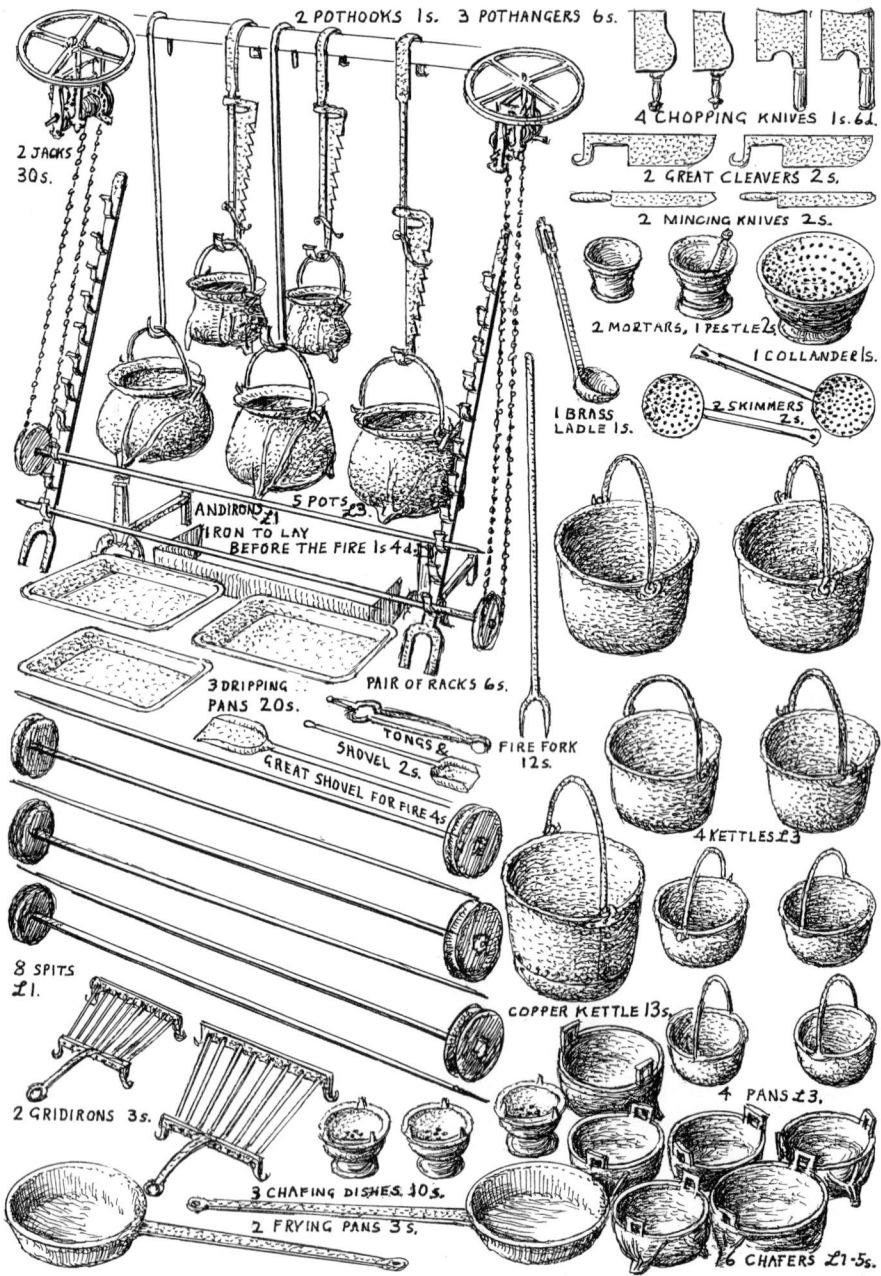

Fig 7   The contents of Thomas Owen's kitchen at Condover Court in 1599.

(For caption see overleaf)

Prayers to St Anthony, the leading 'Desert Father' of the early church in Egypt, cured not only the inflammatory disease in humans called 'St Anthony's Fire', but also disorders of domestic animals. In England up to the 16th century a sickly pig might have its ear slit and a bell hung round its neck, being allowed to feed wherever it chose, having become the common property of the parish. One such pig accompanies St Anthony in this late medieval window in Munslow church.

(Caption from previous page)

From the medieval period pigs provided an important source of meat in Shropshire. These 14th century illustrations from the Luttrell Psalter show them (1) feeding on acorns (2) being stunned prior to slaughter and hung up. Sucking pigs were roasted as a great delicacy (3). In the kitchen (4) one cook uses a skimmer and a flesh-hook to stew beef in three large 'standards', while another chops cooked vegetables to add to the stock. The third cook pounds wheat for furmity, a dish still being cooked for Market Drayton wakes in the 19th century.

This Shropshire pig, owned by Sir Charles Boughton of Downton Hall near Ludlow, weighed an amazing 47 stone before it was two years old. The painting by W. Gwynne was engraved by W. Wright and published at Corve Street, Ludlow in the 1830s.

A Shropshire ram, 'Grandson of Old Black knee'. Painting by Thomas Weaver, Shrewsbury, 1831.

Cattle at Buildwas Abbey, 1841. Thomas Jones, tenant farmer, and his landlord, Walter Moseley with improved Herefords of this period. Painting by James Pardon.

Ale or milk jug made at the Herculaneum pottery on the banks of the River Mersey in Liverpool about 1820. It shows a view of Shrewsbury, transfer printed in underglaze blue. Height 9".

Two frying pans and two gridirons were used for frying and grilling, but the presence of five pots, five kettles, four pans and two skimmers shows that boiling remained the main method of cookery. Six chafers, standing on their short legs at the edge of the fire, were ideal for stews and cereal dishes, which required a gentler heat and more frequent stirring. The striking thing about Thomas Owen's kitchen is its very conservative nature; any cook of the fourteenth century would have found virtually everything unchanged from his day over two hundred years earlier, except for the new jacks.

During the seventeenth century, the social changes which had introduced new planning requirements to houses such as Wilderhope, moved relentlessly forward to meet three new criteria. Externally, the old lob-sided house fronts, their doors to one side to enable direct entry into a screens-passage at the bottom end of the hall, went completely out of fashion. Now every façade had to display a classical symmetry, usually with the door in the middle. Once inside, the screens passage disappeared, so that all walked directly into the hall. Particularly after the Civil War, when the last of the old family retainers gradually disappeared, the hall ceased to serve as their dining room, their lower-class waged replacements now being moved away from the public parts of the house, into more isolated servants' halls. As a result, halls no longer needed fireplaces, or to be built so large as before. Instead, they became modern entrance halls, from where the family and their guests could proceed either to the reception rooms on the ground floor, or up a formal staircase to the rooms above. The third change came in the arrangement of the kitchens. In smaller houses, they were often retained in a cross-wing to one side of the hall, but in some houses of a more architectural character, such as the square-planned lodges built from the late sixteenth century, they were often moved down to basement level. This provided several advantages, keeping the service rooms and their occupants out of sight and mind, elevating the main rooms, and giving the family the benefit of warm, literally under-floor heating.

If the seventeenth century was the period during which the last vestiges of medieval styles of housekeeping finally disappeared, the eighteenth century was one which rationalised the new order with improved domestic planning and artefacts. This may be illustrated by considering three of Shropshire's great Georgian houses, Francis Smith of Warwick's Kinlet Hall of 1727, George Steuart's Attingham of 1779–85, and Hopton Court, probably designed by John Nash

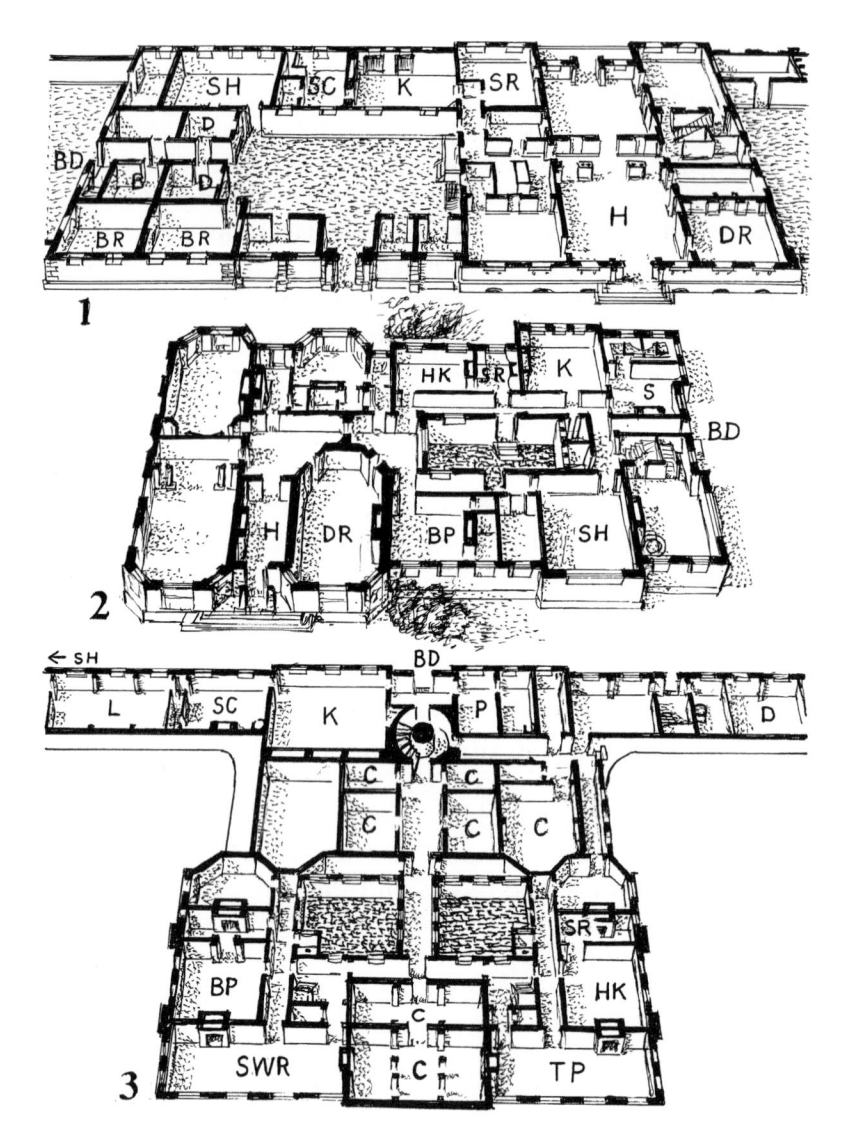

Fig 8 These plans show three different forms of Georgian kitchen offices. Kinlet Hall (1) built to the designs of Francis Smith in 1727, has them in a flanking wing. John Nash placed those in his *c.* 1806 Hopton Court (2) off to one side, where they could be masked by deep shrubberies and trees, while at George Steuart's Attingham (3) of 1779–85, they were relegated into the basement.

K – Kitchen   B – Bakehouse   BD – Back Door   BH – Brewhouse,
BP – Butler's Pantry   C – Cellar   D – Dairy   DR – Dining Room   H – Hall
HK – Housekeeper's Room   L – Larder   P – Pantry   S – Scullery
SH – Servants' Hall   SR – Stillroom,   SWR – Servants' Waiting Room
TP – Tenants' Parlour.

shortly after 1806. All share a number of new features, including the arrangement of the service rooms in a wing running alongside the residential block. They all have a secure back door, controlling the entry and exit of all people and goods, and a 'green baize door' similarly controlling access from the service rooms into the main house. They all reflect the arrival of numerous female servants into what was formerly a largely male establishment. The former butteries and pantries have been combined into the butlers' pantries, from where its occupant supervised the male staff and the adjacent servants' halls. The new housekeepers' rooms, meanwhile, provided combined office-sitting-workrooms for the heads of the female staffs, with adjacent stores for all manner of dry goods and stillrooms where hot drinks, cakes and preserves were prepared. For the cook, there were separate larders for fresh foods, dairies for storing dairy produce, and sculleries where all the dirty processes were completed in order to keep the kitchen as clean and tidy as possible. In terms of architectural arrangement, however, they represent three of the main service arrangements adopted during the eighteenth century. That at Kinlet placed the house between two matching wings, thus presenting a long and extremely impressive façade to both entrance and garden fronts. During the later eighteenth century architects such as John Nash devised a variant of this, by having just one service wing off to the side. As at Hopton Court, this enabled the occupants of the main block to enjoy the benefits of light and open views from three sides, the very existence of the fourth side with its service wing being masked by planting a deep belt of trees and shrubs around it. The house therefore looked as if it was freestanding, the servants now being unseen by the family and their visitors as they approached across the park. At Attingham, the decision was taken to place all the domestic offices in the basements, setting the house on a raised plinth to improve its appearance. Only the upper servants had windows which could look into the park, the lower servants in the kitchens, larders etc. seeing only into the enclosed back yard.

Within such houses, the north-facing kitchens were built much larger and with much better access to natural light than before. Another improvement was their greater height, usually rising up through two storeys. Not only did this enable tall windows to cast their light across the entire room, but it also allowed all hot air, smoke and steam to rise high above the cooks, making their working environment far more comfortable than that of almost every modern catering kitchen.

The fireplace openings, often two or three in number, were usually set along one side of the kitchen, thus keeping the other side pleasantly cool. Wood was still being used as a domestic fuel in some areas, a 'cord', a stack of four-foot long logs four feet high, four feet broad, and eight feet long, costing between eight and nine shillings around 1800. In the south-west of the county some houses were still self-sufficient by using their own wood and peat, but elsewhere coal now predominated, its price being around four to six shillings a ton.[34] By the end of the eighteenth century the Shropshire mines were producing about fifty thousand tons each year, a fifth of the national output. New turnpike roads and canals had reduced its high transport costs, enabling it to develop new markets, so as to supply virtually every town in the region.

To burn the coal, the ranges of the early-mid eighteenth century, such as that in Ludlow Castle, were practical and elegant examples of the blacksmith's craft. Designed to fit within masonry firebacks and hobs, they have fronts and bases of horizontal square-section bars, and side-cheeks or 'niggards' which can be wound in or out by rack and pinion mechanisms at each side. Large wrought-iron knobs top each end-frame, while smaller matching knobs terminate the separate top-bar, which could be slotted on to provide a deeper fire. From around 1700 rectangular pits began to be dug out of the hearth, just in front of the fire. Their tops were then covered with iron plates pierced by a series of parallel slots, in inventories described as 'an Iron Purgatory' (1708) or 'One Cast Iron Purgatory plate 4s' (1747).[35] This purgatory, or 'purgy-hole' received its name from the Roman Catholic belief in a lesser Hell, in which the souls of the deceased were purged of their sins. In practice, their function was to catch all the fine ashes as they fell from the fire, preventing them from scattering across the floor, and also to retain the larger clinkers, which could be returned to the fire until totally consumed.

In a second fireplace opening, or perhaps freestanding beneath a window, stood a stove. This was a table-height masonry bench, its top pierced by a number of circular or square firepits, bridged by closely-spaced iron bars a few inches below. In one of these a charcoal fire provided a clear-burning and controllable source of heat, ideal for stewing, frying, preserving, or making the more complicated sauces and desserts of better-class cookery. Their layout varied from one house to another, but most incorporated arched openings beneath, either to collect the falling fine ash, and/or to serve as bunkers for charcoal. Since any pan placed directly on top of the firepits would stifle the burning charcoal, each was provided with a low iron trivet. This supported its pan an inch or two above the top of the stove, so that there was plenty of room for the hot gases to pass upwards, and for the cook to check the state of the fire.

As for the third fireplace, this might hold a second range or stove, but could also house a pastry oven or a furnace/set pot. The latter was essentially a large old-fashioned boiling pot or kettle enclosed in a masonry case. With a fireplace beneath and a flue rising above, it enabled large-scale boiling operations to be completed cleanly and efficiently.

The inventory of the magnificent half-timbered Park Hall, taken in 1761 on the death of John Charlton, lists everything which a prosperous Georgian gentleman's kitchen should contain.[36] The fire was contained in its iron grate with adjustable niggards or 'wings', a

Fig 9 A charcoal-burning stewing stove in a house near Oswestry. Each grate is lined with a firebasket, the opening in front providing access for air, and a means of collecting the ashes. The space beneath served as a bunker for the fuel.

27

pit-plate across its purgatory, and fenders to hold back the cinders. All the expected roasting equipment was present, but now with some new features. Two pig plates, two hanging plates and a standing plate were all designed to shield the thinner parts of the joints from the radiant heat, while allowing the thicker parts to cook through. This was particularly important with pigs, since the thin flesh over the central ribs cooked far more quickly than the shoulders and legs at each end. There was also a baster, a long-handled spoon, its copper bowl probably pierced along one side to filter the fats as they were poured back over the joints. A dredger, meanwhile, allowed savoury dry breadcrumbs or flour mixtures to be shaken over them when almost completed, in order to build up a 'frothing' or crispy coating. Now that a large brass boiler had been installed, there were only four kettles or pots needed to hang over the fire. Similarly, the presence of a stove and a chafing dish meant that there was no need for the former chafers. Instead there were a number of new utensils designed for more delicate cookery. These included four saucepans, four skillets, a fish kettle, a frying pan, two sauté or tossing pans and a preserving pan, along with two stands to hold them over the burning charcoal. As the kitchens now tended to be at greater distances from the dining room, new devices had now been introduced to ensure that everything was served as hot as possible. Plate warmers, for example, were tinplate boxes with shelves inside to hold piles of dinner-plates. Put in front of the kitchen fire until their contents were heated through, they were then transferred to the dining room fireplace ready for use. The 'brass plate warmer' probably took the form of a 'cat', a double-tripod for holding individual plates or dishes before the fire. There were also a pair of tinplate dish-covers ready to insulate the hot foods as the footmen carried them up to the dining table.

During the eighteenth century Shropshire's most important contribution to food and cooking was in the production of cast iron cooking pots on a truly industrial scale. Born near Dudley in 1678, Abraham Darby had completed his apprenticeship in Birmingham by 1699, shortly afterwards moving to Bristol, where he took an interest in the prosperous local trade of brass pot founding. Due to the high cost of their raw materials, these had always been amongst the most expensive of all culinary utensils. Since most families still cooked in pots hung over open fires, the demand for them was great, only their high price limiting the level of their sales. Anyone who could make them efficiently in the much cheaper cast iron could be assured of commercial success. Having set up an iron foundry in Cheese Lane, Bristol, he apparently began to make the experiments which enabled him to take out a patent on casting iron pots in sand in 1707. Two years later he re-started the 1638 blast furnace in Coalbrookdale, completely transforming the future of the iron industry by using coke rather than charcoal as his principal fuel.

From the very start the pig iron he produced was mainly used for casting large-bellied iron pots. Most were intended for domestic use, but as early as 1709–10 he had supplied one of 104 gallons for a soap-maker. In addition, he made grates, kettles, smoothing irons etc. which, with numerous pots, he sold to country ironmongers throughout the Borders. After Abraham Darby's death in 1717 his Coalbrookdale works were taken into the control of Richard Ford and Thomas Godney, who further promoted the pot trade. By the early 1720s they were distributing their pots etc. throughout Lancashire, Cheshire, north Staffordshire, Derbyshire and the West Midlands. Others were carried down the Severn to Bristol, where merchants such as Nehemiah Champion was placing orders for £200-worth of goods, presumably for export. From here they were also being carried around the coast, and up the Trent to serve customers as far away as Gainsborough. Up to around 1750 the Coalbrookdale Company was primarily a pot-works, and even though it then moved on to produce an amazing range of engineering and decorative ironwork, it still continued to make cooking pots into the twentieth century, their sides bearing cast marks such as 'C-B-DALE/10 GALLS'.[37]

The cast iron cook-ware made by the Coalbrookdale foundry comprised a fairly limited number of shapes, each being made in a range of sizes to suit the individual needs of any particular family. Sold throughout the Midlands and Wales and later to many distant parts of the Empire, they were strong, hard-wearing, good conductors of heat, and, especially when compared to bronze and copper, relatively inexpensive. They were also ideal for all the basic cooking methods used in preparing traditional Shropshire recipes.

The most common vessels made from the early eighteenth century clearly continued the forms and functions of their cast bronze predecessors. Common cooking pots had the familiar flaring rims, two suspension loops and three legs, for example, but now the shape was more spherical, and the raised bands ran all around their sides at regular intervals. They were made in sizes rising in 2pt/1·2l

SHROPSHIRE COOKBOOK

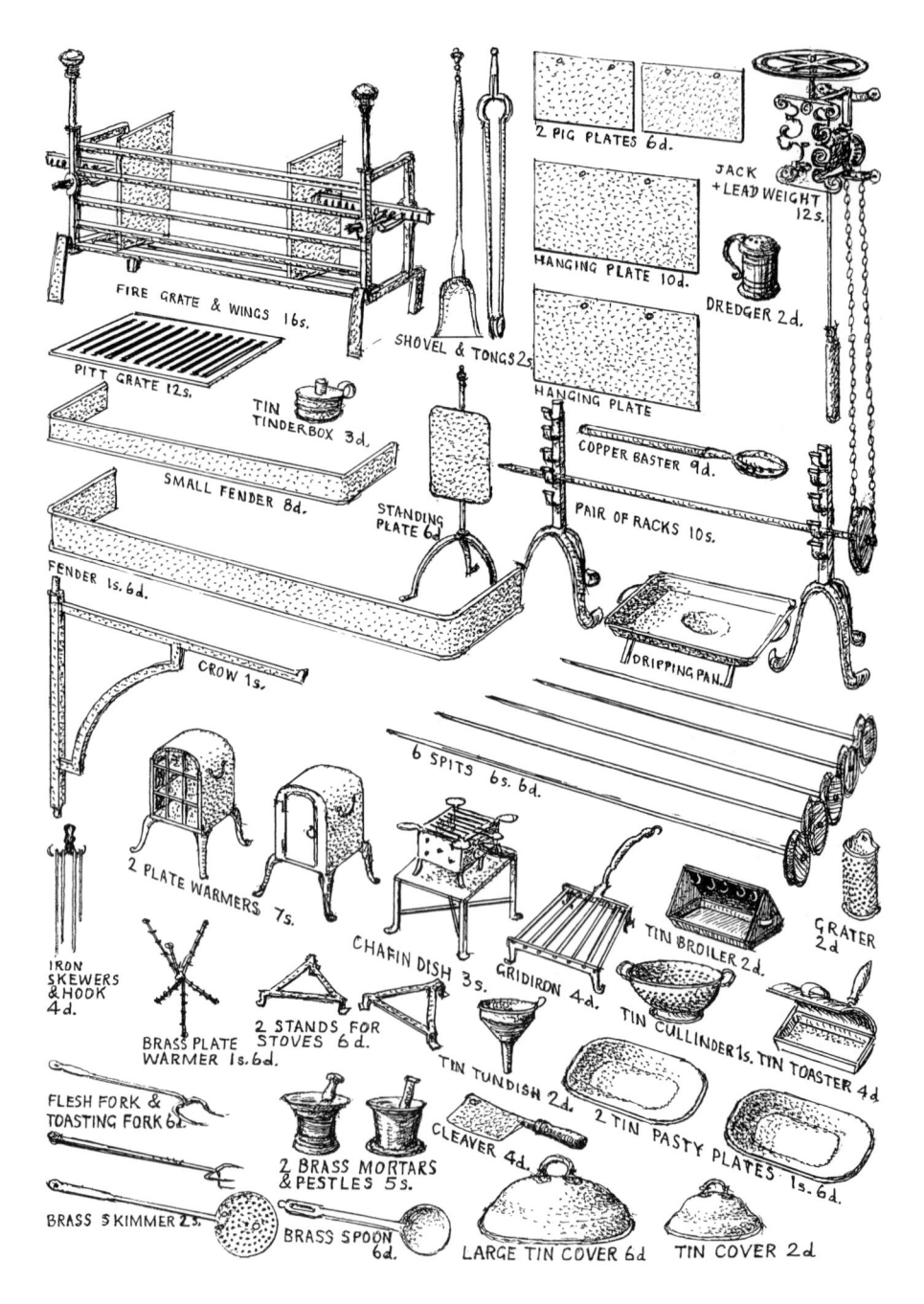

Fig 10   The contents of John Charlton's kitchen at Park Hall in 1761.

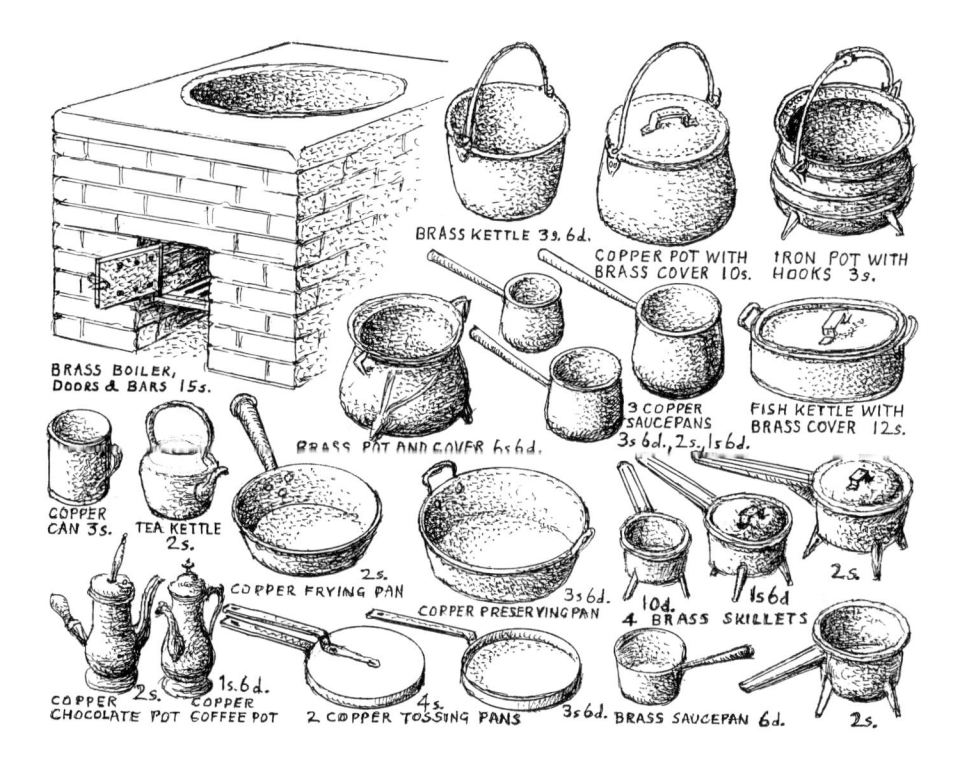

Fig 10   *Continued.*

capacities from 2pt/1·2l up to 22pt/13·2l, and then by the gallon for all the larger examples. The round-bottomed, almost vertical-sided iron kettles with their three legs and two handles, also closely followed the seventeenth century bronze chafer's form, an example in the Museum of Iron at Coalbrookdale being of this type, cast with the initials H W / E and date of 1714. By 1860 they were being made to the same capacities as the pots, starting at 2pt/1·2l and working up to a full 16 gallons/96l, some being deep for boiling and others rather shallower and more suitable for stewing. The early nineteenth century also saw the introduction of flat-bottomed, convex sided oval boiling pots, ideal both for hanging over the fire to boil, or for standing on the hob or the hinged top bar of the range for more gentle simmering.

Cast iron proved to be an ideal material from which to make frying pans too, for if kept in regular use and never severely scoured, they built up one of the first ever 'non-stick' surfaces, the thickness of the iron also spreading the heat and so reducing the

Fig 11 Coalbrookdale cast iron cooking vessels were ideal for preparing all the local traditional foods. They include a shallow kettle of 1714 (1) and a number of mid-19th century forms:

2. deep kettle
3. oval pot
4. stewpan
5. camp oven
6. deep pudding pan with ears
7. frying pan with cast handle
8. frying pans with bail & swivel
9. bake plate

risk of food being spoiled by burning. Either lightweight or heavy, with an integral projecting handle and a pouring spout, they were made both round and oval to stand on top of the fire. Others had a 'bail' or bow handle arched across them from one side to the other, a swivel hook at its top enabling such pans to be suspended from chimney-cranes.

In many Shropshire cottages the everyday breads such as oatcakes, pikelets or buckwheat cakes were made by pouring their yeasted batters across the lightly-greased surface of an iron girdle or bake-plate, both of which were made at Coalbrookdale. The girdles had their circular flat plates cast either plain or with a slightly raised rim, a small 'ear' extending on each opposed side supporting a wrought iron bail handle topped by a swivel hook for hanging over the fire. Others, meanwhile, were given three short cylindrical legs so that they could be stood in the embers in order to achieve their working temperatures. To serve the needs of cottagers who wished to bake loaves of bread, cakes and pies, but had no access to a masonry oven, Coalbrookdale produced camp ovens. These were almost cylindrical vessels, being a little broader at the rim than at the base, and with a diameter almost double their height. Beneath they might have three short legs to support them amid the embers on the hearth, while their close-fitting lids were flat, decorated with raised concentric bands, and provided with a central wrought-iron handle. They ranged from 7 to 20ins top diameter, 6 to 17ins base diameter, and $3\frac{3}{4}$ to $8\frac{1}{4}$ ins internal depth, their volume in gallons sometimes being indicated by a number cast into the top of their lids. With practice, these gave excellent results, especially in areas where peat was still the most economical and available fuel, for these ovens could stand within a peat fire, with further smouldering peats around the sides and on top of the lid, to ensure a good all-round heat. However, since the body of the ovens could easily become so hot that they burned their contents, rather than baked them, the company made false bottoms to stand inside, so that the food cooked at a far more even temperature, with no direct contact with the hot exterior.

The use of cast and sheet iron to make ranges which incorporated ovens, stoves and boilers with a coal-burning firegrate was first introduced to foundries in different parts of the country during the second half of the eighteenth century. As different regions developed their distinctive styles of range, so they gave their names to each particular design. One of the most successful was the Yorkshire Range, which had a large grate to burn that county's cheap and plentiful coal, a large oven to one side, a boiler at the other, and then a large hotplate running across the top of the oven, grate and boiler, providing a graduation of temperatures, hot enough to boil at one end, and cool enough to warm plates at the other. They were large and relatively expensive pieces, averaging at least 4ft in height and width. The most popular range made at

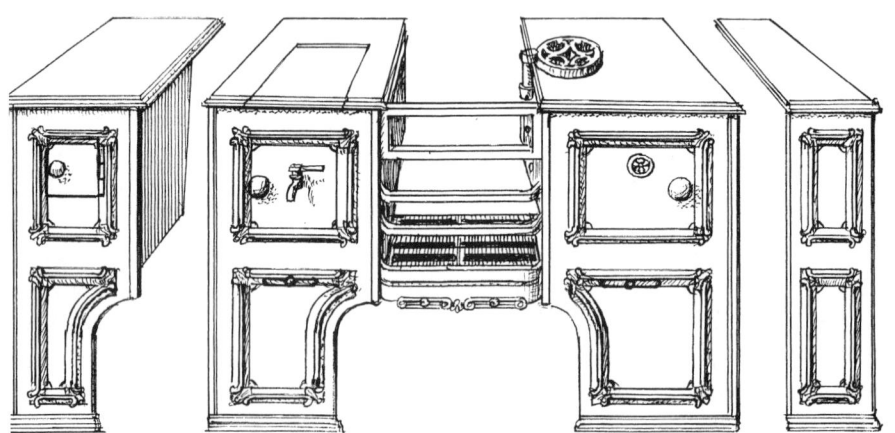

Fig 12 The squatter cottage now at Bliste Hill, Ironbridge, was occupied by Michael Corbett, his wife, six children and a visitor in 1861, their food being cooked on one of Coalbrookdale's 'Yorkshire' ranges. Their range no. 1, seen below, usually had a boiler and an oven to each side of the fire, but these might be substituted by a stove (left) or a sham front (right).

Coalbrookdale was called the Yorkshire Range, even though it would never have been recognised as such in that county. It was much, much smaller, for example, with its central firegrate flanked by two low hobs, and an ashpit which spread wider as it approached the hearth. Instead of having its oven set higher than the fire, to enable hot gases efficiently to circulate round four of its sides, like a true Yorkshire range, Coalbrookdale's 'Yorkshires', had their ovens at the same height as the fire, often heated just from one side, and hence being far less predictable. Some were even provided with rotating oven-shelves, so that when a loaf or cake was baked at one side, they could be easily turned round to bake on the other. However, such Shropshire 'Yorkshire Ranges' were ideal for local use, being easily fitted into any existing hearth, practical for the use of small households, capable of continuing the traditions of cooking over and in front of the fire, and also relatively cheap. In the 1860s, for example, one of these ranges would cost around £2, while a true Yorkshire range (such as the model Coalbrookdale perversely called a 'Shropshire Range') might cost anything between £11 and £16.

The Shropshire 'Yorkshire' ranges were usually between 3ft and 4ft in length, always with a central firegrate with horizontal castiron firebars to the front and base, a brick fireback, and an open top. An oven lay to one side, while the other might have, according to personal choice, another oven, a stove, a boiler, or a solid brick hob covered with a cast iron 'sham front'. The stove had a small door set into the upper part of its hob, this giving access to a small grate-bottomed firebox. Once its separate fire had been kindled, it heated the iron plate on top sufficiently to boil, simmer or fry, ideal for hot summer days when it was unnecessary to keep the main fire going, but still cook a small family meal. The boiler, meanwhile, was like a second oven, except that its hinged lid was at the top, for cold water to be poured in, and it had a brass tap on the front, to draw off hot water as required. Some of the better models incorporated an arched iron plate which bridged the hob, drawing the flames and smoke back from the grate into the chimney, keeping the kitchen/living room much cleaner and fresher than with a simple open-topped range.

Such ranges remained in production through to the late nineteenth century, but, like manufacturers elsewhere, Coalbrookdale went on to make much superior models for large houses and institutions. By the 1870s these included close-fire ranges, in which the top and most of the front of the firegrate were enclosed by boiling rings and doors respectively, these making them much cleaner, more practical and fuel-efficient than before. Other models adopted features from the extremely popular 'Eagle' range, with firebars which could be raised to give more heat with less fuel, and 'bonnets' or hoods which hinged out over the fire to provide an extremely effective grill for cooking steaks etc. on a gridiron. Between 1910 and 1930 Coalbrookdale also made a number of extremely fine ranges for country houses, restaurants etc., one of the most popular being one patented by J.E. Gibson & Co. of Falkirk. This had a particularly efficient boiler, which, like a kettle, was set over the centre of the fire, hence it was called the 'Kettle-Boiler', or 'K B Range'. Even today

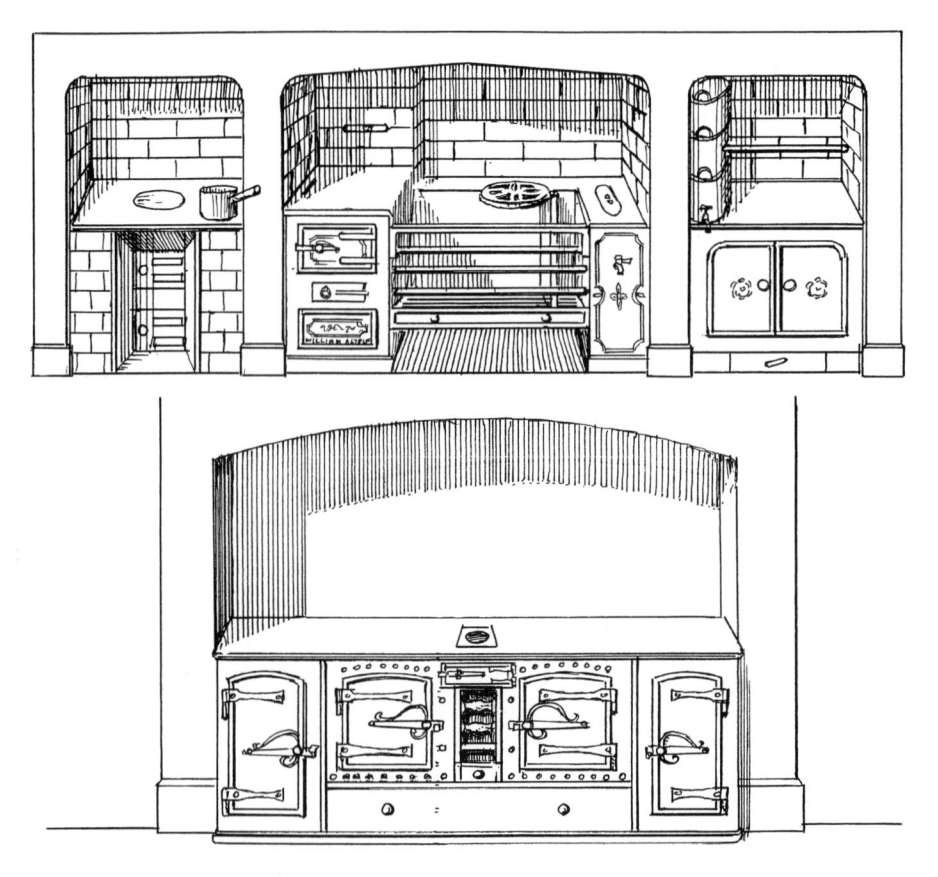

Fig 13   These ranges were being made in Shrewsbury in 1861, the top example with its hotplate/stove (left), 'Yorkshire' range (centre) and hot closet with steamers (right) was by William Alltree of Castle Street, while the closed range below, with its flanking ovens and hot closets, all beneath a hotplate, was by William Easthorpe.

some of the world's best-known closed ranges are made in Coalbrookdale, production of solid fuel or oil-fired Agas and Rayburns having transferred to Shropshire in 1947.

Coalbrookdale was certainly the most important producer of ranges in Shropshire, but it was not unique in the county. In the mid nineteenth century, large 'improved cooking apparatuses' suitable for medium to large-scale establishments were also being manufactured in Shrewsbury in the 1850s and '60s, for example. Here William Alltree of Castle Street and William Easthorpe designed and made versions which incorporated open or closed fires, boilers to provide both hot water and steam, baking ovens, stoves, hotplates and hot-closets for keeping food warm, everything which one of their contemporary cooks could ever wish for.

By the 1830s, the use of ranges was moving down the social scale to enter many of the smaller households, where they made an enormous improvement to the daily lives of numerous wives who were still cooking over fires little changed from those of the medieval period. At first they were viewed as great curiosities. In 1838–9 Thomas, a footman for the Duke of Sutherland, saw one for the first time in one of the lodges at Lilleshall, where he had been invited for a meal of peas, cold mutton, gin and water. Here he was intrigued by its novel sort of grate with a 'fireplace in the middle and a boiler at one end and an oven at the other so as the fire would keep both hot at one time'.[38] It was probably one of Coalbrookdale's 'Yorkshire Ranges'. As they entered more widespread use, the old round-bottomed cooking vessels began to be replaced by new ones with flat bases, including kettles, saucepans, boiling pots etc., which would stand much more securely on level hobs and firebars.

These technological developments formed only a part of a whole series of changes which transformed domestic life here in the nineteenth century. The building of the world's first steam locomotive by Richard Trevithick at Coalbrookdale in 1802 instigated an unimaginable transformation of many aspects of human life across the entire world. In Shropshire the arrival of the main railway line between 1848 and the 1860s revolutionised the transport of both goods and people. Coal, agricultural produce, and every other commodity could now be moved around the country much quicker and cheaper than ever before, promoting the development of every aspect of trade and industry, except for the rapidly superseded road, river and canal systems. As a result, all the larger towns sprouted industrial suburbs, with factories, workshops and workers' houses.

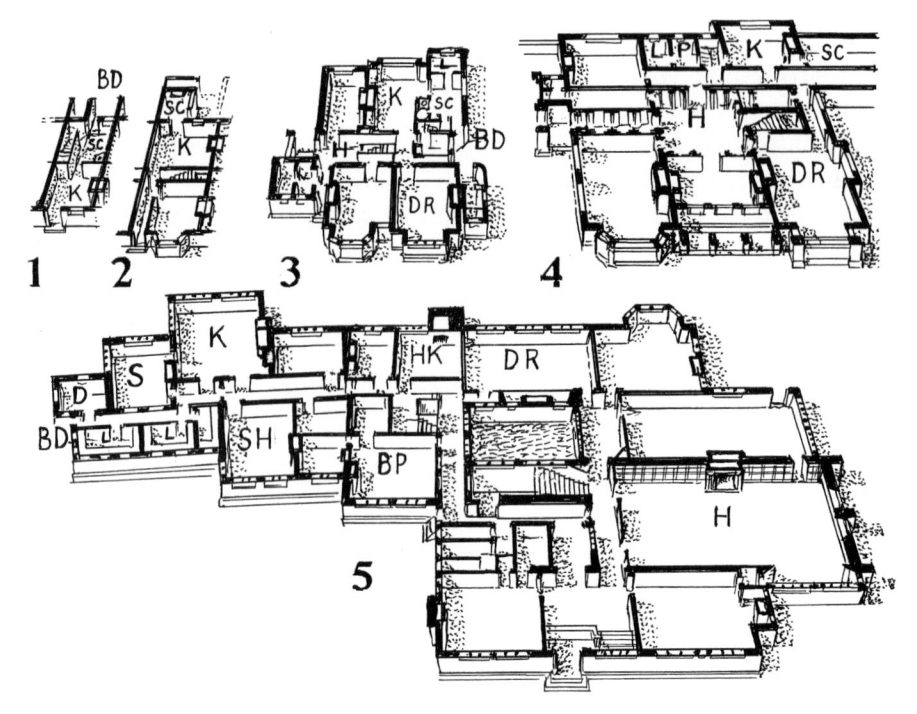

Fig 14 Victorian kitchens varied enormously according to the prosperity of their occupants. Here we can see, all drawn to the same scale:

1. 69-75 Trinity St. Shrewsbury 1878
2. 23 Cleveland Street, Shrewsbury 1881
3. 29 Kennedy Road, Shrewsbury, 1884
4. Lywyn House, Oswestry, 1860
5. Adcote Hall, 1879

BD – Back Door   BP – Butler's Pantry   D – Dairy   DR – Dining Room
H – Hall   K – Kitchen   P – Pantry   SC – Scullery   SH – Servants Hall

In contrast, the towns which had become prosperous as social centres and as overnight stops for long-distance travellers lost most of their prestigious and lucrative customers, who now only experienced the county from the windows of speeding railway carriages. The Talbot at Atcham declined from being a first-class coaching inn to a private house, its drive walled up and turfed over, food being now so scarce that 'even the last rat and mouse committed suicide in the Severn'. Similarly at The Lion in Shrewsbury, the great kitchens which 'once conveyed their abundant meals to a vanished population of John Bulls' were deserted, and the coach dining room converted into a billiard room.[39] Only the development of motorised transport after the Great War enabled such establishments to regain their original prosperity and high reputation. Outside the county, the massive railway-led expansion of cities such as Birmingham and Manchester brought with it such awful levels of pollution, disease and crime that those who could afford to do so retreated to the country, building new country houses and villas in Shropshire, where they still remain.

The new terraces, semi-detached villas and country houses built to accommodate Victorian Salopians are typical of those erected in most other parts of England. Each represents the relative wealth and social status of its intended occupant to a remarkably accurate degree, from tiny cottages with one living room/kitchen and a scullery for factory workers, through to great mansions with fifteen or more similar-sized or larger rooms in their kitchen wings alone, just to serve the needs of one wealthy family. Great attention was paid to producing the most efficient layout at every level, villas and country houses trying to shorten the distances between their kitchens and dining rooms, and keeping them on the same level, in order to ensure that all meals were served piping hot.

Within the larger kitchens, no expense was spared in providing cooks with every facility required to prepare the finest meals available in any part of the world. With its unprecedented wealth and access to different foods either home-produced or imported from Europe and the Empire, England produced food of the finest quality. If this should ever be doubted, just read through the menu reproduced on page 192–3. To prepare every elaborately cooked and garnished dish for a ten-course dinner in the fashionable *service à la Russe* demanded a considerable investment in ranges, stoves, ovens etc as well as in utensils and cookware. Here there would be none of the cast iron vessels cheaply cast in Coalbrookdale, but instead a complete *batterie de cuisine* of expensive hand-made tin-lined copperware probably purchased from one of the great London suppliers such as Jeakes' or Benham's. No better domestic kitchens have been set up either before or since, as may be seen in the following illustrations of the contents of Attingham Park's new kitchen, as set up in 1861.

SHROPSHIRE COOKBOOK

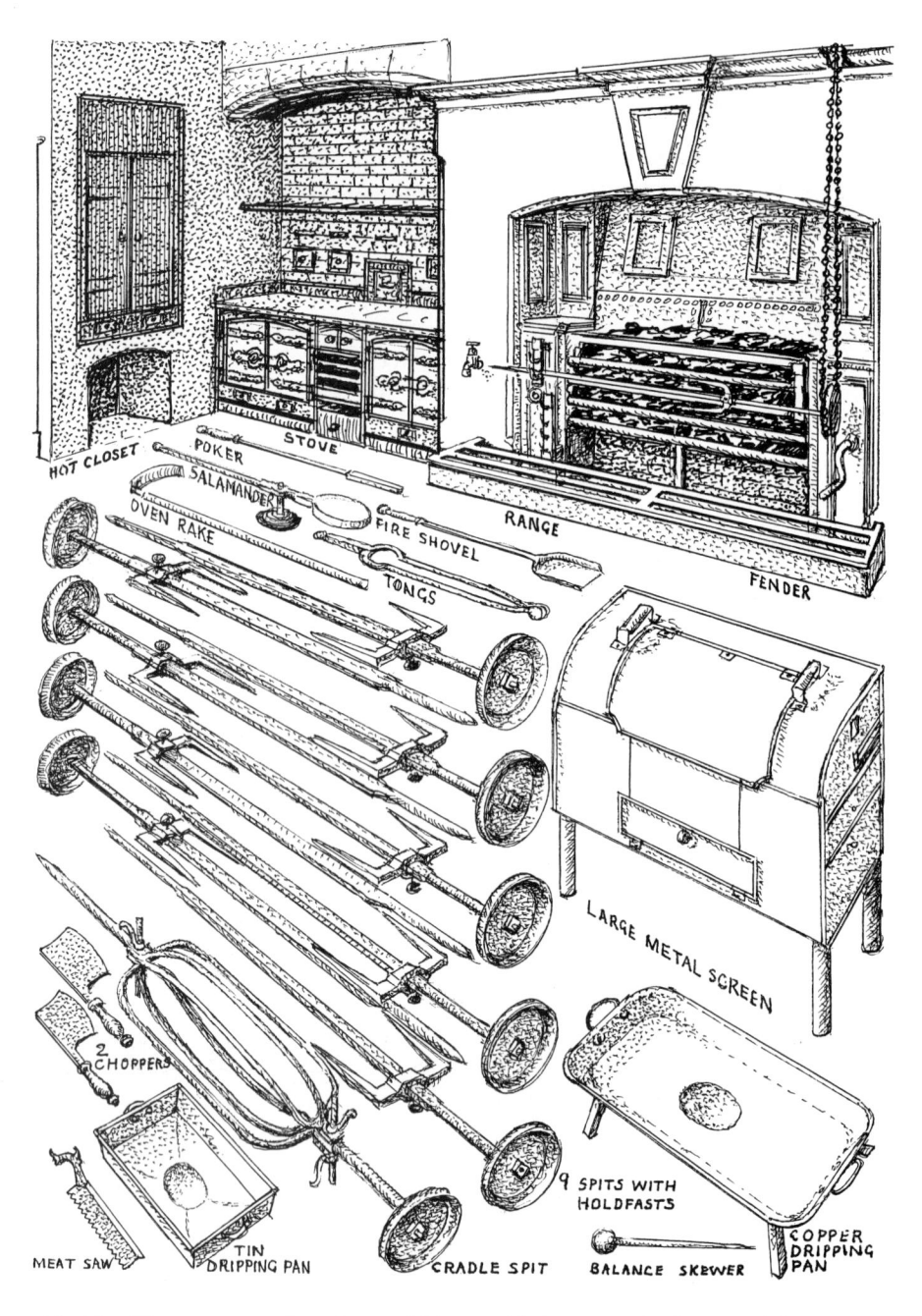

Fig 15   The contents of Lord Berwick's new kitchen at Attingham Park in 1861.

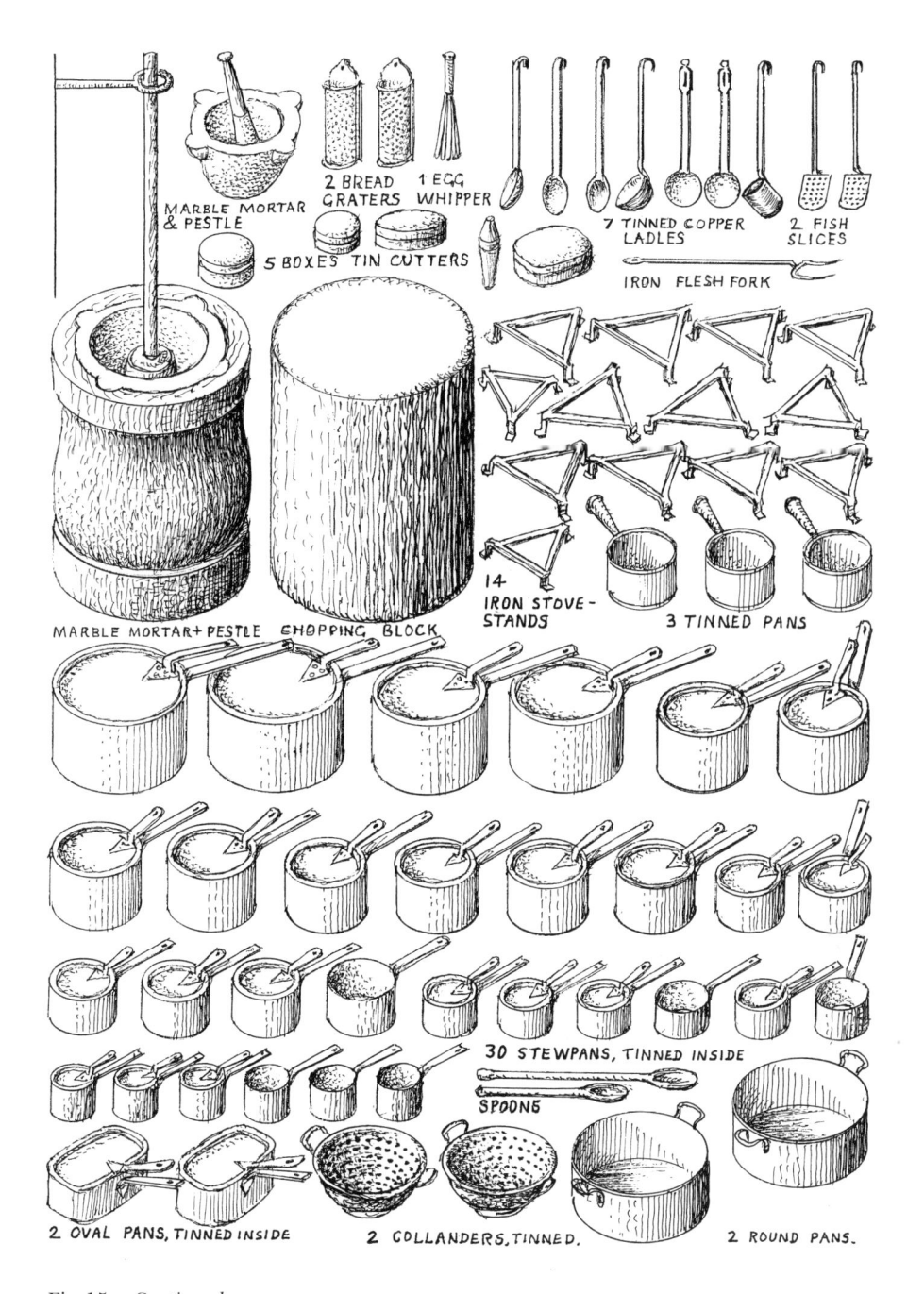

Fig 15   *Continued.*

SHROPSHIRE COOKBOOK

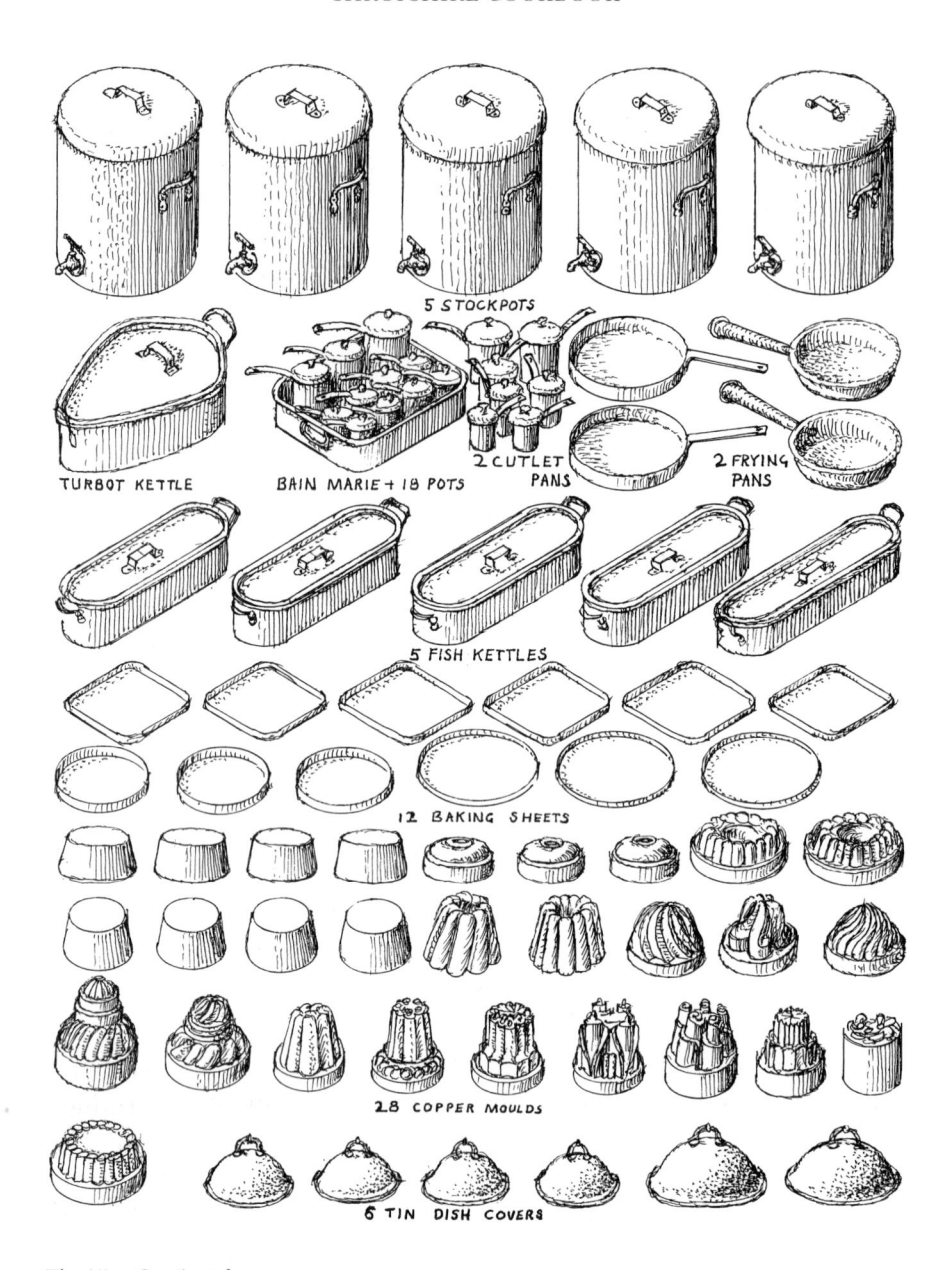

Fig 15 *Continued*.

CHAPTER 2

EVERYDAY FARE

Virtually every visitor to Shropshire over the last four hundred years has been impressed by its fertile countryside and prosperous market towns. It appeared to be a land flowing not only with milk and honey, but also with ample sources of meat, corn, fruit and vegetables. Although it was easy to see the vicious, crippling poverty of the distant industrial conurbations, and to understand how it came about, surely there could be nothing comparable here? In fact, rural poverty was just as prevalent, but much better hidden. The reasons for this were twofold. Firstly, the county's economy was led by agriculture, which meant that it was susceptible to the influences of everything from bad harvests to the effects of national/international trade and government legislation. Secondly, the purpose of farming was to produce income. Rents had to be paid, and so it was more important to sell food rather than to eat it. As Mrs Beguildy explained in *Precious Bane*, 'the mill's no place for good bread, no more than a farm's a place for good butter, seeing it means cash, and the home folk get the leavings. I've [not] any May butter, nor June nor July butter neither, when we sell every morsel of butter we make almost afore it be out of the churn, and never taste nought but lard!'[1]

The balance between having sufficient food and having virtually none had always been extremely close. Once the bulk of the produce had been sold off at the markets, only enough was retained to last through to the next harvest. If that harvest was late, however, or if it failed, the prices rose rapidly, leaving many of the ordinary people unable to buy in what they needed to sustain their families. In the late sixteenth century Richard Gardiner, a prosperous Shrewsbury dyer, anticipated their needs by pioneering the planting of vegetables as a field crop, rather than as garden produce. By growing four acres of carrots and cabbages, selling the latter at 6lb. for a penny, he was able to supply many hundreds of poor people for some three weeks when bread was in short supply before harvest.[2]

>The poore which late were like to pine,
>>and could not buy them bread;
>In greater time of penury,
>>were by his labours fed.
>And that in reasonable rate,
>>when Corne and coin was scant
>With Parsnep and with Carret rootes
>>he did supply their want.

Over the following centuries the lack of such arrangements led to food riots. In April, 1693, even after two bad harvests, there was still corn to be found in Bridgnorth. One Francis Oakes was holding twelve tons in his house, ready for delivery to London, for example, while wagon-loads and pack-horse loads were still coming into the markets for sale to visiting merchants who could pay the high prices. This proved too much for the local poor and hungry to bear, so they just took what they needed, robbing the wagons and slitting the pack-horse sacks, carrying off what they could in their aprons.[3] A similar situation arose in the south-eastern mining district in November 1756. In Wellington 'The great Price of Corn in these parts has almost starved the Colliers and Common People, who have

Fig 16 Paul Sandby's view of Bridgnorth shows ox-wagons loading sacks of grain into a Severn trow which has probably just brought a mixed cargo up from Bristol and Gloucester.

actually eaten nothing but Greens and salt for many Days. To endure hunger is terrible when our great Farmers' Barns and Yards abound with Corn, and the Colliers last week have rose in great Bodies and ransacked Towns around us.' At Much Wenlock, they forced the farmers to reduce the prices of wheat and butter by about a quarter, but even this was not enough. Over a three day period the mob attacked Shifnal, Broseley and Wellington, breaking into shops and houses and stripping them of all bacon, butter, cheese, grain and flour. It was only suppressed when the local gentry assembled a force of fifteen hundred armed farmers, tenants, servants and townsmen, who dispersed the rioters and seized their ringleaders, who were then committed to Shrewsbury Gaol.[4] In October 1782 rioting broke out in the Wednesbury and Stourbridge area, again prompted by the unaffordably high price of grain, but this time the local establishment was able to maintain control through a combination of force and relief. A troop of mounted soldiery was sent for, a number of ale-houses closed down, and a subscription raised to purchase a supply of flour and rice from Liverpool, this being protected by armed guards as it was brought in by barge on the canal. In July 1795 it was realised that there was insufficient grain left in Shropshire to feed the population through to harvest time, and so subscriptions were raised to reduce its price, and to bring in large additional quantities from Liverpool, as before. Some impression of the severity of the situation may be gained from the fact that the leading local gentry, iron companies and iron masters paid subscriptions of 100 guineas each in order to retain the peace. The only riot to break out was quickly suppressed by the Wrekin Company of the Shropshire Yeomanry Cavalry at Madeley Wood. The following years of 1796 and 1800 brought even more severe problems, with the major subscribers donating up to £1500 or even £2000, massive sums for that period, to provide sufficient food for the working population.[5]

It was about this time that the grandfather of Mr John Bowen of St. Mary's Place, Shrewsbury, remembered seeing a strange sight at the market. There members of the county families were standing on a balcony on the front of the Raven Inn, all eating potatoes. In this way they hoped to show that this new food was not only safe to eat, but also fit to be eaten by the gentry.[6] In the event, any misgivings were soon dispelled by necessity, as for many families there was now nothing else to eat. Between 1790 and 1803 rural wages had risen by almost 70%, but what use was this when food prices had risen by

400%? In addition, the 1790s had seen great rises in rents for the ordinary cottagers, Prees finding that instead of paying ten shillings a year, they now had to pay £4. As a result, they, along with numerous others in similar circumstances elsewhere, had to sell their hay to pay the rent, which meant that they could no longer feed their pigs, their major source of meat. After the end of the Napoleonic Wars in 1815, it got even worse, as wages dropped by a third. Throughout rural Shropshire many families were reduced to a diet of bread, potatoes and a little cheese, on which they were expected to give the same work-output as before.[7] Even more distressing, this was not a short term problem, but one which, along with mud-walled cottages, survived throughout the nineteenth century.

In addition to providing food-relief from subscriptions, attempts were made to improve the lives of the working populations by encouraging them to become more self-sufficient and better cooks. A society with these objectives was set up in Oswestry in 1812, when 'much of the corn yielded but an unwholesome and scarcely eatable bread; trade suddenly checked and the prices of home produce lowered in the markets exceedingly', while there was also 'a sudden discharge of many from great manufactories'. The society offered cash prizes to individuals who saved part of their income, kept the neatest cottages and gardens, or designed improved cottages, and it also set up an insurance scheme for cottagers' house-cows. It strongly recommended the growing of onions, carrots, parsnips, cabbages, parsley, thyme, sweet marjoram, rosemary, mint and savory in cottage gardens, but rather interestingly, it omitted potatoes. These were still a relatively unusual crop here, but, along with rice, they were being introduced to supplement the traditional diet in order to prevent people relying on 'rambling about the county in the illegal employment of beggary, or in quest of the precarious and scanty assistance of the Parish' in order to feed themselves.[8]

Contemporary working housewives 'had no notion of using rice or anything else in place of bread, and indeed would not do so if it were recommended to her.'[9] To remedy this attitude, the Oswestry society published *The Family Receipt Book or the Cottager's Cook, Doctor and Friend* in 1817. Having stated that rice contained six times as much nourishment as wheat (an absurdly optimistic claim) it went on to give instructions for stewing rice with bacon, meat or cheese, or making;

MACARONI RICE[10]

1lb/450g rice
5pt/3l cold water
2pt/1·2l milk

2oz/50g strong Cheshire cheese
salt and pepper

Boil the rice in the water for 2 hours, add the milk, finely-grated cheese and seasoning, and boil for a further hour to give 9lb/4kg macaroni rice.

SWEET RICE PUDDING[11]

As above, but replacing the cheese, salt and pepper with 4oz/100g black treacle.

As for potatoes, these were to be plain boiled, and then perhaps sliced and fried in butter before being served with salt and pepper. They could also make;

BAKED POTATO PUDDING[12]

1lb/450g mashed potato
1oz/25g suet

1oz/25g grated cheese
2tbs milk

Mix all the ingredients, [with a little salt & pepper], pack into an earthenware baking dish, and bake at 170°C, 325°F, Gas mark 3 for about 30 minutes.

Another newly introduced vegetable was the Swedish turnip, or swede, which was to be simply boiled, drained, and mashed with a little skim milk and either salt or brown sugar.[13]

Even when times were not particularly hard, the everyday meals in most Shropshire homes were relatively plain and simple, but still quite healthy, and apparently capable of supporting notable longevity. Thomas Parr was born at Winnington, Alberbury, in 1483, worked as an agricultural labourer, married first at eighty and secondly at a hundred and twenty, before dying at the age of one hundred and fifty-two in 1635. John Taylor, the Water Poet, described his diet in the following lines;[14]

> He was of old Pythagoras' opinion
> That green cheese was most wholesome (with an onion),
> Coarse Meslin bread: and for his daily swig,
> Milk, butter-Milk and Water, Whey and Whig'
> Sometimes Metheglin, and by fortune happy,
> He sometimes sipp'd a Cup of Ale most nappy,
> Cider or Perry when he did repair
> T'a Whitsun Ale, Wake, Wedding or Fair,
> Or when at Christmas time he was a Guest
> At his good Land-lord's house amongst the rest ...
> His physic was good butter which the soil of Salop
>   yields ... more sweet than Candy oil.

This represents the kind of 'white-food', dairy-based diet common to many English labourers of the medieval period. In addition, we might expect other basics such as porridge, vegetables, bacon and offal to remain staples up to around 1800, after which the keeping of a pig differentiated between well-off and poverty-stricken families. Whenever a sow farrowed, one or two would be kept for fattening, the rest sold either to others for the same purpose, or to the gentry to roast as sucking pigs. After a pig-killing, meanwhile, the hams and sometimes even the bacon-sides were usually sold as a cash-crop, the head and offal being retained for home consumption. In this it followed the common practice of selling off the best home-produced foods, and living off whatever remained.

As to meals, these were three each day, breakfast in the early morning, dinner probably after finishing work in the afternoon, and supper taken in the evening, before going to bed. Then as now, their contents would vary from one home to another. At one farm, the cow-man's breakfast was sufficiently large to draw the comment that he was 'a rar' cratcher (a big eater), whad'n 'ee think 'e put out o' sight this mornin'? – first 'e ate a cantle o' suppin (a can of milk and water porridge), then a 'eeler (a heel of crisp crust) o' bread an' cheese, an after that a apple-fut, rump an' stump.'[15] Most had just oatmeal or oat and barley meal porridge, or a meaty broth thickened with either oatmeal or flour.[16] For the womenfolk, there was apparently a hierarchy of breakfast dishes, each marking their place in society;[17]

> Dame an' porridge,
> Missis an' broth,
> Madam an' tay

The men were more interested in the quality of what they received, sometimes complaining of their porridge that;[18]

> It's saut, sour and salty,
> Thick growed, an' lumpy,
> Like the Devil's own porritch.'

The contents of the broth, hopefully from boiled meat in a farmhouse, was of great importance; 'The Missis come i' the kitchen to get the chap's breakfast, an' 'er took water an' bacon liquor (i.e. fat from the frying pan) an' brathed it ooth (i.e. thickened it with) flour; but the chaps they couldna bare it, an' my brother 'e comen wham!' Brewis might also be served, just sliced bread scalded with boiling water, with a lump of butter, a shred of onion, and pepper and salt stirred in.[19] Up to the late eighteenth-early nineteenth century these were usually served in wooden bowls called piggins, which were soon replaced by coarse glazed earthenware mugs called pollingers; to 'Always bread the men's pollingers, an' put the bread an' cheese o' the table o'er night' was good practice in many busy farms. By the mid nineteenth century ordinary white factory-made earthenware basins had been adopted as the usual bowl for eating breakfast.[20]

Outdoor meals taken during the working day were called either noon-spell or four-o'clock, depending on the approximate times at which they took place.[21] They were usually quite simple, comprising bread, cheese and beer. Various types of bread were made in the county, including the oatcake now usually associated with Staffordshire and Derbyshire. To make this a backstone, originally a fireproof stone slab, but later a circular iron plate we would now call a girdle, was supported over the range on a stand called either a maid or a lazyback.[22] Once lightly greased and heated through, a yeasted oatmeal batter was poured onto its surface, as described in the following Shropshire recipe of the 1830s – 40s;

OAT CAKES[23]

1lb/450g fine oatmeal   1 tsp sugar
1pt/600ml water at 37°C,   1 tsp dried yeast
  100°F

Sift the oatmeal into a bowl, and make a well in the centre. Dissolve the sugar and yeast in the water and mix in the oatmeal from the sides to form a smooth batter. Cover, and leave in a warm place for an hour to ferment.

Heat the backstone until a little flour sprinkled on it slowly browns, rather than smoulders, then wipe it clean, and lightly grease with a little butter wrapped in muslin.

If necessary, add a little more warm water to the batter to produce a pouring consistency, and pour a large circle onto the bakestone. Once its upper surface has dried off and set, and the edges have risen up, a spatula should be passed beneath it, and the oatcake turned over to cook on its underside. Finally remove on to a clean cloth, and leave to cool. As with many apparently straightforward recipes, the baking of oatcakes benefits from long practice.

The ordinary household bread used in the county up to the mid nineteenth century was made of muncorn, a wholemeal blend of wheat and rye which had been grown and ground together. It had a good flavour, and did not go stale so quickly as white bread. The following recipe probably has less rye than the original loaves, but gives good results;

MUNCORN BREAD[24]

10oz/275g strong wholewheat flour
2oz/50g rye meal
1 tsp dried yeast
8fl.oz/240ml tepid water
1 tsp salt
1 tsp sugar

Mix the flour, meal and salt, make a well in the centre, and pour in the yeast and sugar beaten into the water, stir in the flour from the sides, then turn onto a floured board and knead for 5 minutes. Place in a bowl, cover, and leave in a warm place until doubled in volume.

Turn out onto the board and knead again, then place either on a greased baking sheet or a 1·5l capacity tin, cover and return to the warm until it has risen once more. Bake at 230°C, 450°F, Gas mark 8 for 15 minutes, then reducing to 190°C, 375°F, Gas mark 5 for a further 15 minutes and finally (having removed it from the tin, if used) for 15 minutes more at 170°C, 330°F, Gas mark 3, before removing and leaving to cool.

This was probably identical to 'Brown George', the name given to the coarsest local brown bread.[25] Wheatmeal and white breads would also be home-baked, using recipes common to the rest of the country. In farmhouses they usually took the form of cottage loaves, with a large round loaf topped by a smaller one. Single loaves, meanwhile, were called 'batch cakes', these being useful to supply household needs before it was necessary to cut into a new cottage loaf. Coal cakes were much smaller, being quickly cooked at the mouth of the oven, before the loaves were placed within it. Eaten hot with a lump of butter, they made an excellent treat for everyone present at that time.[26]

In Ludlow there was also a tradition of making small white rolls called either can-doughs or whitecakes. In the nineteenth century they were oblong, in the 1930s long diamonds with blunt corners, and by the late 1980s oval or bridge-roll shaped, and dusted with flour. Made by bakers such as Harris at 6 Church Street in the 1870s, Henry Tantrum in the early twentieth century, and Gerald Preece, who was producing a hundred dozen every weekend in the 1980s, they were usually eaten at breakfast. Having been re-heated to crisp their crusts, they were split open longways, a knob of butter put inside, and re-closed to allow it to soak into the soft crumb. Only then could they be re-opened for the insertion of marmalade or jam just before being eaten.[27] Whatever the size and shape of the loaves, they had to be marked with the sign of the cross in order to avoid witchcraft. Some did this with a fork, but around Pulverbatch and Ruyton it had to be done with a skewer, for;[28]

> She that pricks bread with fork or knife
> Will never be happy, maid or wife.

For those without an oven, some early forms of baking continued well into the nineteenth century. Pot cakes, for example, were loaves baked in a cooking pot hung over the fire, while scratching cakes, made by mixing crisp pork scratchings with flour and water and rolling out to one inch./2·5cm thick, could be baked either in a pot, on a backstone, or in a conventional oven. They formed part of a group of crock or flead cakes, as made in Dorset, Surrey, and other parts of the country.[29]

Where an oven was available, it was of the traditional 'beehive' type. Its masonry dome had a flat floor at table-height, and a single doorway for access, this usually being set within one side of a wide fireplace in order to carry away the smoke. It would be heated by using a long-handled iron-pronged fire-fork to thrust a burning faggot as far back into it as possible, so that its flames licked the underside of the dome before issuing from the door. When it was sufficiently hot, a ling broom, called a 'grig-besom' was used to sweep out the embers, this being followed by a wet oven mop called a malkin; 'I like a grig-besom fur sweepin' the embers out o' the oven, an' then a clane mauken to finish op 'ooth'.[30] The bread was then inserted on a long-handled oven-slice called a peel, the doorway sealed with a wooden or iron door, and then left to bake in the remaining heat. This method gave excellent results, but was time consuming, introduced unwelcome dirt into the kitchen, and was an intermittent rather than a continuous process. For these reasons most 'beehive' ovens fell out of use once ranges with fire-side ovens became available in cottages.

It might be thought that, as today, baking in ovens was always a relatively safe practice, but this certainly was not the case in the past. The obvious problem was the provision and storage of fuel, which, if accidentally ignited, could lead to the destruction of entire houses, their contents, and potentially their inhabitants. In 1558, for example, a terrible fire had swept through parts of Shrewsbury. To avoid this happening again, the corporation ordered that great quantities of gorse and broom faggots should no longer be stored in, or within sixty yards of any house, except those required for immediate use, twenty for a baker's oven, and six for all others.[31]

Sometimes the fuel could prove to be even more dangerous, as one Reece of Haremeare found to his cost. He had developed a bad reputation for petty theft, and particularly for damaging his neighbour's hedges by taking their wood to fire his oven. Richard Mercer, being 'a very waggish fellow' therefore bored a hole in one of his hedge-stakes, filled it with gunpowder, stopped it with a peg, and set it in place. Sure enough, Reece stole it and thrust it in his oven, the ensuing explosion blasting out the top of the dome and setting fire to the end of his house. Hideous cries of 'Fire! Fire!' brought Mercer and his master not only to inspect the damage, but apparently to present a show of innocent surprise. Presumably their hedges suffered fewer depredations over the following years.[32]

The main meal of the day, usually taken after everyone had returned home from work, was dinner. Here the medieval tradition of having a broth stewed in the pot over the fire continued well into the nineteenth century, before transforming itself into soups. If resources allowed, joints of meat would be cooked in the pot, then removed with an iron flesh-fork, and allowed to rest a short while in order to become firm enough to be carved at the table. In the meantime the broth, appropriately enriched with chopped vegetables and seasoned with herbs, salt and pepper, could be either eaten as a starter, or reserved for next day's breakfast. The next two versions of 1817 come from Oswestry;[33]

BEEF POTTAGE ($\frac{1}{4}$ recipe, 6 pints for 5 people)

12oz/325g shin beef or similar *2oz/50g bacon rashers*
1lb/450g pearl barley *2oz/50g onion, sliced*
1½lb/675g potatoes *2oz/50g leeks, sliced*
1 tsp parsley or thyme *1 tsp salt*

Simmer the meat in $5\frac{1}{2}$pt/3·5l water for 2 hours, add the remaining ingredients, and simmer for a further 4 hours.

BAKED SOUP

1lb/450g sliced meat *1pt/600ml peas*
2 onions, sliced *pepper & salt to taste*
2 carrots, sliced

Put all the ingredients into a large casserole with 8pts/4·8l water, and bake at 170°C, 325°F, Gas mark 3 for about 2 hours.

The following recipe was clearly designed to form a rabbit into the ideal shape for cooking in a pot hung over the fire;

SAVOURY RABBIT[34]

1 cleaned rabbit
8oz/225g fresh white breadcrumbs
1 onion, very finely chopped
1 tbs sage, finely chopped
1 tbs plain flour
½ tsp salt
⅛ tsp ground pepper
8oz/225g sliced bacon
3–4 tbs milk

Mix the breadcrumbs, onion, sage, salt and pepper with 3–4 tbs milk, to form a forcemeat.

Form the rabbit into a round shape, passing a skewer through the front and back legs to hold it in position. Pack the forcemeat inside, pushing it up the chest and down into the pelvis, and filling up the whole body, while leaving a hole through the middle. Secure the flesh of the flanks across the top and bottom of the forcemeat, to enclose it as completely

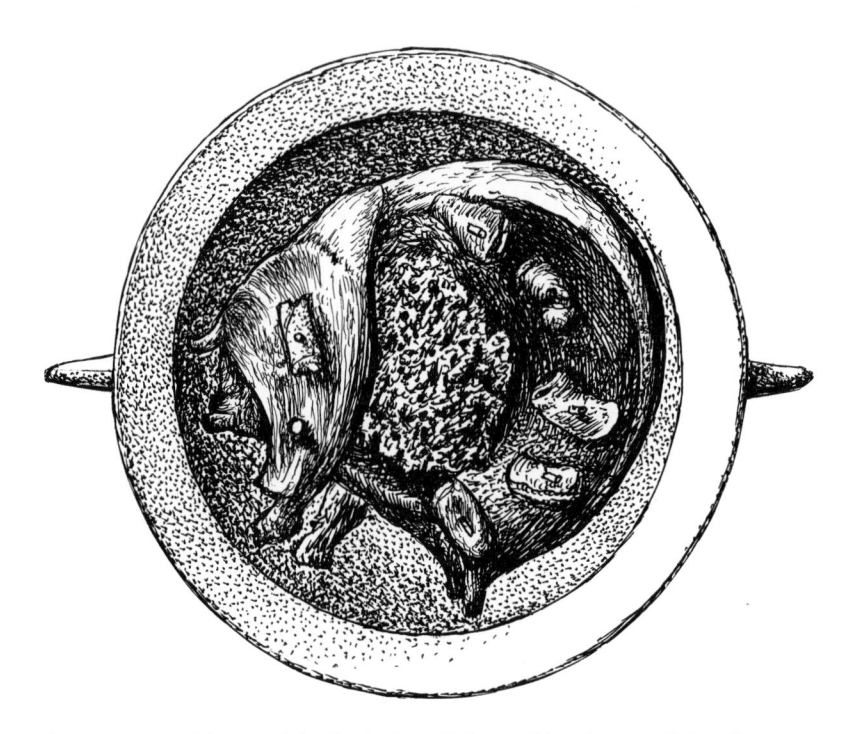

Fig 17   Savoury rabbit was ideally designed for cooking in a traditional cast metal pot.

as possible. Fold each slice of bacon into a neat zig-zag, pass a skewer through to hold it in place, and stick them into the top of the rabbit.

Place a couple of wooden rods across the bottom of a large casserole, place the rabbit on top, then pour in the milk with sufficient water added to come half-way up the rabbit. Put on the lid and bake at 150°C, 350°F, Gas mark 4 for some 2 hours until tender, having removed the lid for the last 20 min.

Lift the rabbit out onto a hot dish, mix the flour to a smooth paste with a little cold water, stir into the remaining stock, bring to the boil while stirring, pour over the rabbit, and serve hot.

Very similar dishes were still popular in the twentieth century, continuing this long-tradition. It is an excellent way of preparing hot, satisfying and economical dinners with minimum effort.[35]

MUTTON SOUP (for 6 people)

1¼ lb/550g fat mutton *1 small turnip*
7 potatoes *3oz/75g split peas*
8 onions *½ tsp chopped thyme*
1 stick celery *½ tsp chopped marjoram*
1 tsp salt, pinch of pepper

Chop the mutton very finely, and the other vegetables coarsely, and simmer all but the herbs for 2 hours, in 10pt/6l water. Stir in the herbs, and continue to simmer for a further 30 minutes before serving.

SHEEP'S HEAD BROTH

1 sheep's head, briefly scalded, or clipped-closely and singed, to remove the wool, and then scrubbed clean
1 onion *1 bayleaf*
1 clove *1 hard-boiled egg*
few pieces macaroni *1 carrot, pre-cooked & diced*

Put the head in a large pan of cold water with the onion, clove, macaroni and bayleaf, cover and simmer for 6 hours. Skim off the fat and stir in the carrot and egg, just before serving with toast, and a white sauce.

[if preferred, the meat could be stripped from the head, cut in squares, and layered with sliced hard-boiled eggs and mushrooms in a pie dish, covered with the reduced stock, and baked under a pastry crust].

RABBIT SOUP

1 rabbit, prepared and jointed
1lb/450g shin beef, chopped small
3oz/75g bacon, chopped small
1 small onion
1 clove
2oz/50g flour
¼pt/150ml milk
salt & pepper to taste

Put the rabbit, beef, bacon, onion and clove into a pan, cover with boiling water, and simmer gently for 30 minutes. Remove the rabbit joints, trim all the meat from the bones (easier done now than when raw), chop it in small pieces, and return to the pan. Continue simmering for a further 45 minutes until all the meat is tender, then beat the milk into the flour, stir into the soup, season to taste, and bring to the boil, stirring continuously until it has thickened.

Other soups relied largely on vegetables.

ONION SOUP

4 large onions, sliced
2oz/50g dripping
2–3pts/1·2–1·8l vegetable stock, cabbage water or milk
salt & pepper
1 tbs grated Cheshire cheese
a few pieces of stale bread

Melt the dripping in a large saucepan, add the onions, cover, and leave on a very low heat for an hour until cooked down, but not burnt. Stir in the stock, bread, and seasoning, cover, and simmer gently for 1 hour before rubbing through a sieve, boiling up once more, and stirring in the cheese just before serving.

POTATO SOUP

1lb/450g potatoes, diced
1 head celery, diced
1 large onion, chopped small

1pt/600ml vegetable or chicken stock
½pt/300ml milk
salt & pepper to taste

Simmer the vegetables in the stock for 30 minutes until tender, rub through a sieve, return to the pan with the milk, season to taste, bring to the boil, and serve with diced toast. 1 tbs cornflour may be beaten into a little of the milk before it is added, to produce a smoother soup.

GREEN PEA SOUP

2lb/900g peas/pea pods
1 tsp sugar
5fl.oz/150ml single cream

2 large sprigs fresh mint, chopped
salt & pepper
1 tsp dried mint

Boil the peas and pods in 2pts/1·2l water for about 30 minutes until tender, then drain (retaining the stock), rub through a sieve, and return to the stock with the cream, fresh mint, and seasoning to taste. Bring almost back to the boil, and serve sprinkled with the dry mint.

In this great dairying county, it is not surprising to find recipes for milk and cheese soup, which could be made in a few minutes;

MILK & CHEESE SOUP

1½pts/900ml milk
1½tbs butter
1½tbs flour

4 oz/100g grated Cheshire cheese
salt & pepper
1 slice fried bread, drained

Melt the butter in a saucepan, stir in the flour until absorbed, but not browned, then the milk little by little, until it is all in.

Bring to the boil while stirring, remove from the heat, and stir in the cheese just before serving with the bread.

Following the broth or soup came the boiled or roast joint, if one could be afforded. This was usually a Sunday dinner speciality, after which it provided a whole series of meals throughout the coming week;

> SUNDAY Is a feast day boasted;
>   I like a leg of mutton roasted.
> MONDAY I my taste to tickle,
>   eat it cold with Indian Pickle.
> TUESDAY Hash it and gravy make;
>   then sippets round a dish are laid.
> WEDNESDAY Boil, and with due care,
>   some mashed potatoes I prepare.
> THURSDAY I make a savoury pie;
>   or else some slices nicely fry.
> FRIDAY I proclaim a fast,
>   in order for to make it last.
> SATURDAY When cash runs narrow,
>   I crack the bones and eat the marrow.
> And then that none is thrown away,
> the rest I mean to give to my dog Tay.

Local varieties of shepherd's pie were ideal for using up the remains of the joint, this one coming from Mrs E. Batho of Moreton Villas, Whittington;

MONDAY PIE[36]

1 small onion, chopped
2oz/50g mushrooms, sliced
½oz/12g dripping
1lb/450g cooked lamb, minced
½ tsp Worcester sauce
½pt/300ml gravy or stock
1lb/450g mashed potatoes
1 egg, beaten
salt & pepper

Fry the onion and mushrooms in the dripping until cooked, then mix with everything except the potatoes and egg. Place in an ovenproof dish, cover with the potatoes, roughing their top with a fork, brush with the egg, and bake at 200°C, 400°F, Gas mark 6 for 40 minutes.

All of the dishes described above would be accompanied by boiled vegetables. In the medieval period most people appear to have plain-boiled them, only then draining and chopping them for addition to the stocks in which meat had been boiled. The idea of cooking vegetables and meat together, the classic English stew or casserole, was only introduced from France in late Elizabethan and Jacobean times. Writing around 1600, the aptly-named Richard Gardiner of Shrewsbury still considered that carrots were to be used in flavouring and enriching broths from which the meat had already been removed. However, he also saw their potential for being boiled with salt beef, where they would absorb the excessive saltiness, and also being cooked, left to chill, and served as a vinegared and peppered salad to accompany roast meats. His is probably the best description of how carrots were then being used in both peasant and polite households;[37]

> The better sort of Cookes will take Carrots devided in peeces and boile them in season their stewed broth and doth wonderfull well therein as dayly is known in service to the better sort. Also Carret rootes are boiled with powdered beefe, and eaten therewith; and as some doe report a fewe Carrets do save one quarter of beefe in the eating of the whole beefe; and to be boyled and eaten with Porke, and all other boiled meat of flesh amongst the common sort of peoples, & amongst the poorer sort also; Carrots of red colours are desired of many to make dainty sallets for roast Mutton or Lambe with Vinegar and Pepper. Also Carrets shred or cut small, one or two of them, and boiled in pottage of any kinde, doth effectually make these pottage good for use of the common sort.

He then describes how both the long yellow carrot and the great short carrot are far superior to the small, long, pale yellow common or wild carrot, only the red apparently being reserved for salads. As for other vegetables, he recommended the use of the following, described in verse by Edward Thorne;[38]

> Of carrots first, and Cabbage close
>   And how to keepe them sound;
> And Parsnip's also to preserve,
>   And turnip's fair and round.
> Of Lettice next and garden Beanes
>   And onions of the best;
> Of Cucumbers and Artichokes
>   And Radish with the rest.

> These and such other hearbes and seedes
>   hath Gardner, in good will;
> Unto Sallopian neighbours he's
>   entreated of with skill.

The same vegetables, along with field-beans, peas, and later the potatoes and Swedish turnips introduced around 1800, all remained in constant use through to modern times, either on their own, or forming a part of a meat or vegetable dish. Some of the ways in which potatoes were cooked have already been described, the following recipes showing how other crops were cooked in the county.

PEAS & CARROTS[39]

8oz/225g par-boiled carrots   *1 tbs flour*
8oz/225g par-boiled peas   *1 tbs dripping*

Chop the carrots into pea-sized cubes, mix with the peas in a pan, and almost cover with the waters in which they were par-boiled. Melt the dripping in a separate small pan, add the flour, with a little salt and pepper, and stir together over a gentle heat until cooked, but not browned. Bring the peas and carrots to the boil, stir in the contents of the smaller pan, simmer for 10 minutes, stirring as it thickens, and then serve.

MASHED SWEDE[40]

Cut the pared swede into large pieces, cover with water and boil for some 20 minutes until tender, then drain, mash with a little milk, and either salt or brown sugar to taste.

BRAISED SWEDE[41]

Cut the pared swede into four, put into a baking dish or casserole with about ½ins/12mm water, and rashers of bacon on top, cover and cook at 190°C, 375°F, Gas mark 5 for about an hour, until tender, then drain, and dish with the bacon.

SAVOURY CABBAGE[42]

½ a cabbage, boiled
2–3 carrots, boiled
4 rashers bacon
bacon fat or butter

Mix the vegetables on a board and chop them together finely, seasoning them with a little salt and pepper. Fry the bacon in a large frying pan, then remove it, and stir-fry the vegetables in the remaining fat, supplementing it with more bacon fat or butter as necessary. Just as they start to brown, turn the vegetables into a hot bowl, top with the bacon, and serve.

ONION DUMPLINGS[43]

For each dumpling take;

1 onion, peeled
4oz/100g plain flour
1oz/25g dripping
salt & pepper

Rub the dripping into the flour, work in 3–4 tbs cold water with a round-bladed knife, and knead to form a large circle. Dust this with salt and ground black pepper, place the onion in the middle, totally enclose it within the pastry, and tie in a freshly rinsed and squeezed piece of muslin, some 18ins/45cm square. Plunge into a deep pan of boiling water, cover, and boil for some 45–50 minutes until the onion is tender when tried with a skewer. As it cooks, top up the water as required.

Many of the dinner-time foods described above could be found in other Midland counties, but there were two others, for which Shropshire was pre-eminent, and these were bacon and offal. When Arthur Young visited Coalbrookdale in 1776 he had found that 'There was not a single cottage in which a fine hog did not seem to make a part of every family; not a door without a stone trough with a pig eating his supper'.[44] Similarly in 1803 the Rev. Plymley noted that Shropshire labourers kept pigs, but since some now bought ready-milled flour or ready-made bread, instead of wheat, they had lost the bran on which to fatten them.[45] Even so, pig-breeding remained popular at all levels of society. It was by no accident that P.G. Wodehouse set *Pigs have Wings* in this county, with its account of the triumph of *The Empress of Blandings* over Matchingham's *Queen* as winner of the top prize for a Fat Pig at the Shropshire Show.[46] In fact, the pig here approaches deification, appearing on the altar rail from the old screen at Llanvairwaterdine church, with St. Anthony in a sixteenth century window in Munslow church, or with the Prodigal Son on the reading desk at Atcham church.[47]

Great care had to be taken when killing a pig, for if the moon was on the wane, the bacon would shrink and lose all its fat when boiled, and so an almanac had to be consulted beforehand.[48] Immediately after being 'strucken', the carcase was hung up and cleaned using two quite different techniques. In the north of the county it was scalded, scraped and hung up by the heels on a bar called a gambrel, with its back to the wall. In contrast, those in the south and east lay the pig in straw, set fire to it to remove the bristles, and then hung up by its nose, the belly towards the wall.[49]

As it bled, the blood was carefully collected and stirred to reduce clotting in readiness for making black hog's puddings. In the early eighteenth century these were made to the following recipe;

BLACK HOG'S PUDDINGS[50]

4pt/2·4l strained blood
6lb/2·7 kilo cooked pig fat,
  cubed
6pt/3·6l pinhead oatmeal,
  soaked overnight

2 leeks, very finely shredded
salt and pepper
cleaned small intestine
pennyroyal & thyme, finely
  chopped

Having been mixed together, this was packed loosely into the small intestines, made up into links, and gently simmered for an hour.

The innards of all farmed beasts enjoyed considerable popularity, Mary Webb describing the scenes she knew so well in Shrewsbury market, but have now disappeared completely 'Men shouted stentoriously, brandishing stained carving knives; an unbearable stench arose from the offal, and women with pretty clothes and refined manners bought the guts of animals under such names as "sweetbreads", or "prime fat kidneys", and thrust their hands into the disembowelled bodies of rabbits to test their freshness'.[51] Somehow, the modern equivalent of checking the sell-by date gives not quite the same experience. Some of the pig's offal had simply to be washed and boiled to make it palatable. Chopped lengths of small intestine called chitterlings pre-prepared in this way could be nibbled with mustard and vinegar, fried as a supper dish, or cooked with onions; 'Mary [ate] pig's chitterlings and onions, As nobody thought of chitterlings with anything but respect, nobody thought Marigold was doing violence to her beauty.'[52] Large chitterlings might also be finely minced with boiled groats, small pieces of pork fat, finely minced sweet herbs, currants, sugar and spices, packed into large skins, and boiled for twenty minutes, to appear as white puddings.

The combination of heart, liver and lights (lungs), with the windpipe, collectively known as the fry, was simply boiled to form men's dinners around Pulverbatch and Clun, but it was more usual to mince them, season them with herbs etc., and bake them into a rounded meat-loaf called harslet, ideal for slicing when cold.[53] This is still made by many local butchers and is of excellent quality. Alternatively the fry could be made into;

SHROPSHIRE FAGGOTS[54]

1lb/450g pig's fry
3 onions, sliced small
3oz/75g fresh breadcrumbs
  or mashed potatoes
1 pig's caul
salt & pepper

Soak the caul in tepid water, and the bread-crumbs in a little stock, before squeezing dry.

Mince the fry and the onions, season with salt and pepper, and place spoonfuls in the centre of 4 inch/10cm squares of caul. Fold them up, pack closely together in a baking tin, and cook at 190°C, 375°F, Gas mark 5 for some 30 minutes until cooked through.

These are very plain faggots however, those currently sold by the present day butchers usually being of a richer and more highly seasoned mixture. As for the kidneys, they formed the basis of;

HEART AND KIDNEY PUDDING[55]

8oz/225g self-raising flour *2 pig's kidneys*
4oz/100g suet *salt & pepper*
1 pig's heart

Mix the flour, suet and ½ tsp salt, and use a round-bladed knife to work in about ¼pt/150ml cold water to produce a light, elastic dough. Knead lightly, and use two-thirds to line a 1½pt/900ml pudding basin.

Cut the heart and kidneys into small pieces, removing the 'deaf ears' (valves), skin etc. Roll in a little flour seasoned with salt and pepper, put into the lined basin with sufficient water to almost cover them, and seal down with a lid made from the remaining pastry. Take a square of greaseproof paper, fold two pleats across it at right-angles, and tie it over the pudding (or cover with cooking foil, squeezed tightly around the rim), and steam for 3 hours.

KIDNEY AND BACON[56]

1 small onion, chopped *1 tbs lard or dripping*
8oz/225g (about 4) kidneys *1½ tbs plain flour*
2oz/50g ham or bacon *pepper and salt*

Place the onions in a small pan, just cover with water, and simmer, covered for 10 min.

Remove the stringy cores from the kidneys, cut the rest into small cubes, stir into the onions after their 10 min., and simmer for a further 5 min. until tender.

Cut the ham or bacon into small squares, fry in the dripping until just browned, remove from the heat, and stir in the flour.

Pour the onion and kidney mixture into the ham or bacon, return to the heat, and stir until it has thickened. Add salt and pepper to taste, then serve on slices of hot toast.

Perhaps the most useful of all the offal was the liver. There was a tradition of baking it whole, first having stuffed it with forcemeat and wrapped it in rashers of bacon, but it was easier to deal with when sliced.[57] Mrs M.N. of Shrewsbury, writing in the 1730s, considered this recipe to be highly esteemed by the gentry families of the county;

THE SHROPSHIRE & WORCESTERSHIRE DISH[58]

6 rashers dry-cured bacon *1–2oz/25–50g lard*
1lb/450g lamb's liver, sliced *pepper & salt*
1 onion, finely chopped *1 tbs lemon juice*
6oz/175g spinach & lettuce, chopped

Place a large dish, covered with a pan lid, over a pan of gently simmering water, to serve as a hotplate.

Using a large frying pan, fry the bacon in the lard, remove the bacon then fry the liver in the same fat until just tender, placing them both in the hot dish.

Add the spinach and lettuce to the pan, adding a little more fat if necessary, and stir-fry until they are browned. Add salt and pepper to taste, heap the vegetables over the liver and bacon, and serve directly from the hot dish.

The frying of herbs with bacon was also a very convenient and popular means by which a cottager's wife could quickly make a good meal in a frying pan, using the minimum amount of fuel. A working knowledge of the local botany was an essential prerequisite, however, otherwise there could be disastrous results. In 1837 G. Hulbert recalled 'The wife of one Matthews, who dwelt near Shrewsbury, gathered some herbs, and having boiled them, fried them with bacon; but in the night following [they] fell very sick, vomited and purged, and then fell asleep, and could not be waked for twenty-four hours. Two of [the children] then vomited, and it saved their lives: the third slept on, and only opened its eyes and died.'[59] Unwittingly their mother had included Dog Mercury in her herbs, thus producing these fatal results. Rather safer liver dishes included;

BAKED LIVER & BACON[60]

1lb/450g liver in large slices
4 rashers streaky bacon
1 small onion, chopped finely
4 mushrooms, finely chopped
1oz/25g fresh white breadcrumbs

1 tbs fresh parsley, chopped
$\frac{1}{2}$ tsp salt
large pinch ground pepper
large pinch ground nutmeg
1 tbs Worcester sauce

Dry the liver on kitchen paper, and arrange in a greased roasting tin. Mix the remaining dry ingredients (except the bacon) in a bowl, and knead firmly so that the breadcrumbs absorb the moisture of the onions. (N.B. The addition of 1–2 tbs plain flour will help to hold it together). Cover each piece of liver with this mixture, with a piece of bacon on top, pour $\frac{1}{2}$pt/300ml water around them, and bake at 150°C, 300°F, Gas mark 2 for about 45 min., until both the liver and its coating are cooked through.

Lift the pieces of liver onto a hot plate, add the Worcester sauce to the remaining juices, bring to the boil, and pour around them just before serving.

LIVER ROLL[61]

1lb/450g liver
8oz/225g fat ham or bacon
8oz/225g fresh white breadcrumbs
1 tbs sage & thyme, chopped

1 tsp salt
$\frac{1}{4}$ tsp ground pepper
large pinch ground nutmeg
a little plain flour

Finely mince (or liquidise) the liver, and chop the bacon into small squares. Mix with the remaining ingredients to form a smooth mixture, if necessary adding a little milk or water to ensure it holds together.

Take a piece of muslin about 18ins./50cm square, plunge it in water, squeeze dry, lay flat on a board, and dust it with flour. Arrange the mixture as a 3ins/7cm roll along one edge, roll up, twist each end, and tie with string.

Plunge into a large pan of boiling water, cover, and boil for 2 hours, then drain, unwrap, and leave to cool. Slice cold with tomatoes or salad.

WHITE HOG'S PUDDING (1720s)[62]

1lb/450g pig's liver
5oz/150g fresh white breadcrumbs
$\frac{1}{4}$ pt/150ml milk
6oz/175g currants
6oz/175g suet

$1\frac{1}{2}$ oz/40g sugar
1 egg, beaten
1 tbs sherry
1 tbs rosewater
$\frac{1}{4}$ tsp ground clove & mace

Simmer the liver until cooked tender, drain, leave until cold, grate (or chop and blend) until smooth, mix with the milk and breadcrumbs, then refrigerate overnight.

Next morning mix in the remaining ingredients. These were originally packed into lengths of intestine, but today they may be cooked as in the previous recipe.

Whereas pigs were usually killed by the families who had raised them, cattle were almost always dealt with by professional slaughtermen and butchers who then, as now, processed their meat and their offal. Boiling tripe was a long and troublesome process, and so was rarely done domestically, it being far easier to purchase ready-prepared from the markets, as you can still do today. Late Victorian Shrewsbury even had its own self-proclaimed 'Tripe King', who also produced violin-strings and gut for 'tennis bats' from other animal parts. Moving on from offal, the rest of a pig's carcase had now to be dealt with by dividing it up into head, shoulders, sides, hams and trotters.

As this was done, the leaf, or inner layer of fat, was removed, cut up, and rendered down to make lard, the remaining crispy scratchings being either eaten with bread or baked as scratching cake.[63] Every other morsel was saved for conversion into;

SAUSAGES[64]

1lb/450g mixed lean and fat fresh pork
4oz/110g fresh white breadcrumbs

SAUSAGE SEASONING

6 tbs salt
2 tbs ground white pepper
¼ tsp powered sage
¼ tsp ground cayenne pepper
¼ tsp ground mace

Mince the pork finely, and mix thoroughly with the bread and about 1 tsp of the seasoning, according to taste. The mixture may then be either filled into pre-soaked skins, or made up into flat cakes and fried.

For everyday use, the head could provide pigs' cheeks for curing like bacon, or else it could be made into brawn;

GRANNY MORGAN'S BRAWN[65]

1 pig's head
1 pig's tongue
1 pig's liver
1 pig's heart
6 black peppercorns, 6 cloves
¼ pt/150ml vinegar
1 small onion, chopped finely
1 tbs rolled sage

Clean the pig's head, and soak in brine for 2–3 days, wash it in cold water, then simmer in a covered pan until the meat falls from the bones. Meanwhile simmer the liver, tongue and heart in a separate pan until tender. When all is cooked, strain both stocks into a clean pan, and boil rapidly with the spices until reduced to 1pt/600ml, and stir in the vinegar.

Chop all the meat, and pass through a mincer, with the (optional) onion and sage, mix together, and season with salt and pepper to taste. Pack the meat into basins, cover with the re-heated stock, cover with a plate and a weight, and either a cloth or a piece of kitchen paper, before leaving in a cool place to set. Traditionally it was left for a week before being used, but it may be turned out and sliced the following day.

The hams would be sold off by most cottagers as a means of raising useful cash, the sides then being home-cured to provide a year-long supply of bacon. This was by far the most important meat in the everyday economy. Bacon and eggs appears to have risen to the status of a national dish in this particular county. Yorkshire might have its pudding, and Norfolk its dumplings, but only Shropshire has given its name to an entire meal. 'The Shropshire' is just bacon and eggs. 'Waggoners and such folk, stopping for refreshment at a public house will say 'Can ye gie us any 'S'ropshire?', 'W'enn nothin but eggs an' bacon – owd S'ropshire fare' – to offer yo.'[66] As already described, bacon was also widely used here as an important ingredient in many other dishes. Some appear to have been specifically designed as a means of making it go as far as possible, giving the impression of ample meat in a meal, without really using very much at all. Of these, the best known are the fitchett pie and the herb roll.

'Fitchett' is the alternative English name for the polecat, the largest native member of the weasel family. It grew up to around a foot and a half in length, and was notorious for its foul smell. Though it is hard to believe today, there is some evidence that it was sometimes cooked and eaten, a Cheshire man once exclaiming 'I ketchit a fitchet, an' I'm gooin' have a pie made on him.'[67] By the early nineteenth century fitchett pie was a very well-established dish in Shropshire farmhouses and cottages, the dyspeptic Mr Hartshorne defining it in 1841 as 'FITCHUK PIE, an unsavoury compound of bacon, apples and onions; by labouring men it is considered a dainty kind of pie, but it smells rank unto the senses of those who are habituated to delicate feeding, since some ill-natured Apician conceived its name from those offensive odours which are emitted by the Pole Cat.'[68] Despite his jaundiced opinion, the fitchett pie remained very popular. Not only was it a complete meal in one dish, and extremely economical, but it was truly delicious, its various elements combining to provide an particularly well-flavoured and satisfying dish, its scent having not the slightest hint of polecat.

FITCHETT PIE[69]

12oz/325g bacon or ham, diced or in ¼ ins/0·5cm slices
1lb/450g potatoes
1lb/450g apples
salt & pepper

8oz/225g plain flour
4oz/100g lard
2 medium onions
½ pt/300ml stock

Rub the lard into the flour, with a pinch of salt, and work in 3–4 tbs cold water to form the pastry, knead this lightly, and set aside to rest. Peel and slice the potatoes, apples and onion, and build up layers of potatoes, apples, bacon or ham, and onions in that order in a deep pie-dish, seasoning these with salt and pepper. Pour in the stock, roll out the pastry, cover the pie, making a steam-hole in the centre, then bake at 200°C, 400°F, Gas mark 6 for 20 min., then reducing to 180°C, 350°F, Gas mark 4 for a further 50–60min, before serving hot.

VARIATIONS

Some recipes leave out the onions, while others replace the bacon or ham with either scrag end mutton chops, or cheese.

SHROPSHIRE HERB ROLL[70]

8oz/225g plain flour
4oz/100g suet
½ tsp salt
1 egg, beaten
2oz/50g mixed parsley, thyme, savoury and marjoram, finely chopped

4oz/100g bacon and/or rabbit
1 onion, finely chopped
4 fl.oz/120ml milk
3oz/75g lard

Mince the bacon and/or rabbit.

Mix the flour, suet and salt, and use a round-bladed knife to work in sufficient milk to form a firm dough. Turn out onto a floured board, knead lightly, and roll out about a third of an inch, barely 1cm thick, in a rectangular shape.

Mix the onion and herbs with most of the egg, and spread over the dough, leaving a margin of at least 1 ins./2·5cm all round. Spread the meat on top, and press it down firmly using a wet hand.

Brush the margins with some of the remaining egg, and roll up tightly, turning in the edges at each turn, finally sealing down the long seam, and brush the whole with the remaining egg. Place, join downwards, in a roasting tin, with the lard, and bake in an oven pre-heated to 180°C, 350°F, Gas mark 4 for an hour, basting from time to time.

Serve hot, with a jug of gravy.

Even more economical with the bacon came

BLANKS & PRIZES[71]

2–3 rashers of bacon, cut into small dice
1lb/450g pre-soaked and cooked butter beans

When the beans are hot and almost ready, fry the bacon, and pour it, along with its 'liquor' or fat, into them. Stir all together with a little ground pepper, and serve.

The 'Blanks' were the beans, the bacon representing the much more savoury 'Prizes'. Only Yorkshire folk claimed to make more use of the pig than those of Shropshire by selling the squeals to the Scots, for putting into their bagpipes.

The Shropshire Pie first appeared in print in Richard Bradley's *Country Housewife and Lady's Director* (part II) of 1732. In its basic form, it was a very simple combination of pieces of rabbit and pork in a mixture of red wine and water, all baked in a pastry pie-crust. The result was quite delicious, however, the combined flavour avoiding the drier, gamey, nature of the rabbit, and the fattier, bland flavour of the pork, to produce a very satisfying, well-flavoured dish. By the 1860s, puff-paste was being specified for the lid, while by 1932 the meat was being rolled in flour before baking, to thicken its stock. The earlier, unflavoured versions are far better, however, for the stock remains virtually clear, yet so rich that it forms a jelly when cold.

SHROPSHIRE PIE (BASIC RECIPE)[72]

cubed flesh of 2 rabbits (c. 1lb 8oz/675g)
2lb/900g cubed pork, including the fat
salt & pepper
1oz/25g butter
½ pt/300ml red wine
½ nutmeg
1lb/450g puff paste
1 egg, beaten

Thoroughly mix the rabbit and pork with a seasoning of salt and pepper, arrange in the bottom of a pie dish, and dot with the butter. Mix the wine with an equal quantity of water, pour over the meat, then grate on the nutmeg. Having rolled out the puff paste and allowed it to rest in a cold place for 30 min., cut off a long strip, and stick it to the pie-dish with a little beaten egg. Brush the top of the strip with the egg, lay on the lid, trim its edges, and cut a round hole in the centre. Roll out the trimmings and apply borders around the rim and central hole. Brush with the egg, carefully avoiding the cut edges, then bake at 200°C, 400°F, Gas mark 6 for 20 min., then reduce to 180°C, 350°F, Gas mark 4 for a further 1 hour 40 min., then serve hot.

SHROPSHIRE PIE (RICHER VERSION)

This was the version which 'Lady H' gave to Richard Bradley. It is exactly the same as the recipe above, but includes the following in its filling;

1. *3 or 4 globe artichoke bottoms, parboiled and diced.*
2. *Cocks-combs, artificially made by cutting away the spongy side of prepared tripe, and cutting the firmer part beneath into the shapes of cock's combs.*
3. *forcemeat balls, made with:*

   2 rabbit livers
   2 rashers streaky bacon
   1 tsp/5ml dried marjoram
   salt & pepper
   1 egg yolk

Cover the liver with water in a small pan, bring to the boil, simmer 1 min., and drain. Finely chop the livers and bacon, then grind to a smooth paste either by blending, or in a pestle and mortar. Work in the marjoram, salt, pepper and sufficient yolk to produce a soft paste. Roll this into balls, and space around the meat in the pie-dish.

In addition to bacon, and rabbits, rooks might appear on the cottager's table, particularly when baked as pies. The following recipe, used by Mrs Henry Holland of Wilton House, Market Drayton, was collected by Meg Pybus in 1985;

ROOK PIE[73]

6 young rooks
12oz/325g shin beef, cubed
1 onion
1 bay leaf
6 slices fat streaky bacon
4 hard boiled eggs, sliced
8oz/225g flour
4oz/100g lard

Cut off the wings and legs, nick under the breast, peel off the skin and draw the entrails. Skin the thighs, discarding the rest of the leg. Wash the flesh, and stew with the onion and bay leaf for about 20 minutes until tender. Leave to cool, meanwhile using the flour and lard, with a pinch of salt, to make shortcrust pastry. Remove the flesh from the bones, sprinkle with salt and pepper, arrange it in a pie dish, with the eggs and bacon on top, almost cover with stock, then add the shortcrust lid, and bake at 220°C, 425°F, Gas mark 7 for 15 minutes, then reduce to 180°C, 350°F, Gas mark 4 for a further hour. It is best eaten cold, when the stock has jellied.

As any of these meat and bacon dishes could become monotonous during the course of a year, they were enlivened by the use of pickles. In addition to the usual onions, chutneys etc, the local speciality of pickled damsons was particularly good;

PICKLED DAMSONS[74]

4lb/1·8kg large damsons
1pt/600ml vinegar
1½lb/675g sugar
1oz/25g mixed pickling spice

Prick the damsons with a needle. Heat the remaining ingredients until the sugar has dissolved, add the damsons, and cook until tender but not broken. Use a pierced spoon to transfer the damsons into sterilised jars, then reduce the remaining syrup by rapid boiling, before pouring it over the damsons, sealing down while still hot, and keeping for use.

If possible, dinner would include a pudding. On Sundays and other special days it might be an 'honest solid mass of raisins, suet, eggs, treacle and flour [which] only in the vast leisure of Sunday it might be digested', but on other days it was usually much plainer.[75] The simplest boiled puddings were just egg-sized pieces of bread-dough plunged into a pan of boiling water. Once having risen to the surface, these 'pot-balls' were dished up with hot treacle.[76] Other dumplings relied on the use of suet crusts;

APPLE – GOB[77]

4 apples, peeled & cored *4 cloves*
6oz/175g flour *sugar*
3oz/75g suet

Mix the flour, suet and salt, and use a round-bladed knife to stir in about 3–4fl.oz/100ml cold water to form a dough. Turn this out onto a floured board, knead smooth, divide it into four, form each into a ball, and roll out as a broad disc. Place an apple on the centre of each, fill its centre with sugar and a clove, then wet the edges of the pastry, and work them up around the apple until it is completely sealed. Rinse and flour four 12ins/30cm squares of muslin, place a dumpling on each, gather the muslin around it, and tie off with string.

Plunge into a pan of boiling water, and then simmer for about 1½ hours.

They could also be made with shortcrust pastry, placed joint downwards (left unwrapped) on a greased baking sheet, brushed with beaten egg, and baked at 190°C, 375°F, Gas mark 5 for about 1 hour.

The boiled apple-gob recipe above, if made with dried figs, soaked and chopped, made in a basin, covered and steamed, produced the local speciality, the Figgetty Dumpling.[78] Figs were also used to make;

EVERYDAY FARE

FIG PUDDING[79]

4oz/100g dried figs
3oz/75g suet
2oz/50g fresh white breadcrumbs
2oz/50g flour
2oz/50g sugar
pinch of salt & of nutmeg
1 egg, beaten
about 4–5 tbs milk

Make sure all the stalks have been removed from the figs, then chop them coarsely and mix them with the dry ingredients. Mix in the egg sufficient milk to make a moderately stiff mixture, put into a well-greased 1½pt/900ml basin, cover with a piece of cooking foil pressed down over the rim, and steam for 2½ hours.

Serve with a sweet white sauce.

As well as the plain suet puddings Spotted Dicks etc., made both here and in other parts of the country, there were regional specialities such as;

CARROT PUDDING[80]

4oz/100g grated carrot
4oz/100g self-raising flour
4oz/100g currants
4oz/100g raisins
2oz/50g suet
2oz/50g candied peel
½ tsp mixed spice
¼ pt/150ml milk

Mix the dry ingredients, and mix in just sufficient milk to form a stiff mixture. Pack this into a well-greased mould or basin, using a piece of kitchen foil pressed down over the rim to serve as a lid. Either steam, or place in a lidded pan half filled with boiling water, cover, and cook for 2½ hours, topping up with more boiling water as necessary.

At first sight the following pudding is very plain, but the combination of its lemon flavour with its rich clear sauce is very successful.

SHROPSHIRE PUDDING[81]

8oz/225g wholemeal breadcrumbs	*2 eggs*
	1 tbs brandy
2oz/50g suet	*½ nutmeg, grated*
6 tbs soft brown sugar	*juice and grated rind of 1 lemon*

Mix all the ingredients, pack into a greased mould or basin, and cook as in the recipe above.

SHROPSHIRE PUDDING SAUCE

¼ pt/150ml brandy	*4oz/100g sugar*
4oz/100g butter	

Heat the ingredients in a lidded pan until completely dissolved and almost boiling. Serve in a hot jug to accompany the pudding.

In most counties a bread-and-butter pudding is essentially a combination of bread, butter, sugar and dried fruits baked in a rich custard batter, to give a soft and luscious hot dessert. The Midlands variety is quite different, being much stiffer and more cake like. As well as being served hot, a square or two might be kept for eating later.

BAKED BREAD PUDDING[82]

8oz/225g stale white bread	*2oz/50g suet*
4oz/100g currants or mixed dried fruit	*¼ tsp grated nutmeg*
	1 egg, beaten
2oz/50g brown sugar	*a little milk*

Break the bread into small morsels, soak in cold water for 30 minutes, pour into a strainer, and squeeze dry. Beat out all lumps with a fork, then mix in all the ingredients, with just enough milk to give a stiff dropping consistency. Pour into a well-greased baking dish or tin, and bake for 1 hour at 190°C, 375°F, Gas mark 5.

Sprinkle the top with a little more sugar just before serving.

In warmer weather baked custards and pies were more suitable. The richest custards were made with beestings, the milk drawn from the cow just after it had calved. When flavoured with a little ground spice and sugar, it was poured into a pastry-lined pie-dish and baked in the oven. Around Pulverbatch the pastry was left out, leaving the custard 'bare-footed'. 'We'n mak' a dish o' bar-fut custard ooth bystin for the men's supper; it'll be a trate for 'em'.[83] As for pies, there were the usual apple pies, pear pies, etc., but those with the best flavours were made with 'faiberries' (gooseberries), raspberries and wimberries, (otherwise called either bilberries or blaeberries). Wimberries grow plentifully on the southern hills and western borders, where they were gathered by women from late July.

As Mary Webb enthused; 'Of all wild fruits the wimberry, or cloudberry, should rank first. Its colour is the bloomy purple of distant hills ... it will grow only in beautiful and mysterious places. High on the airy hill ... the fruit is not ready for picking until after St. Swithins. From that date until late September a tide of life, gipsy and cottager and dweller of the plain, flows up into our hills, to the Stiperstones, to the Longmynd to the lonely stretches of the Clun Forest, come the stooping neutral-tinted figures. Alone beside the family kettle amid the day's provisions sits the baby, gazing trustfully at the blue, arching sky, so deeply saturated in wimberry juice that one doubts if many Saturday tubs will clean him. Twice a week [the wimberry higgler] appears with his cart and rough pony, and over the green deeply-rutted tracks, down the valleys brimful of shadow and along precipitous roads the wimberries go on their journey to the cities of England.'[84]

She then saw them arrive in Shrewsbury; 'The Saturday was a great wimberry market. The berries were brought in hampers that needed two men to lift them, and the purple juices dripped from them as from a wine-vat. Other fruit lay in large masses of purple, gold and crimson. The air was full of aroma'. Among the other fruits sold here were raspberries, each small mound being cradled in the basin-like hollow of a cabbage leaf, (an ideally 'green' form of packaging); 'They wur sellin' rasb'ries at 4d. A lef I' Sosebry a' Saturday; they binna tied to mizzer by the lef, but they bin genarily about a pint, an' I should think these one nigh a quart'.[85]

The harder fruits, such as gooseberries and pears, might be bottled for use throughout the coming year, and all the surplus soft fruits made into jams. This midsummer period was the best time to enjoy the fresh fruits as pies, the best of all being made of wimberries.

WIMBERRY PIE[86]

4oz/100g wimberries, (or two pints wimberries to one of peeled, cored and finely chopped cooking apple)
2 tbs honey or sugar   pinch of cinnamon
2oz/50g lard and/or butter   4oz/100g flour

Use the flour, fat and about 1–2 tbs cold water to make shortcrust pastry. Divide this into two, and roll each out to form the lining and lid of a small ovenproof pie tin or pie dish. Arrange the fruit in the lined dish, with the honey or sugar and cinnamon, dampen the edges of the pastry, add the lid, and trim its edges. Having cut a round hole in the centre of the lid, bake at 200°C, 400°F, Gas mark 6 for 20–25 minutes until the pastry has lightly browned. The pie may be sprinkled with sugar for serving.

Later in the evening supper would be served, usually a light snack of bread, cheese, and sometimes onions. As a youngster I used to share this with my grandparents, old, dry Cheshire cheese and slices of raw English onion, which combined to produce dreams of the most alarming character. In Shropshire, where the county's own cheeses were marketed as 'Cheshire', two other varieties were also made. Towards the end of the season dried and sifted sage leaves were mixed into the curd before pressing, since they imparted a good flavour, and also helped to dry out the finished cheeses. As well as this sage cheese, there was marigold cheese. To make this, fresh marigold petals were mixed into the curds, after which they were made up like cream cheeses, being eaten as soon as they were ripe.[87]

In the long, cold nights of the winter months, when everyone huddled around the kitchen fire, many Shropshire families used a number of traditional recipes to make their usually uncooked cheese into dishes which were warm and comforting to both mind and stomach. They were all easily prepared by the fire, so that no-one had to go into the cold, or miss out on the conversation.

A SHROPSHIRE SUPPER DISH[88]

1 large mild onion
4oz/100g Cheshire cheese, grated
½pt/300ml milk
½oz/15g butter
1 tbs plain flour
pepper and salt to taste
toast

Peel and slice the onion, just cover with water, and simmer for some 20 minutes until tender.

While the onion is cooking, beat the flour into the milk, add the butter, pepper and salt, bring to the boil while stirring, and set aside.

When the onions are ready, drain them, stir in the cheese until it has melted, then add the milk, and stir over a gentle heat until the milk and cheese are incorporated.

Pour into cups or bowls, and eat with a spoon, with the toast handed separately.

One of the great benefits of following traditional recipes, is that they often reveal methods of cookery which, although appearing almost pathetically simple and unrefined, reveal the deepest knowledge of how to make the very best of basic ingredients. The following supper dish is an excellent example, using a highly unusual but very effective method to convert Cheshire cheese into a hot, comforting dish of the greatest delicacy.

CHEESE CURD[89]

8oz/225g Cheshire cheese
½pt/300ml milk
1 egg, beaten
toast & bacon

Grate the cheese very finely into the milk and beat them together for a few minutes. Pour into an ovenproof dish, and bake at 170°C, 325°F, Gas mark 3 for about 20 minutes, but without boiling. Remove from the oven, when it will be seen that the cheese and milk have broken down to a delicate curd floating on a whey. Lightly whisk the mixture while pouring in the egg, and return to the oven for a further c.20 minutes until just set, but not boiled.

Pour on to hot toast, accompanied by fried rashers of bacon.

SCRAMBLED CHEESE[90]

2oz/50g Cheshire cheese, grated   *2 eggs, beaten*
2 tbs milk   *pepper and salt*
<u>optional</u> *1 small onion*   *toast*

Melt the cheese and milk in a pan, rapidly stir in the eggs, pepper and salt, and stir over a very gentle heat until it has thickened, but not turned into a curd.

If the onion is to be used, it should be boiled for 20–30 minutes beforehand, then peeled and finely chopped before adding to the cheese and milk at the same time as the eggs.

Pour the scrambled cheese over the toast. It has a creamy texture and a delicate flavour.

In addition to whole-milk Cheshire cheese, a harder variety was made from skim-milk, this being known as Legh cheese, from the village of that name near Knutsford.[91] It too could be cooked, but required the addition of cream to make it palatable. The following recipe was intended to be toasted in a dish before the fire, but may now be heated under a grill.

TOASTED CHEESE[92]

To each 4oz/100g Cheshire cheese, allow 3–4 tbs double cream.

Grate or coarsely chop the cheese and mix it with the cream in a heatproof, (preferably enamel or stainless steel) dish to form a layer about ½ ins/1·5cm deep.

Place under a hot grill for some 10–15 minutes until the cheese has melted, and the surface is bubbling and browned. Scoop up with fingers of hot toast.

The following recipe is from the late twentieth century, but shows how this cooked cheese tradition was so deeply rooted in the county.

CHEESE AND TOMATO SUPPER DISH[93]

8oz/225g cheese (any kind of leftovers will do)
4 tomatoes, sliced OR a tin of tomatoes, drained
3 eggs, beaten   salt & pepper

Grate the cheese and layer with the tomatoes in a baking dish. Pour the eggs on top, season with salt and pepper, and bake at 220°C, 425°F, Gas mark 7 for about 45 minutes.

Before closing this chapter, some mention should be made of flummery. Numerous Georgian recipes with this name refer to luxurious, sweet almond-milk jellies to be served as fashionable desserts. As made in working homes in Shropshire it was much plainer, following its ancient Welsh roots. This flummery, Welsh *llymru*, is unlike any food made today, being a cold oatmeal jelly with a sourness reminiscent of yoghurt, and a reputation of being filling rather than nourishing. Even so, it made a refreshing dish in summertime;

FLUMMERY[94]

5oz/150g coarse oatmeal   3fl.oz/90ml buttermilk (if available,
2pt/1·2l water   but not essential)

Soak the oatmeal in the liquids for 3 to 4 days until it has gone sour, then strain through a very fine sieve. Boil the liquid briskly, stirring continuously until it forms a stream the size of a rat's tail when the stirring stick is raised a few inches above the surface. Pour into rinsed bowls or dishes, and leave in a cool place to set.

Most people ate their flummery with milk or beer, the better-off in Shrewsbury replacing these with wine.

CHAPTER 3

SOMETHING FOR TEA

In medieval England there were none of the sweet biscuits and cakes which we know today. They entered our culinary repertoire in the Elizabethan period, when even noble ladies took great pride in using the very best flour, sugar, dried fruits and spices, among the most expensive of ingredients, to make fine confectionery. Since such drinks as tea and coffee were still unknown, their biscuits and cakes were designed to be eaten with wine, a tradition which continued into the 20th century with madeira cakes etc. Even today, we still enjoy a glass of fortified wine with our slice of Christmas cake. As tea and coffee were originally prohibitively expensive and solely affordable by the wealthy and fashionable, it was only in the loftiest of circles that they began to replace wine as an accompaniment to cakes etc. However, as increasing trade and falling taxes made tea-drinking more economical, so the enjoyment of tea-and-cakes afternoon refreshments rapidly descended the social scale.

In the houses of the Shropshire well-to-do and gentry, evidence for the drinking of tea starts in the early 18th century, John Eyton of Wellington having a copper teapot in his kitchen in 1709, and Thomas Newell of Donnington a coffee pot in his in 1731. Other 1730s households list most of the other required equipage, including coffee mills, tea-boards and tea tables.[1] Around the middle of the century there are also references to more elaborate tea-wares, such as the japanned (i.e. enamelled) tea kettle mounted over its matching lamp and large waiter or tray used at Park Hall in 1761.[2] This would have been filled with boiling water in the housekeeper's room, the lamp lit beneath it to maintain its heat, and then carried to the kettle-stand or tea-table in the drawing room. Here, the mistress of the house would unlock her tea caddy, select her finest green or black tea, spoon it into her teapot, and finally scald it with boiling water from her tea-kettle, ensuring its freshness. From this

Fig 18 Stanley and Mary Leighton taking tea with Jane Disbrowe during a game of croquet at Loton Park in 1863. By now it had become the national beverage of choice, accompanying almost every social event.

period fine ceramic teaware began to be made in the new factory potteries, but in the great houses it was often of silver or silver-gilt of the most exquisite quality. Perhaps the finest currently on show in the county is the magnificent Neo-classical service made for the 3rd Lord Berwick by Benjamin and James Smith around 1810, and still at Attingham Park.

Given this high-status usage, it is not surprising that others wished to drink tea, rather than their usual small beer. Their problem was its high cost, which included a 100% import tax. Within a year of William Pitt's decision to reduce this to 12·5% in the 1780s, annual imports rose from six to sixteen million pounds. The East India Company was bringing in thirty million pounds in 1830, rising to forty nine million pounds in 1836.[3] These changes at national level were soon being felt in Shropshire. As early as 1795 it was reported that in Madeley;

> since the use of Tea is becoming so prevalent, on a moderate calculation, each family consumes 3½lbs. of flour each week more than formerly by instituting a fourth meal every day. In the days of yore, Breakfast, Dinner and Supper were esteemed sufficient, but now it must be Breakfast, Dinner, Tea and Supper, which wastes both meal and time, and makes a difference each week in the parish of Madeley of 3,234lbs. of flour.[4]

Similarly in Oswestry in 1817, the poor were being advised that;

> A great deal of money is often spent in tea and butter, which might be better disposed on meat and home-brewed beer. Two pound of fresh meat costs less than one pound of fresh butter and gives five times the nourishment, and tea is very expensive, unwholesome slop, and requires a great deal of sugar and cream, without which, it acts as a slow poison, injures the stomach, produces pain, and then recourse is too often had to the gin shop.[5] (The gentry who wrote this were, apparently, impervious to tea poisoning, being rendered immune by reason of their breeding and affluence!)

By the mid nineteenth century tea had largely replaced beer as the main everyday drink in most ordinary households. Now in plentiful supply and much cheaper (even if this was partially due to adulteration with a variety of cheap but potentially dangerous additives), it was hot, comforting, and easily and quickly made using the minimum of fuel and equipment. To convert it from being a drink into a light mid/late afternoon meal, it needed to be accompanied by some similarly inexpensive simple and quickly-made cakes. Ideally they too should be hot, finished at the fireside so as to be served as fresh and perhaps as crisp as possible. It took only a few minutes to convert sliced bread into toast, for example, without interrupting conversation, but in Shropshire a number of alternatives were usually preferred.

In the poorest homes simple cakes could be quickly made using little more than fat and flour, made into a dough, and cooked in a frying pan. Similar items made in great manufacturing cities were sometimes known as 'poverty cakes', and seen as food of last resort, but in Shropshire the addition of a little sugar and milk converted them into a teatime delicacy. If well-made, they were short and crumbly on the outside, with a soft, hot interior;[6]

Fig 19 In 1813, the working classes were being instructed to avoid tea, because it was a slow poison. They knew better, however, and drank even more of the cup which refreshes, but does not inebriate. Here in a Lightmore cottage in the 1950s the kettle sings over the fire, the caddy stands on the mantelpiece, and the teapot and pint pot lie ready on the table.

SHROPSHIRE FRIED CAKES

8oz/225g self-raising flour   *4–5 tbs milk*
2oz/50g butter or lard   *bacon fat for frying*
2oz/50g sugar

Sift the flour, rub in the butter or lard, add the sugar, and work in the milk with a round-bladed knife to form a firm dough. Knead lightly, roll out about a third of an inch, 1cm in thickness, and cut in 3ins, 10cm, rounds.

Melt the fat in the frying pan, so it is at a medium heat and about an eighth of an inch, 4cm, deep. Put in a number of the cakes, and leave them to cook without shaking for up to a minute, then turn over and cook on the other side. They should be of a golden brown colour and not charred, so adjust the cooking time and temperature accordingly. Eat while still hot. Although a spreading of jam or honey is not strictly traditional, it should certainly be tried.

A rather more popular treat was the pikelet, described by the dyspeptic C.H. Hartshorne in 1841 as 'a small indigestible circular piece of half-baked dough, which being covered with butter is esteemed dainty tea fare'.[7] Within the county they were better known as either 'lightcakes' or 'flaps'. In the 1830s Molly Preece of Church Pulverbatch acquired the nick-name of 'Polly Flap' from her profession of pikelet-maker, for example.[8] They were made by pouring a yeast-raised batter of white wheat flour onto the lightly-greased surface of a bakestone or girdle;

PIKELETS OR FLAPS

14oz/400g strong white flour
¼ tsp salt
1tsp dried yeast
¼ tsp sugar
½ pt/300ml tepid water
or milk and water

Sift the dry ingredients into a bowl, make a well in the centre, pour in the liquid, and beat together, rapidly to form a smooth batter. Cover, and leave in a warm place for 45–60 minutes, until it has fermented and has a frothy appearance.

Heat an iron bakestone/girdle on the stove until a little flour sprinkled on it slowly browns, then sweep it clean, and grease it with a little butter wrapped in a small piece of cloth or muslin.

Pour a pool of the batter onto this bakestone/girdle, and leave until the upper surface has set dry, its bubbles have burst, and the edges have risen up, then turn it over and allow it to bake for a minute or so on the other side, before removing on to a hot plate.

These 'Flaps' were then buttered and eaten fresh and hot; 'I went to see the poor owd Missis las' wik, an' fund 'er busy makin' flaps, so I buttered 'em off the bak' stwun, and we'd a rare joram' (i.e. lots of them). They were probably only toasted to heat them through if baked beforehand. For a special treat, they might also be spread with cranberry jelly. When Robert and Gillian sat in the tearoom at 'The Junction ' (Craven Arms), 'There were cakes of many shapes; there was a brown teapot with raised forget-me-nots on it; there were pikelets and jelly, and pink willow cups' as well as 'a large cake with icing that stood on a doiley smelling of mice'![9]

Shropshire buckwheat-cakes or French-wheat-cakes were similar to flaps, but were pale brown in colour, finer in texture, and had a much more interesting and attractive taste. Today buckwheat flour is chiefly associated with the making of Russian blinis and sweet American buckwheat cakes, but it was formerly used to make a completely different kind of Shropshire 'pancake' or 'crumpet'. The plant itself is not a true grain, but a relative of docks and rhubarb which produces clusters of seeds shaped like tiny triangular pyramids. Introduced into Europe from eastern Asia, it was already well-known in England by the 1540s, where its modern name 'buck-wheat' probably originated, its seeds resembling those of 'buck' or beech trees. As a field crop it was particularly useful, flourishing

Fig 20   A relative of the dock, buckwheat provided a useful substitute for corn on poorer soils. After being harvested and threshed, it was ground so that its flour could be used to make Shropshire buckwheat cakes.

where cool climates and light soils were unsuitable for cereal grains. Buckwheat cakes were almost certainly being baked in Georgian Shropshire, but may have an even older local pedigree. Two versions are given here; the first being for the plain local cake, and the second for a richer version published in Elizabeth Hammond's *Modern Domestic Cookery and Useful Receipt Book* of 1817. She called hers 'Bockings'. Bocking was a flannel material woven at the Essex village of that name giving some impression of how the finished cake should look.

Buckwheat is now available from most health- food shops. It is naturally gluten-free, making it particularly suitable for those allergic to wheat products.

SHREWSBURY BUCKWHEAT CAKES[10]

10oz/275g buckwheat flour *1 tsp dried yeast*
1pt/600ml lukewarm water *butter for cooking*
pinch of salt

Beat the flour, salt and yeast into the water, and leave in a warm place for about 3 hours to rise. Pour large ladlefuls into a barely buttered bakestone/girdle over a gentle heat. When the edges rise, the bubbles have burst, and the surface has gone from glossy to dull, toss or turn over for a few moments to dry off.

Butter while hot, and serve piled high in the centre of a hot dish, pan-side downwards.

BUCKWHEAT CAKES (2)[11]

3oz/75g buckwheat flour *3 eggs, beaten*
½pt/300ml lukewarm milk *butter for cooking*
½ tsp dried yeast

Beat the flour and yeast into the milk, and stand in a warm place for an hour, during which time it will double in volume. Mix in the eggs, with further milk, if necessary, to make a pouring batter, as for pancakes, and cook as in the previous recipe.

The toasting of buckwheat cakes was considered to be a matter of great skill and dexterity, for each one had to be turned nine times to obtain the correct result. It is recorded that Betty Morgan, who died in Ellesmere about 1846, was the local expert in this process.[12]

In order to keep the toasts, flaps and buckwheat cakes really hot, most cottages and farmhouses in Shropshire used a cat.[13] This was not a mouse-devouring feline however, but a wooden ball perhaps a couple of inches (5cm) in diameter, from which extended six ornamentally turned or carved legs. Like its namesake, it always landed securely on its feet, but in addition it had three legs projecting upwards between which a plate could be propped either level, or at a convenient angle. When stood on the hearth before the wood fire, it ensured that all its well-buttered contents remained in

Fig 21   Shropshire buckwheat cakes and flaps (the local type of pikelet) were baked on a cast iron bakeplate hung over the fire. They could then be kept warm on a plate supported on a six-legged 'cat' both before and after toasting.

perfect condition as the meal progressed. From the early 19th century the gradual introduction of cast-iron ranges saw cats fall out of use, only occasional examples being seen in use by the 1870s.

In *Seven for a Secret* Mary Webb described how Gillian Lovekin made the everyday tea served to Robert Rideout, her father's cowman-shepherd, as attractive as possible, in order to gain his affection. Coming in from the dark, snowy yard he found that she had 'set the table with the best china, brought out cranberry jelly, new bread, lemon cheese', treats usually reserved for visitors.[14] The preserves would almost certainly have been home-made, cranberries being gathered from the wet, boggy and acid heaths of the county.

CRANBERRY JELLY

cranberries   *sugar*

Weigh the cranberries, and put into a large jar with ½ pt/ 300ml water per 1lb/450g of berries. Loosely cover the jar with a piece of cooking foil, and stand it in a pan of simmering water for about 2 hours, until all the juice has been extracted.

Pour the pulp into a square of fine cloth or muslin, tie up, and leave overnight for the juice to drip into a measuring jug.

Pour the juice into a pan, with 1lb/450g sugar to each pt/600ml of juice, bring it to the boil, skim, and boil for about another 30 min. until a sample will set on a cold saucer. Pour into sterilised jars, and seal down.

For making both orange and lemon cheese, the fruit would have to be bought from the greengrocers or market traders in town. Since they were relatively expensive, the pulp of the oranges was eaten fresh, and the juice of the lemons probably used in bakery and hot drinks on cold nights. It was the left-over peels that were used to make fruit cheeses, an economical practice we can still follow today.[15]

ORANGE OR LEMON CHEESE

6oz/175g orange or lemon peel 6 egg yolks
4oz/100g sugar 8oz/225g butter

Coarsely chop the peel, place in a pan, cover with water, put on the lid, and simmer for about an hour, until very tender.

Drain the peel, blend until perfectly smooth, then blend in the sugar, the warmed butter cut in small pieces, and finally the yolks.

Transfer the mixture to a saucepan, stir it constantly over a gentle heat until it has thickened and is hot, but not boiling, then pour into sterilised jars, seal down, and store in a cool place.

This made a delicious cold spread for bread and butter, but either the fresh uncooked mixture or the finished preserve could be used to fill tarts of shortcrust pastry, and baked at 220°C, 475°F, Gas mark 7 for 10 minutes. The quality of the pastry was a matter of considerable pride. When Sarah brought her cheesecakes out of the oven at *The House in Dormer Forest* she broke off a piece for Enoch, the oddman. "When I wed," she said dreamily, "'im as I choose shall get a plenty of these – a plenty." "Dear now!", said he, in the middle of chumbling, "It eats short"[16] A completely different experience met Gillian Lovekin when she opened her oven at 'Dysgwlfas-on-the-Wild-Moors', for every one of her cheesecakes had burnt as black as ebony. Her father was horrified by this needless waste. "How much stuff went to 'em?" he asked; "Pound o' flour, half dripping, three oranges, sugar, two eggs" she replied. He estimated that this had cost the household a shilling, since the eggs had come from her own poultry. This was the exact sum, now forfeited, which was to pay for her next, eagerly-awaited music lesson. Realising that it would have to be cancelled, she then burst into tears.[17] Strict economy was the practice in almost every Shropshire farmhouse.

Most fresh and preserved fruit was served in tarts to form the pudding course at dinner in Shropshire, but an apple turnover called an apple foot (plural apple feet) might be made either for tea, or to serve as a snack. One might form part of the farm-workers' 'bait' to be taken into the fields, or be carried off by others to be eaten later.[18]

APPLE FEET

8oz/225g plain flour *1½lb/625g cooking apples*
4oz/100g butter or lard *4 tbs sugar*
pinch of salt

Rub the butter or lard into the flour and salt, sprinkle on 3–4 tbs cold water, stir in with a round-bladed knife, until it forms large lumps, then use the hand to gently form it into a ball. Knead lightly for a few seconds, cover and set aside in a cool place.

Peel, core and slice the apples, and dust with the sugar. Roll out the pastry, cut into 5ins/13cm circles, and arrange the apple on one half of each, leaving a ½ins/1cm vacant border around the edge. Brush the edges with water, fold over and pinch the edges to form a semi-circular pasty, and stab the top with either the point of a knife or a fork.

Arrange on a greased baking sheet, and bake at 425°F, 220°C, Gas mark 7, for about 25 min.

This is the basic recipe, but it may be changed by adding ½ tsp ground cinnamon to the sugar, or by brushing their tops with milk, and sprinkling over a little sugar before baking.

For special teas etc., that great regional speciality, the Shrewsbury Cake, might be home-made, or much more probably bought from one of the confectioners in the county town.[19] At a national level, this cake is of considerable interest. It is one of the country's first cakes to be identified with a particular place, and one which has remained in continuous production, first as an accompaniment to wine, and then as a delicacy for tea or any other light meal.

In medieval England a 'cake' was 'brede baked and tornyd and wende at fyre'[20] In other words, it was a small yeast-raised wheat loaf, flat, round or oval in shape, baked on one side, and then on the other, using a bakestone set over the fire. In more recent times they became known as oven-bottom cakes, or oven-cakes. Following the same tradition, we still have tea-cakes today, even though they are made from bread dough. The 'cakes' provided by the bailiffs of Shrewsbury to Lady Hare, wife of the chief justice of Chester in 1540, may have been of this type, even though they were to accompany her claret and sack. When Lord Stafford visited the town in 1561, the bailiff gave him 'a dossen of fyen kakys. 2s.' Costing 2d each, these were clearly made of ingredients far more expensive than plain bread-flour, and suggest that what were to become known as Shrewsbury Cakes had already come into existence.

Later in Elizabeth's reign every visitor of any importance was presented with dozens of these twopenny 'fine cakes'. They ranged from her favourite, the Earl of Essex, the Lord President of the Council of the Marches, Sir Henry Sydney, and the Lord Chancellor's son, Henry Bromley, to Sir William Pellam, members of the Council for the Marches, and 'Mr Osley and Capten Buchas and other Landowners'. The method of delivering their cakes is detailed in a petition of 1582 to the bailiffs of Shrewsbury from their baker, Roger Phillips. His request was for compensation 'for a diaper napkin and a box which were sent with fine cakes to their worships [probably Sir Henry Sydney's party], and which though often demanded cannot be obtained'. The gifts which accompanied the cakes; sugar, quince marmalade, wine, sack (a sweetish white wine from Spain and the Canaries), and hippocras, show that they were to be served as part of an exclusive sweetmeat banquet, an entertainment usually held at quite separate times and locations than those of the main meals of the day. The hippocras was a sweet, strong spiced wine, which took its name from the conical shape of its filter bag, this supposedly resembling the sleeve of the celebrated Greek physician Hippocrates.

HIPPOCRAS (1580s) [21]

2pt/1150ml red or white wine *2 tsp ground cinnamon*
½ tsp each of ground clove, *¼ tsp ground ginger*
nutmeg & galingale *8oz/225g sugar*

Stir the spices into the wine, and leave overnight. Next morning run it through a coffee-filter paper, passing it through the same filter a second time if at all cloudy.

Stir the sugar into the filtered wine, after which it is ready for consumption.

N.B. Although the above recipe is relatively quick, it is better to use bruised or coarsely chopped spices, and soak them in the wine in very lightly corked bottles left in a cool place for about a week. This makes filtering far easier, and reduces the chance of ropy colloids, which are virtually impossible to filter.

By now Shrewsbury's 'fine cakes' were a well-established product of the towns' bakers, along with the ordinary bread 'cakes' for general use. In 1596, however, the bailiffs of the corporation had to forbid the making of all cakes, since there was a nation-wide shortage of grain, and many people were facing starvation. Local circumstances were so bad that a famine relief quota of 3,200 bushels, some 85 tons, of wheat and rye had to be shipped up the Severn from Bristol. In such conditions it was important to ensure that all bread was baked strictly according to the weights stated in the assize of bread, as agreed by the magistrates. The production of unregulated 'cakes' would clearly lead to unfair distribution, and had to be banned. This severely damaged the bakers' interests, and so John Higgins and William Fox 'wardens of this fellowship of bakers within the towne and liberties' of Shrewsbury appealed against the bailiffs' decision. In their petition, they claimed to have made cakes from time immemorial, and prayed that they might continue to make penny and halfpenny (bread) cakes as before, "but no fyne cakes unless the causers thereof [i.e. customers] do bring butter with them to make them withall." The result of this petition is not recorded, but we may assume that 'fyne cakes' were soon back in production once the crisis was over.

In 1600 Shrewsbury's 'fine cakes' were well known to the town's visitors and inhabitants, but to few others. Only now did their reputation start to expand beyond the immediate area. On 16th August 1602, the twenty-year-old Lord Herbert of Cherbury wrote the following lines from Eyton-upon-Severn to his guardian, Sir George More; 'Lest you think this country is ruder than it is, I have sent you some of the bread, which I am sure will be dainty, howsoever it be not pleasinge; it is a kind of cake which our countrey people use and made in no place in England but in Shrewsbury; if you vouchsafe to taste of them, you will enworthy the countrey and sender. Measure not my love in substance of it, which is brittle, but the form of it, which is circular'. This first physical description of the fine cakes is particularly reassuring in confirming their 'short' texture and circular shape, here taken to indicate eternity. A traditional verse epitomised this as;

> The ring is round that has no end,
> So is my love for thee, my friend.

As such gifts of 'fine cakes' spread around England, they now required a name which would distinguish them from any of the other regional varieties of fine cakes. The first published recipe appeared in John Murrell's *A Delightfull Daily exercise for Ladies and Gentlewomen* of 1617;[22]

TO MAKE SHREWSBERY CAKES

8oz/225g flour *¼ nutmeg, grated*
2oz/50g caster sugar *1tbs rosewater*
3oz/75g butter

Mix the dry ingredients, rub in the butter, work in the rosewater, and knead for 10–15 min until it forms a very smooth dough.

Roll out $\frac{3}{16}$ ins/4mm thick on a floured board, cut into 3 or 4 ins rounds, place on a sheet of plain paper on a baking sheet, and bake at 170°C, 325°F, Gas mark 3 for some 15 min until just starting to change colour, but not browned. Remove from the oven, stack in a tall column, and leave to cool.

Although simple and almost four hundred years old, this Jacobean recipe still produces good results. By the mid seventeenth century the 'Shropshire Cakes' made by ladies such as Madam Avery had become rather richer and much more ornamental in appearance.[23]

TO MAKE A SHROPSHIRE CAKE

'Take two pound of dryed flour after it has been searced fine, one pound of good sugar dried and searced, also a little beaten sinamon, or some nottmegg greeted and steeped in rose water; so streene two eggs, white and all, not beaten to it, as much melted butter as will work it to a paste; so mold it and roule it into longe roules, and cutt off as much at a time as will make a cake, two ounces is enough for one cake: then roule it in a ball between your hands: so flat it on a little white paper cut for a cake, and with your hand beat it as big as a cheese trencher and a little thicker than a paste board: then prick them with a comb not too deep in squares like diamon and prick every cake in every diamon to the bottom; so bake them in an oven not too hot: when they rise up white let them soake a little, then draw. If the sugar be dry enough you need not dry but searce it; you must brake in your eggs after you have wroat in some of your butter into your flower: prick and mark them when they are cold: this quantity will make a dozen and two or three, which is enough for my own at a time, take off the papers when they are cold.'

The value of this recipe is that it was clearly noted down by someone who had never come across such a cake before, and wished to record every detail, to make sure of getting things right. It is extremely unusual to be given the weight of any cake at this period, but here it is stated as 2oz/50g. Similarly the sizes are rarely, if ever, given, but here they are the size of a cheese-trencher. Since these still exist in museum collections, we know that the cakes were almost 5ins/13cm in diameter. Their decoration of a diamond pattern of comb perforations, each with a hole pricked through its centre, adds a further interest, since it shows how such large cakes could be broken up into dainty squares (like a modern chocolate bar) for elegant eating. Polite Cavalier ladies would not wish to be seen gnawing at a five-inch shortcake! The existence of this pattern on a mid seventeenth century Shropshire cake also helps us to date the start of the identical design seen on top of Victorian Shrewsbury Simnels. They are quite straightforward to make today;

MADAME SUSAN AVERY'S SHROPSHEERE CAKES

1lb/450g plain flour
8oz/225g butter
8oz/225g caster sugar
½ tsp ground cinnamon or grated nutmeg

1 medium egg
1 tsp rosewater
non-stick baking parchment

Rub the butter into the dry ingredients, then use a round-bladed knife to work in the egg and rosewater, finally kneading lightly to form a very stiff dough.

Divide the dough into 16 pieces, roll each into a ball, place on the baking parchment, and pat out to about 5ins/13cm diameter, and about ⅛ins/4mm in thickness.

Using a comb, mark each cake in a pattern of small diamonds, going half-way through, then use a wooden skewer to pierce a hole in the centre of each diamond.

Bake at 180°C, 350°F, Gas mark 4, for some 10–15 minutes, until cooked, but not browned. Allow to cool before removing from the parchment.

The first published recipe 'To make Shrewsbury Cakes', using the new name for the old 'fine cakes', appears in 'W.M.' 's *The Compleat Cook* published in London in 1655.[24] It is very similar to that given above, but uses ground ginger for its flavouring, has rather more egg, and hygienically recommends the use of 'a Comb that hath not been used'. During the later seventeenth century the recipes for Shrewsbury Cakes appear in a number of manuscript recipe books, showing that they were now being baked in fashionable households in distant parts of the country. In London, for example, the Restoration scholar and virtuoso John Evelyn recorded three versions in his recipe book, one flavouring them with ground coriander seeds, and another using 'the great teeth of a comb that is new and kept for that use'. All were rolled out as a sheet 'of reasonable thickness' before being cut to shape using the rim of a wineglass, showing that here they were being much reduced in

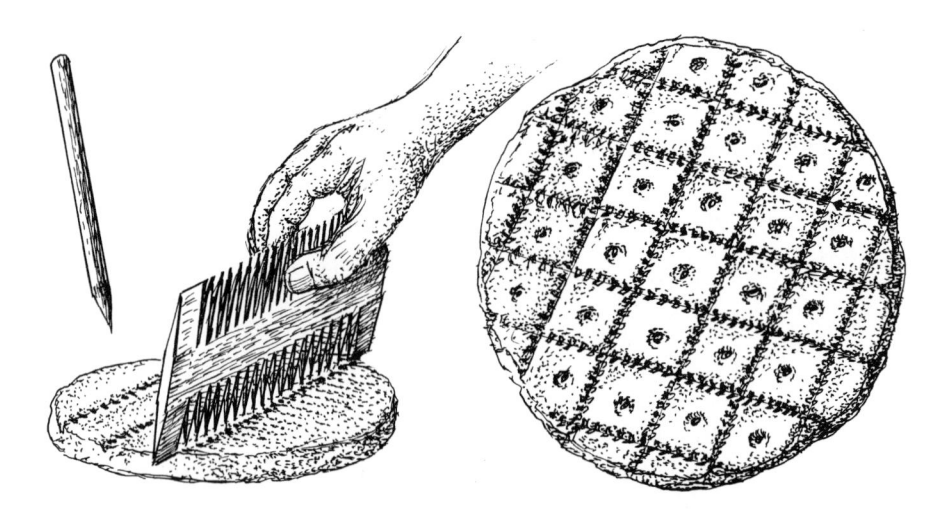

Fig 21   Mid-17th century Shropshire cakes were impressed with a comb and a skewer to produce not only an attractive design, but a means of snapping them into small squares for elegant eating.

size.[25] Meanwhile at Westbury in Buckinghamshire Rebecca Price recorded Mrs Burnford's recipe for 'Shroesbery Cakes' which incorporated both cream and orange-flower water, and were simply made 'in what fashion you please' before being pricked and put into the oven. Already 'Shrewsbury Cakes' were becoming the generic name for a variety of rich, crisp shortbreads.[26]

Back in Shrewsbury, however, the cakes were being made to recipes such as this, taken from the 1630–1750 family recipe book of Colonel Plomer.

SHREWSBURY CAKES[27]

9oz/250g plain flour
6oz/175g butter
1 tbs caraway seeds
½ tsp ground nutmeg

6oz/175g sugar
1 medium egg, beaten
1 tbs sherry
1 tbs rosewater

Mix the dry ingredients, rub in the butter, and work in the mixed egg, sherry and rosewater to form a dough. Knead lightly, roll out, about ¼ins/·7cm thick, cut in 3ins/10cm rounds, prick the surface, and bake at 140°C, 275°F, Gas mark 1 for some 20 min until just starting to brown.

In the eighteenth century Shrewsbury Cakes retained their popularity, and featured in the popular literature of the day. The lines composed by various writers tell us of their short texture, their price, or their place of origin, as may be seen in the following examples;

> Why, brother Wilful of Salop, you might be as short
> as a Shrewsbury cake if you please
> (William Congreve, *The Way of the World* 1700)
> Right Shrewsbury Cakes! They are so fine,
> They're fit to eat alone or with wine.
> Twelve a penny
> By four is too many,
> Gentlemen, will ye please to buy any?
> (Dr. William Hayes, organist at St. Mary's Shrewsbury, 1729–1731)
> Enter to them FOG crying Gingerbread who salutes the Doctor
> and asks him if, since his preferment has led him into Salop,
> he has brought any Shrewsbury Cakes. The Doctor waives
> the question.

(Anon. *Droll or humour of Bartholomew Fair* 1733)
And here each season do these cakes abide
Whose honoured name the inventive city own,
Rendering through Britain's isle Salopia's praises known.'
... Ah, 'midst the rest, may flowers adorn his grave
Whose art did first these dulcet cakes display;
A motive fair to learning's imps he gave
Who, cheerless o'er her darkling region stray,
Till reason's morn arise and light them on their way.
(William Shenstone of Leasowes, (1714–63) *The Schoolmistress*)

In the late Georgian period a number of Shrewsbury confectioners enjoyed an excellent reputation for making Shrewsbury Cakes, their names including Blakemore, Pidduck, Davies and Williams. Minshull's *Salopian Directory* of 1786 also lists 'Hill, baker and confectioner, Raven Street.' This was the same person as the Mrs.Hill, Confectioner, Castle Street, Salop,' noted on a bill dated 20th May 1793, 'Raven Street' being the former name of Castle Street. By 1804, Minshull's *Directory* was listing 'James Palin, confectioner and stationer' at the same location, showing that there had been a change of ownership. The appearance of Palin at this date is of particular interest, since he still enjoys a totally undeserved reputation as the originator of Shrewsbury Cakes. Anyone walking along Castle Street today will see the modern shop building at the junction with School Gardens, its wall bearing a bronze plaque inscribed;

> This shop occupies the site of a building where Pailin first made the unique Shrewsbury Cakes to his original recipe in the year 1760 ...

It would be hard to find any plaque which manages to convey so much mis-information in so few words. Even his surname is spelt incorrectly.

In 1760 Palin appears to have been the two-year old son of a Chester grocer; he never trained as a confectioner, and it is extremely unlikely that he ever baked a Shrewsbury Cake in his life, let alone develop their unique original recipe. How could he – they had already been in production for two hundred years! The truth about Palin's place in the story of the Shrewsbury Cake was first revealed by A.J. And L.C. Lloyd in the 1930s.

After being apprenticed to a bookseller, James Palin was made a freeman of Chester in 1784. About 1790 he migrated to Shrewsbury, settling in the parish of St. Chad's. The following year he married

By Special Appointment.

VINCENT CRUMP,
CONFECTIONER
TO HER MAJESTY THE QUEEN,
WYLE COP & PRIDE HILL, SHREWSBURY.

ROYAL SHREWSBURY CAKES.
Bride, Citron, and Dessert Cakes.   Simnels in the Season.
DEALER IN BRITISH WINES.

SHREWSBURY.

THE CELEBRATED
Shrewsbury Cake and British Wine Establishment.
ESTABLISHED 1760.

T. PLIMMER,
Wholesale and Retail Confectioner,
FANCY BREAD AND BISCUIT BAKER,
CASTLE STREET, (Corner of School Lane,)
SHREWSBURY.
N.B.—AGENT FOR THE BRITISH HONG-KONG TEA COMPANY.

Fig 23   1861 advertisements for Shrewsbury Cakes.

Frances Hill at her parish church of St. Mary's, only a short distance from her mother's confectionery shop in Castle Street. As we have seen, Mrs Hill still continued to sell her bakery from here well into the 1790s, her daughter, almost certainly trained up in the business, probably continuing this side of the enterprise, while James concentrated on selling stationery and books. In 1815–16 he was elected Warden, or head, of the Shrewsbury Booksellers Company. This was the trade he knew, and which he followed into the 1820s, his death at the age of 71 being recorded in the local newspaper in 1829. So how did a bookseller gain a reputation as a confectioner?

The answer is poetry. The Rev. Richard Harris Barham (1788–1845), writing under the nom-de-plume of Thomas Ingoldsby, had a great facility for inventing ancient legends told in verse. These were published *c.* 1840 as the *Ingoldsby Legends*, their humorous Gothick Horror style exactly fitting the mood of the time, so that they enjoyed great success. 'The legend of Bloudie Jacke' was, if he was to be believed, drawn from that of 'The Shropshire Bluebeard' collected from a Mrs Botherby, a native of the county, and alluded to by Ralph de Diceto, Dean of St. Paul's in 1183. It tells of young Mary-Anne entering Bloudie Jacke's tower, where she sees him dragging her stone-dead sister by the hair. As she cowers under a stair, she is discovered by a horrid great dog, which is about to tear her limb from limb. Being a properly prepared young lady, she whips out a Shrewsbury Cake, which the savage beast apparently finds delicious, and allows her to escape;

> She has given him a bun and a roll
> Bloudie Jacke,
> She has given him a roll and a bun
> And a Shrewsbury cake
> Of Pailin's own make
> Which she happened to take ere her run
> She begun –
> She'd been used to a luncheon at One

She then ran into Shrewsbury, rallied the people and the authorities, who then found Bloudie Jacke, chopped him into pieces, and stuck his head on a pole at 'Wylde Coppe'. The moral of the tale was clear; young ladies should never associate with scary young men;

> Or sometime or another they'll make
> A mistake
> And lose more than a Shrewsberrie cake.

A footnote to the poem adds the line;

> Oh Pailin! Prince of cake compounders!
> The mouth liquifies at thy very name-
> but there!'

Barham clearly had a knowledge of the town, and would have found the Palins' bookshop-cum-confectioners uniquely suited to meet his intellectual and gustatory needs. This probably explains his inclusion of Palins' name and products in his poetry. Certainly there could be no financial motivation, for Palin had been dead some ten years before the *Legends* were published. By 1828 the shop and confectionery business was being operated by Thomas Owen. He was still there in 1851, but by 1868 it was in the hands of Thomas Plimmer. He was the first to take full advantage of the Pailin/Ingoldsby Legend connection, developing a circular trademark which featured the three loggerheads of the town's coat of arms encircled by appropriate lines from the 'Legend of Bloudie Jacke'. This was first used in June or July 1875, becoming a registered trade mark on 17th April 1878. It is interesting to note that it followed Barham's misspelling of Palin's name, rendering it as 'Pailin', and claimed that its cakes were made from his original recipe (although we now know that it was probably Hill's recipe which had been followed from the foundation of the business, some forty years before he ever came to Shrewsbury). However, the publicity worked so well, that the Plimmer's 'Pailin's Original Shrewsbury Cakes' became widely accepted as the town's premier brand, greatly appreciated for their short texture and rich, buttery taste.

In 1938 the business was taken over by Phillip's Stores Ltd, a large-scale concern which continued to make 'Pailin's Original Shrewsbury Cakes' at 16–17 Castle Street, but now selling them at its six other shops in the town, and thirteen others in the county and beyond. As in 1596, a national emergency, this time the Second World War and rationing, forced them to go out of production. By the 1950s, however, 'Pailin's' still with their characteristic trademark, returned to the shelves, continuing to be made in the same shop as they had been for two hundred years, until the site was cleared for redevelopment.

Although the 'Pailin's' brand of Shrewsbury Cakes had the protection of a registered trade mark, there were many other producers operating in the town in Georgian, Victorian and more

Price per tin :

6 Cakes 2/6 12 Cakes 4/6

Postage Extra

Fig 24 This trade mark for Palin's Shrewsbury Cakes was introduced by Thomas Plimmer in 1875, and registered three years later.

modern times. All followed very similar recipes, as may be seen from the following examples, taken from the popular cookery books of their day;

Mrs Raffald's Shrewsbury Cakes, 1769[28]
Take half a pound of butter, beat it to a cream. Then put in half a pound of flour, one egg, six ounces of loaf sugar beat and sifted, half an ounce of carraway seeds mixed into a paste. Roll them thin and cut them round with a small glass or little tins. Prick them and lay them on sheets of tin and bake them in a slow oven.

Dr. William Kitchiner's Shrewsbury Cakes, 1817[29]
Rub well together one pound of pounded Sugar, one pound of fresh Butter, and one pound and a half of sifted Flour – mix it into a paste, with half a gill of milk and cream, and one egg, – let it lie

half an hour, roll it out thin, cut it into small cakes with a tin cutter, about three inches over, and bake them on a clean baking plate in a moderate oven.

Theodore Garrett's great *Encyclopaedia of Practical Cookery* of 1893 gave eight versions, all contributed by the leading cooks and confectioners of the day, who still continued to include rosewater, caraway seed, cinnamon or nutmeg, as in the seventeenth century.[30]

Almost every visitor to the town found them advertised in the bakers' and confectioners' shops, tried them, and found them delicious;

> Nathaniel Hawthorne, 5th September, 1855;[31]
> we went into a shop to buy some Royal Shrewsbury cakes, which we had seen advertised at several shops. They are very rich cakes, with plenty of eggs, sugar and butter, and very little flour.

> An American visitor, summer 1867;[32]
> I wanted to prove Congreve's simile, and got some Shrewsbury cakes, 'short' indeed; like what we call Scotch cakes.

> William Dean Howells, 1890s;
> The city is the home of those Shrewsbury cakes famed in 'The Ingoldsby Legends', and once offered to distinguished visitors, who thought them delicious; but if they were no better than now, we can imagine how poor the living of the proudest was in olden times.

> C.G. Harper, 1902;
> One thing certainly the visitor to Shrewsbury cannot, nay, must not fail of doing. He must not neglect the delicacy peculiar to the town in the making of cakes goes on unfailingly, and the eating of them is a rite, a canonical observance almost.

Today's visitors to Shrewsbury might easily walk around its bright shopping centres and historic streets without seeing any trace of its once-famous cakes, until they enter Mardol. Here, at no. 73 Christopher's Fine Foods still continue to make them by hand to an old recipe.

It would be almost impossible to give a standard recipe for Shrewsbury Cakes, but the following gives good results, and the opportunity to try their different traditional flavours. It uses the probably older rubbing-in method, rather than the creaming method given in more recent versions:

SHREWSBURY CAKES

10oz/225g plain flour
6oz/175g butter
choice of; 1 tbs carraway seeds/
  ½ tsp ground cinnamon/
  ½ tsp ground nutmeg/
  2 tbs chopped candied peel/
  grated zest of a lemon

5oz/150g caster sugar
1 medium egg, beaten

Rub the butter into the flour, then mix in the caster sugar and spices.

Make a well in the centre, pour in the egg, mix in with a round-ended knife, then knead until all the dry ingredients have been incorporated into a firm dough.

Form the dough into a ball, turn it onto a floured board, and pat out to form a thick slab, before rolling to about ¼ ins/ c. ·7cm thick, then cut into 3 or 4 ins/8 or 10·5cm rounds.

Prick the cakes, arrange them on a baking sheet, and bake at 180°C, 350°F, Gas mark 4 for about 20 min.

Although not so well known as the Shrewsbury Cake, Shropshire has an equally distinctive item of regional confectionery, the Market Drayton gingerbread. There are innumerable traditional gingerbreads in England, all of which fall into five main categories; unbaked and moulded gingerbreads, moulded and baked gingerbreads, cakes called gingerbreads, parkins, and flat biscuits called gingerbreads. Those associated with Market Drayton fall outside all of these groups, being $3 \times \frac{1}{2} \times \frac{3}{8}$ ins deep/ $80 \times 12 \times 10$ mm each, with ridged tops, and sold in blocks of seven. They first appear around 1817, in the last years of King George III, their subsequent history having been fully researched by Meg Pybus in *Under the Buttercross*, her book on Market Drayton.[33]

The date of their introduction is quite significant. After the upheaval of the French Revolution and the final defeat of Napoleon at Waterloo in 1815, a number of top-rank Italian and French cooks and confectioners left their native countries, and began to work in England, either independently, or for noble families. Among the techniques the popularised was that of pushing with a syringe. This required the use of a tinplate cylinder, similar to a modern icing syringe, but rather longer. Metal plates pierced by round, lobed or star-shaped holes fitted over one end, while a wooden plunger slid into the other.[34] Holding it by a pair of handles on the sides, the operator pulled it towards him, the end of the plunger pressing against his chest, so that the biscuit-paste within was squeezed out through the plate, to form a long, shaped strip on the baking sheet below. Later versions were mechanised, being worked by screw-threads, in order to extrude very stiff doughs.[35]

In Newport, John Bullock was making biscuits apparently of this type in 1847.[36] They can easily be made by rolling the dough into long, narrow rods, instead of using a biscuit-forcer;

FINGER BISCUITS

8oz/225g flour
2oz/50g butter
4oz/100g sugar
1 tsp ground ginger
1 tsp ground cinnamon
1tsp ground nutmeg
5oz/150g golden syrup
1–2 tsp orange flour water or milk

Rub the butter into the flour, mix in the sugar and spices, make a well in the centre, place the bowl on the scales, and weigh in the syrup.

Stir in the syrup, then use the hand to work it into a dough, sprinkling in just sufficient orange flour water or milk to make it workable, but still quite stiff.

Use the hands to roll lumps of the dough into ½ins/12mm diameter rods on a floured board and cut in 4ins/10cm lengths. Space about 1ins/2·5cm apart on a greased baking sheet, and bake at 180°C, 350°F, Gas mark 4 for 15 min. allowing to cool before removing from the baking sheet.

The Market Drayton gingerbreads recipe made by Mr Thomas was passed on to a succession of members of his family, to a nephew W. Harper in 1829, to his son H.H. Harper in 1854, who transferred it to his cousin R. Billington in 1864, his son S.R. Billington and then S.P. Billington in 1898. The Billingtons were very proud of their position as the original makers of Market Drayton gingerbread, using a family tree on their promotional packaging, its branches showing where it was distributed all over the world, including Russia, India, Japan, Australia and North America. This international trade probably represented orders sent out to ex-patriates who wanted to enjoy their favourite local delicacy, rather than a truly world-wide trade, but still reflected a real demand for a popular product. There is no doubt that Billingtons were the leaders in this field for 120 years, but in 1937 they retired and sold their trade assets, including the use of the famous Billingtons name and wrappers, to Mr S.T. Hayward Hughes. He continued to make the gingerbreads in his shop on the High Street in Cheswardine up to the outbreak of war, which interrupted the trade, and terminated all exports. After the war, he was soon back in production, but never again to the earlier levels. His recommendation was to dunk the gingerbreads into either sherry or port, continuing the cakes-with-wine tradition of the seventeenth century.

'N.B. All other members have picked up what they DO know either directly or indirectly from this establishment.' This statement on Billington's publicity had showed that others were moving into their exclusive trade. The chief of these was W.I. Chesters, established in 1850, with shops in the High Street. They too enjoyed considerable success, sending orders out to most parts of the Empire as well as serving an extensive local and national trade, which included Fortnum & Mason in London. Since they could not claim the title 'The Old Original' for their products, their packaging used the term 'Market Drayton Prize Gingerbread', accompanied by drawings of the 'Tudor House' and the thatched cottages in Cheshire Street. The Depression of the 1930s brought real difficulties to the trade, and so on 3rd September, 1937, the business was sold to Reginald Boughey and William Cox, including the exclusive and absolute benefit of the secret process, and the right to manufacture and sell Chesters Prize Gingerbread. Government restrictions on the supply of the essential ingredients put it out of production during the War, but it enjoyed a popular revival in 1954, even exporting to New Zealand, Australia, America and Czechoslovakia, but then closed after Mr Cox's death in 1960.

The appreciation of the town's gingerbreads encouraged housewives to bake it in their own kitchens, even though they had neither the recipe nor the required equipment. The following home version was published in the 1930s, but it produces an extremely hard gingerbread, a real challenge to the teeth, but improved by dunking.[37]

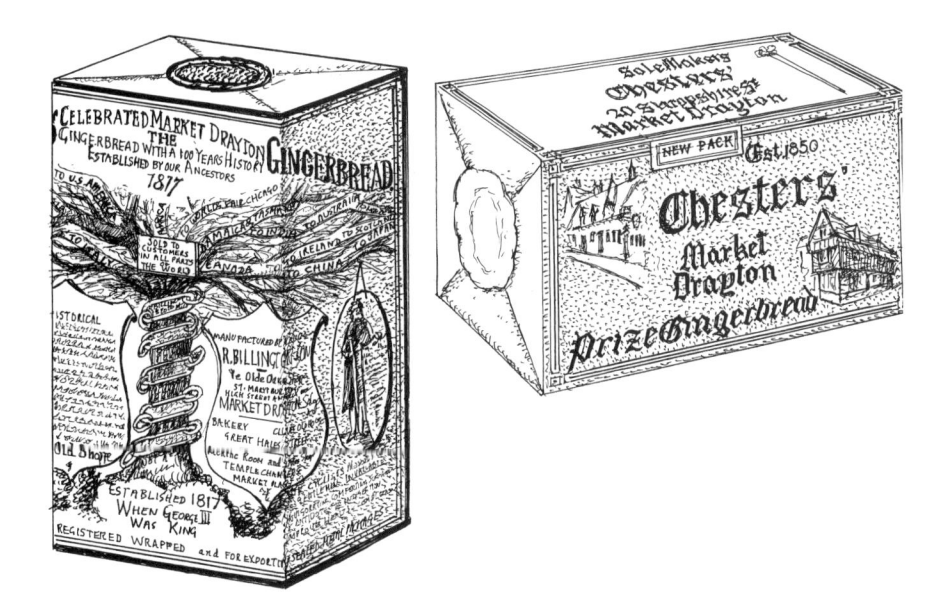

Fig 25   The leading manufacturers of Market Drayton Gingerbread developed very strong brands by the use of distinctive packaging, as seen in these examples from Billingtons (left) and Chesters (right).

GINGERBREAD

1½lb/675g plain flour
8oz/225g butter
8oz/225g sugar
ground ginger
1 tbs brandy

pinch of ground mace
1oz/25g candied peel, finely chopped
1 egg, beaten
8oz/225g Golden Syrup

Rub the butter into the flour, mix in the dry ingredients, make a hole in the centre, and pour in the previously mixed treacle, egg and brandy. Stir these together then knead to form a firm dough. Cover this, and leave overnight.

Form the dough into finger-size rolls, some 3ins/10cm long, and arrange on a buttered baking tray, and bake at 170°C, 325°F, Gas mark 3 for some 20 min, until golden brown, then remove and allow to cool before removing from the tray.

As in other parts of England, girls who went into service in one of the 'Big Houses' acquired the taste, and frequently the skills, to bake many other teatime treats. These would probably include deliciously light and crisp-surfaced fatless spongecakes, seedcakes, fruitcakes, ginger cakes and chocolate cakes. Even though popular in Shropshire, they represented the widespread national culinary tradition, rather than the local one, and so are not described here.

CHAPTER 4

FESTIVE FOODS

In all traditional societies the progress of each year was marked by an apparently unchanging sequence of communal events. Governed both by the seasons and by Christian festivals, the latter frequently continuing many much older practices, they provided everyone with something to look forward to. Sometimes it was a day off work, and a visit to a fair, wake or picnic, but more often it would be a special evening or meal spent at home or with close family, friends and neighbours. At all of these food would play one of the most important parts. Sometimes it was the sole reason for the event, as when a particular food was in plentiful supply. At others it was the centrepiece, in reality being anticipated with just as much, or even more pleasure than the festival itself. The hymns and sermon at the chill Christmas morning service might well feed the immortal soul, but to mortal man, woman and child it was the following dinner which frequently took priority in the mind, – and most certainly in the stomach.

After celebrating Christmas and the New Year around midwinter, there next came a period of frugality. This was the 'Black Quarter' for many cottagers, when the family's cow was 'dry' for calving, the store of bacon was finished, and the new flitches not ready for eating.[1] In addition, the religious period of fasting for Lent was about to commence. Strictly observed by the Roman Catholic church, it was still forcibly maintained in Elizabethan England, the 1562 'Act touching Politick Constitutions for the Maintenance of the Navy' ensuring that no-one was ever allowed to eat 'neither meat nor eggs either' during Lent or on any Wednesday, Friday and Saturday throughout the year. Anyone so offending had to face a fine of £3, or else spend three months in prison. John Buttry of Shrewsbury found himself imprisoned there in 1599 because he had had meat cooked in his house during Lent, purely for the sustenance of his sickly wife. The only way to avoid such problems was to obtain a licence issued by the parish priest, countersigned by his churchwardens, and costing £1 6s 8d for a lord, 13s 4d for a knight, or 6s 8d for an ordinary man, enormous sums for that period. These still had to be obtained up to the period of the Civil Wars. In 1641, for example, Edward Lewis, the vicar of Cherbury, issued one of the last licenses 'to eate flesh, forasmuch as it doth manifestly appear that the gentleman is visited with a dangerous sickness & of long continuaunce . . .'[2]

SHROVE TUESDAY

On this day, immediately before the start of Lent, it was important to ensure that all the perishable forbidden foods were eaten up. Since these included eggs, it was the ideal time to make pancakes: hence Pancake Day. In towns and villages such as Shrewsbury, Newport and Edgmond the Pancake Bell was rung from the Church tower at around 11.30 a.m. marking the start of a holiday for the apprentices, and the making of pancakes in numerous homes.[3]

MOTHERING SUNDAY

Mid Lent Sunday was the traditional day for those who, whatever their age, returned home to visit their mothers, taking with them presents of food for a special meal. At Ludlow large quantities of veal were purchased on the Saturday, for the veal and rice pudding dinners.[4] At Stottesden thick, stiff pancakes called 'fraises' were eaten with a sweet white sauce, while at Pulverbatch a dish of custard eaten with some leftover Christmas mincemeat was the special dish.[5] All of these were most probably introduced during the Georgian period, since they clearly infringed the old Lenten restrictions.

In Shrewsbury, the traditional food-gift for Mothering Sunday was the Shrewsbury Simnel. This was no ordinary cake, but one of Britain's largest most impressive and most expensive items of regional bakery. The first detailed descriptions were written in the 1830s, the following being typical;

'The Simnel is a cake made with a very hard crust, the inside well stored with currants, raisins, candied peel &c.; a coating of saffron, turmeric and the yolks of egg is given to the crust, which imparts to it a rare though not unpleasant flavour.'[6]

Simnel. A plum cake having a raised crust for the exterior . . . exceptionally hard and highly flavoured with saffron. It partakes of the nature of a mince pie, but the contents are packed close together, and consequently rendered still more indigestible.[7]

They are raised cakes, the crust of which is made of fine flour and water, with sufficient saffron to give it a deep yellow colour, and the interior is filled with materials of a very rich plum-cake, with plenty of candied lemon peel, and other good things. They are made up very stiff, tied up in a cloth and boiled for several hours, after which they are brushed over with egg, and then baked. When ready for sale the crust is as hard as if made of wood, a circumstance which has given rise to stories of a lady taking hers for a footstool. They are made in different sizes, and are rather expensive, some large ones selling for as much as half a guinea, or even, we believe, a guinea, while smaller ones may be had for half a crown.[8]

From the 13th century English simnels made from a yeasted dough of the finest sifted wheat flour, in Latin *simila*, were first boiled and then baked. They were rarely made after the 15th century, but in Shrewsbury the name was transferred to a new kind of boiled-then-baked cake. Old recipes, just like old houses, may be approximately dated from a study of their materials and methods of construction. In the case of the Shrewsbury simnel, this places its origins back to sometime around 1600. Its pastry, made by boiling water with saffron, and then poured scalding hot into the flour to form a fatless hot-water pie crust, is a direct survival of much earlier medieval practice. The use of pastry to enclose a rich fruit-cake mixture is totally alien to any form of medieval pastry, however, the technique being first recorded for Banbury cakes in Gervase Markham's *English Hus-wife* of 1615.[9] This was filled with a special yeast-raised currant dough. Later recipes include equal weights of candied orange peel and currants, sweetened with honey and flavoured with cinnamon, allspice, ginger and nutmeg.[10] As to their appearance, we are fortunate to have two drawings, one of 1866 and another of the early 20th century.[11] The latter was probably made by Lady Gomme at a meeting of either the Folk Lore Society or the English Folk Cookery Association. Both show simnels which look exactly like pork pies, their heights being about a quarter of their diameters. Within their zig-zag notched rims, their tops are marked out in diamonds, each pierced by a small hole, and with a larger hole in the middle of the whole lid. This decoration perfectly matches that on the top of 17th century Shrewsbury cakes. Lady Gomme noted the dimensions of hers, some three inches high by fifteen inches in diameter. By combining all the above information, and carrying out a number of practical trials, the following recipe produces good results.

SHREWSBURY SIMNEL CAKE

Pastry case
1½lb/675g plain flour
1pt/ 600ml water
large pinch saffron
1 egg, beaten

Filling
4oz/100g butter
4oz/100g sugar
1 egg, beaten
10oz/275g candied peel
8oz/225g currants
4oz/100g raisins
½ a nutmeg, grated
½ tsp ground cinnamon
¼ tsp ground allspice
¼ tsp ground ginger

Make the pastry by sifting the flour into the bowl. Measure a pint of water into a saucepan, add the saffron, bring to the boil, pour into a well in the flour, mix in, then knead until all the flour has been worked in, knead into a ball, cover, and set it aside.

Make the filling by creaming the butter, creaming in the sugar, and beating in the beaten egg, and the flour, little by little, to form a stiff mixture. Work in the dried fruits, peel and spices, using the hands if necessary, finally forming it into a solid cake some 6ins/15cm diameter, with a flat base and top, and vertical sides.

Place a very large pan on the stove, fill with some 6ins/25cm of water, cover, and leave to come to the boil, having placed a circular trivet in the bottom.

Weigh off 1½lb/675g of the pastry, and raise it by hand until the base and walls are ¼ins/6mm in thickness, the walls are some 2½ins/6cm high, and the inside large enough to receive the round of filling.

FESTIVE FOODS

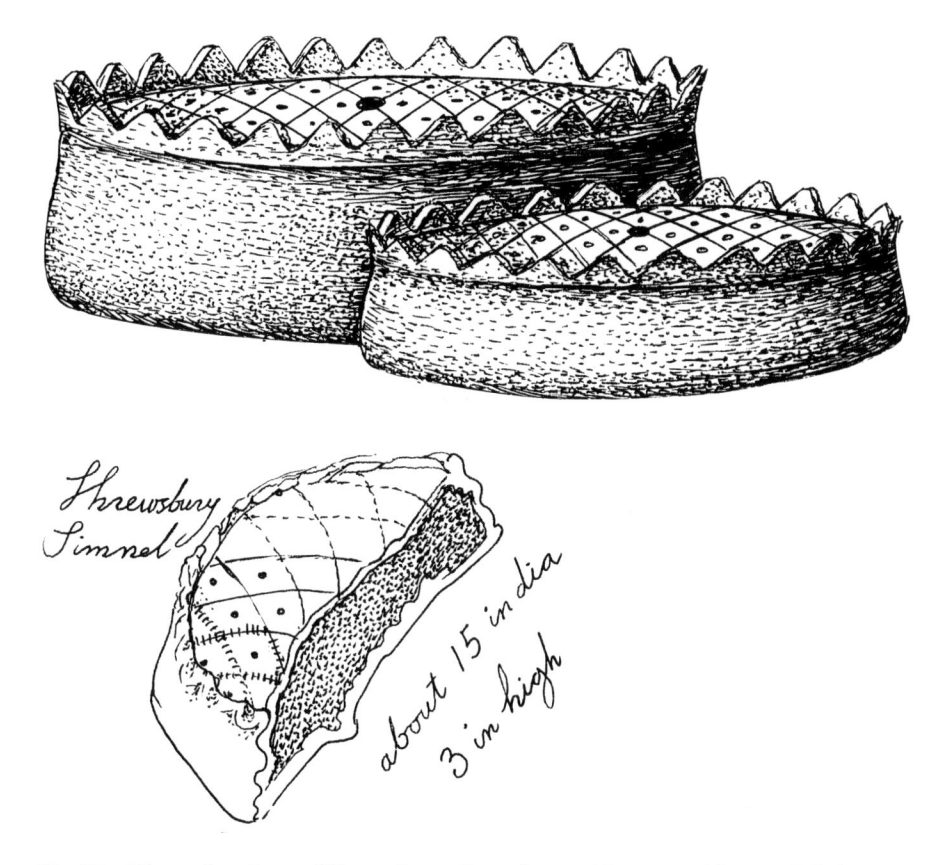

Fig 26   These drawings of Shrewsbury Simnels provide rare evidence of their original appearance. The pair of simnels date from 1868, while the single one was probably drawn by Lady Gomme in the early 20th century, when they were still being made.

Place the filling inside, and work the walls close to it all round. Roll the remaining pastry into a large disc, and decorate it by first marking (not piercing) it in squares using a clean comb, and impressing a hole half-through the centre of each square using any round-pointed implement.

Brush beaten egg around the top of the inside of the raised pastry, set the decorated disc within it as a lid, pinch the top edges together, and pinch and cut them to some ¼ins/6mm in thickness, and ½ins/12mm in height. Cut a ½ins/12mm hole in the middle of the lid.

Cut a piece of muslin some 30ins/75cm square, lift the cake onto the middle, gather the loose muslin on top, and tie it as near to the lid as possible with a piece of string.

Plunge the cake into the boiling water, so that its weight is taken by the trivet, re-cover the pan, and boil for 2 hours.

Pre-heat the oven to 170°C, 325°C Gas mark 3.

Use the handle of a wooden spoon to raise the loose muslin above the level of the boiling water, allow it to drain for a short period, then grasp it within a thick towel, and lift the cake out and on to a greased baking sheet.

Remove the string, open the muslin, pull one edge under the whole, leaving the cake on its own, and mop dry with either a cloth or a pastry brush.

Using both fingers and comb quickly dipped in cold water, pinch the rim back to being vertical, and re-mark the decoration as required. Using a pair of scissors, then cut around the rim to give it a zig-zag outline.

Brush the whole cake with beaten egg, and bake at 170°C, 325°F, Gas mark 3 for 2 hours. Use a skewer to check that the centre of the fruit filling is completely baked, then remove from the oven and allow to cool on its baking sheet.

The result is a $4\frac{1}{2}$lb/2kg cake around 8 inches/20cm in diameter with a hard glossy golden-brown crust and an extremely rich dark interior, as in the original description. The only remaining problem is how to get into it, for the crust is unbelievably hard and tough, and cannot be penetrated with even the sharpest of knives. To cut it into slices requires the use of a vice-like grip and a joiner's hand-saw, which adds a certain drama to the dining table. The only sensible solution appears to be to cut the lid off, within the perimeter of the upstanding rim, lift it off, and then cut the rich interior into radiating slices. The lid may then be replaced to keep the remainder clean and moist.

Having produced their simnels, the Shrewsbury bakers promoted them by issuing an accompanying broadsheet which explained their totally fictitious origins.[12] According to this local folk-story it all started when Simon and Nelly's family all returned home, presumably to celebrate Mothers' Day. Nelly thought it would be a good idea to make them a cake from some of her left-over Lenten dough. Simon, meanwhile, thought they should use up their left-over Christmas pudding. This started an argument which was exacerbated by Nelly wanting to bake it, while Simon said it should be boiled. As their anger increased she picked up her stool and threw it at him, while he used a broom to beat her around the head and shoulders. Seizing the broom, she and Simon continued to struggle until they realised that neither could prevail, leaving compromise as the only solution. It was therefore agreed that the stool should be broken up and its wood used to boil their cake in their big pot, and the broom used to fire up the oven to finally bake it. The eggs which had been broken in the struggle provided a glaze for the cake to provide its fine glossy finish. The new cake proved successful, and so became known as 'Simon and Nelly', subsequently shortened to Sim-Nel, and finally 'Simnel'.

The quality of the Shrewsbury simnels ensured excellent sales both locally and well beyond the county. In the 1830s it was noted that 'This cake is a very general present to London, or other distant friends, and often presented as a token of respect from one neighbouring friend to another. Of late a very rich one was presented by several ladies to Mr. Pelham, the successful candidate for the borough of Shrewsbury.'[13] They also began to expand well beyond their original Mothers' Day season, large numbers being sold in December to serve as Christmas cakes.

Virtually everyone enjoyed their Shrewsbury simnels when served at table, but local middle-class boys who might obtain one devised a unique way of sharing it with their friends. Balancing it on top of a short vertical post set into the ground, they used it like a coconut shy. Taking turns to throw a ball, an apple or stick at it from a predetermined distance, only those who knocked it to the ground were entitled to take a bite out of it, before balancing it on top once more.[14] Only the most solid and robust of cakes could ever have survived such treatment.

SPRING

As in other parts of the country, many people noticed that the lack of fresh greens over the winter months, combined with eating more salt-preserved meats than usual, left them feeling quite jaded. Something was therefore required to 'clean the blood' and clear their accumulation of pimples. The most effective solution was to have either a few meals of boiled dandelion leaves, or to make up one's own tonic;

SPRING MIXTURE[15]

2 lemons, sliced *1oz/25g cream of tartar*
2oz/50g Epsom salts *4oz/100g sugar*

These were placed in a pan with 6pt/3·3l of water, boiled for about half an hour, allowed to go cold, filtered into bottles, and lightly corked. It was recommended that a wineglass-full should be taken every morning.

PALM SUNDAY

'D' you mind the tale of them that found the Golden Arrow, and went with apple-blow scent round 'em, and a mort o' bees, and warmship, and wanted nought of any man? There's no need of fire or can'le for them, my dear, for they'm got their light – the kindly light – and the thorn's white over.' [16] This, the last sentence of Mary Webb's *The Golden Arrow*, explains the benefits of finding the golden arrow of local folk-tales, and why the people living around Pontesford Hill went to look for it on Palm Sunday.[17] It was also the day for 'going palming', gathering the dark stems of the pussy-willow, with its soft silver-grey furry buds, since the real palm-fronds as thrown down before Jesus on his entry into Jerusalem never flourished in England. Having baked their cakes, and packed up their kettles and crockery, they set off and climbed to the top of the hill, there to enjoy a great, convivial picnic, one of the first 'Wakes' of the summer months.

GOOD FRIDAY

As in all parts of England, most bakers made hot-cross buns to mark the day of Christ's death on the cross. Today the large commercialised bakers make them for weeks or months around Easter-time, so that are seen by many as an item of confectionery, rather than as a commemoration of the crucifixion.

Still retaining its original name, Butcher Row in the heart of Shrewsbury was the greatest meat market in the county. Emily Hay's watercolour shows the long-board covered canopies, the meat on hanging rails and the chopping blocks on which joints were cut up for sale.

Richard Glover's pottery at Clee Hill made a range of useful domestic wares, including this jar, in which home-brewed beer was finished and stored. A spile-pin in the upper hole allowed overflowing fermentation to run off, the curved strip below diverting it from the tap in the lower hole.

The wimberry pie, Shropshire's finest treat.

A great wimberry picker of the Shropshire hills. Elsie Rowson of Stiperstones shows how its done.

Where the wimberries grow; the Stiperstones in the dawn light of summer.

Wimberries ripe and ready to gather in late July.

EASTER SUNDAY

For centuries, Easter Day, the day of the Last Supper, was celebrated by each parish having a feast in their church. In some areas it survived the zeal of the Reformation, and continued into the 17th century. In 1637 the inhabitants of Clungunford complained to Archbishop Laud that their rector had refused to follow their traditional Easter Day custom. All his predecessors had provided a church-feast of bread, cheese and beer in the church for all the ancient people who had received sacrament that morning, but the present incumbent would have none of this. In his reply, Laud agreed that no further feasting should be allowed in the church, but that it should continue in the parsonage house, provided that it took place in a decent and neighbourly way.[18] A similar 'love-feast' was held at Berrington up to at least 1713.

Special Easter Day meals also took place in private houses, with joints of roast lamb as in the Jewish Passover supper. God had told the Jews to mark their doorposts with the blood of a lamb so that he might pass over them when destroying the firstborn children and livestock of their Egyptian masters. Here, every churchgoer knew the instructions in Exodus 12:8 – 9, that the lamb should be roasted with fire and eaten with bitter herbs. However, some people felt it necessary to make the point that they were Christians, not Jews, and so replaced the lamb with pork. The usual 'bitter herb' was tansy, but in Ludlow it was 'Robin-run-i'-the-hedge', or ground ivy, *Nepeta glechoma* or *N. lederacea*. This explains why the traditional Easter Day dinner at Ludlow was a leg of pork, stuffed with ground ivy.[19]

WAKES

A few Shropshire wakes were directly related to the seasonal availability of particular foods. In Shrewsbury two such wakes took place in Abbey Foregate. Bowls of cherries from the local orchard were sold at the Cherry Pie Wake on the Sunday before 1st July, while the Eel Pie Wake followed on the Sunday before 12th August.[20] Other wakes were held throughout the warmer months, these being the great summer holiday for local people, who rarely, if ever, left their own particular area. They included;

Norton Hill Wake, 2nd March
Caradoc Wakes, Trinity Sunday (the first after Whit.)
Wrekin May Sunday, first Sunday in May
Drayton Parish Wakes, Assumption Day, 15th August
Titterstone Wakes, last Sunday in August

Sundays had preference since they were the only days-off for the working population. The usual activity was to carry everything required up to the summit of the major local hill for an open-air meal, after which there were all manner of sports and games. Beer and refreshment stalls were often set up, while hawkers attended to sell their various cakes. The poem on Norton Hill Wakes tells how;

> There were some crying Banburys, and some crying cakes,
> My lads and my lasses, lets keep up the Wakes;
> Some crying Banburys as big as the egg of a pout,
> And gingerbread junks as big as my foot.
>
> We eat and we ate, and we ate and we eat,
> Till we could not eat more, they were so good and sweet,
> So Bob treated Ally and Ralph treated Sally,
> And I bought a fig cake for my Nally.[21]

There were also mint-cakes from one Billy Hayward. The 'Banburys' were probably made to their original early 17th century recipe, which was still current two hundred years later. In essence, it was a small version of Shrewsbury Simnel, but in a puff-paste case;

BANBURY CAKES[22]

8oz/225g strong plain flour
½ tsp dried yeast
6fl.oz/180ml tepid milk
4oz/100g candied peel
4oz/100g currants

1 tbs mixed ground allspice,
cinnamon, ginger & nutmeg
4oz/100g honey
1lb/450g puff paste
a little sugar for sprinkling

Beat the yeast and a pinch of sugar into the milk and leave in a warm place for 15 min. until frothy, or, if using instant yeast, sprinkle directly into the flour.

Make a well in the flour, pour in the milk, stir together, then knead for 10 min. on a floured board. Cover with a light cloth, and leave in a warm place for 30 min.

Mix the peel, currants, spices and honey together, and knead it into the dough.

Roll the puff paste into 4 ins/10cm rounds. Lay some of the dough in the centre of each, moisten the edges, and fold in half to resemble a small pasty. Turn over so that the joint is underneath, forming an oval cake with pointed ends, and press flat with the hand.

After sprinkling with sugar, bake at 190°C 375°F, Gas mark 5 for some 15–20 min, until a light brown.

Gingerbreads cut in chunks could have been made from any one of the numerous ginger-cake recipes, but some of these served at the various Shropshire wakes were probably of the very distinctive form of short fingers;

SHROPSHIRE GINGERBREAD[23]

12oz/325g plain flour *4oz/100g butter*
4oz/100g golden syrup *4oz/100g sugar*
2 tbs ground ginger *2 tsp/10ml brandy*
pinch ground mace *½oz/12g candied peel*
½ an egg, beaten

Chop the peel very finely. Rub the butter into the flour, and mix in the dry ingredients.

Make a well in the centre, pour in the golden syrup, egg and brandy, stir into the flour, knead to a firm dough, cover with a cloth and leave overnight in a cool place.

Roll out as a long sausage, as thick as a finger, cut into 3ins/75mm lengths, and space out on a well-greased baking sheet. Bake at 170°C, 325°F, Gas mark 3 for some 25 minutes, until golden brown.

N.B. The golden syrup in the recipe probably replaced honey in earlier versions. In practice clear honey works just as well.

At Market Drayton Wakes wheat would be used to make furmity. Taking its name from the Latin *frumentum*, meaning corn, it was of great antiquity, perhaps representing man's first method of making wild grains more palatable and nutritious. It was also popular in the medieval period, being served everywhere from peasant cottages through to great castles, the wealthy enriching it with saffron as an accompaniment to porpoise or venison. By the eighteenth century it was already out of fashion as an everyday food in most parts of England, but was still retained for harvests, Christmases etc., at which it had been served for centuries. The following is from an early eighteenth century Shropshire recipe book, but with the initial method of preparing the grain modernised to save considerable time and effort.

FURMITY[24]

6oz/175g whole wheat grains   *8oz/225g currants*
2pt/1·2l milk   *4oz/100g sugar*
2 eggs, beaten   *3 tbs rosewater*

Put the grain in a food processor with ¾pt/450ml water, process for 5 minutes, and rinse off the debris through a coarse sieve, [alternatively use 6oz/150g pearl barley instead]

Put the drained grain into a pan with the milk, and simmer very gently for an hour, stirring it to prevent burning, until it has formed a thick glutinous mass [alternatively bring to the boil, remove from the heat, cover, wrap in thick towels, and leave to cook, re-heating every 20 or 30 minutes, which gives good results with less trouble].

Mix the remaining ingredients in a basin, rapidly stir in a little of the stewed grain, then pour this back into the pan, and stir over the heat for 5 minutes. Cover the pan, and leave for a few minutes until it is cool enough to eat, then serve in individual bowls.

The result is a spicy, glutinous milk pudding, appreciated by many, though some find it rather cloying. A similar, but much more recent dish was 'hot-stir', or hasty pudding;

HOT-STIR

1pt/600ml milk *2oz/50g plain flour*
pinch of salt *2oz/50g butter*

Bring the milk and salt to the boil, and as it rises sprinkle the flour in with one hand, while beating the mixture with a fork or whisk held in the other. Stir continuously as it simmers for the next 5 minutes, then stir in the butter.

Pour into basins, and serve immediately. It was usually eaten with treacle, sugar, thick cream or jam.

At Ellesmere Wakes this was not served so much to satisfy hunger, as to provide a source of amusement and a race. Each old man was provided with a basin of it, boiling hot, along with a spoon, the first one who managed to empty his bowl being declared the winner.[25]

In Shrewsbury itself, the great annual celebration was Shrewsbury Show, a survival of pre-Reformation religious and guild festivals.[26] Every year, on the second Monday after Trinity Sunday, each trade guild or Company, all in their liveries, mustered in the courtyard of the Castle, formed up in the Market, and then set off to follow the most circuitous of routes (allowing for most breaks for 'refreshments') up to Kingsland, the high plateau at the opposite side of the river Severn. Each Company was preceded by its banner bearing its coat of arms, that of the Bakers being accompanied by its band, and that of the Butchers by their beadle and two men bearing a sword and a shield of their arms. At Kingsland each Company entered its own arbour. These were rectangular gardens, ditched and fenced around, and provided with an elaborate gateway. Most dated from the 1660–1680 period, and were fine examples of the best local design and craftsmanship. Within stood their respective halls, long wooden buildings with a central table flanked by benches. A buttery for tableware, food and drink was partitioned off at the lower end, while at the upper end an impressive raised chair beneath a canopy of state was provided for the Mayor or the Company's presiding warden. Once the Companies were installed, the Mayor and Corporation set off on horseback, visiting each arbour in turn to enjoy their hospitality as described in *Shrewsbury Quarry* of 1770;[27]

SHROPSHIRE COOKBOOK

Fig 27 At the annual Shrewsbury Show, the town's trade guilds marched in procession, each led by its arms and flags, such as the Baker's (left) and Butcher's (right). On reaching Kingsland, the elevated area beyond the curve of the Severn, they feasted and drank in their respective Arbours, each within its ditched enclosure entered through an elaborate gateway. The arms on the Tailor's Arbour were erected in 1669, while the Shoemaker's gateway is ten years later.

> To KINGSLAND'S Arbours once a year they go,
> In ordered elegance, serene and slow,
> The Bodie's Corporate in classes bright -
> In different classes but in one delight.
> They blend with mystical hands the friendly bowls,
> There blend their wishes with their souls; ...
> With each [the Mayor] quaffs the invigorating cheer,
> To friendship sacred, and the hallow'd year ...

Such communal drinking from large bowls was a medieval practice, but one which continued in trade and craft guilds up into the nineteenth century. The expenses for the ingredients of the bowl, and its accompanying foods, is given in the records of the Taylor's Company in 1687;

'Drinke att Kingland	16s	
Wine att do.	6s	
Bunns 8d, Bread 12d	1s	8d
The woman for looking after ye drinke etc.	2s	
Man for do.	1s	
For moweing ye harbor, and cutting ye hedge	2s	6d

In the mid 19th century the Show entered a period of rapid decline, becoming a public fairground drawing in thousands from the surrounding countryside by train. As a result, it was closed down by the Corporation, all its arbours demolished, and their sites sold off for villa developments. In its heyday, the Show and its arbours were probably unique in England, though they must have closely resembled the great garden houses erected around London by that city's greatest merchants. The only visible reminder of their existence in Shrewsbury today is the 1679 stone gateway of the Shoemakers' Arbour, now preserved in the Dingle garden near St. Chad's Church.

HARVEST

Two ceremonies took place in the harvest field, first 'Cutting the Neck', when the last of the standing corn was reaped or cut, and 'Crying the Mare' when the last sheaves had been gathered in.[28] Both were followed by a drink and a party. The harvest suppers held here for centuries to celebrate the end of harvest, when all was safely gathered in, were rapidly becoming a thing of the past in the 1880s. The Church of England didn't like things it could not control, and worked hard to convert the cheerful eating, drinking, dancing, music and singing in the barns and farmyards into a much more sober service within the church. In this it was very successful, most parishes converting to the Harvest Festival. At the church described in *The Golden Arrow*, its interior was;[29]

> decorated with corn and wild apples, heaps of fruit, yellow fern and nuts. Eli had sent a quantity of eggs ... Mrs. Arden had sent her usual giant loaf, and Mr. Shakeshaft his usual miniature haystack, made by himself, Joe and the farm boy. [Afterwards] there was a great bustle of moving benches and carrying in tables for tea. The women who had been preparing it in a side room came in with tablecloths. Everyone ran about with plates.

It all sounds very familiar to anyone who has been involved with harvest festivals, but it was very new and strange to those who first experienced it in the middle of Victoria's reign.

ALL HALLOWEEN October 31st

The eve of All Saints Day was always celebrated with evening parties, when everyone gathered around the fire and indulged in rituals to divine their futures. In John Arden's cottage in *The Golden Arrow*, Mrs Arden made her plans well in advance; 'We must have a bit of a randy for it, no danger! There'll be the acorns, and the nuts and the apples to sort ... some nice pippins, and [apple] cobs and that, and we'll play All Hallows games.'[30] She then baked a batch of soul-cakes. A large semicircle of acorns was then set out around the bakehouse fire in order to dry them. As in other parts of Britain, these would be placed before the fire, each one representing a particular person, and carefully watched to see how it behaved;[31]

> These glowing nuts are emblems true
> Of what in human life we view;
> The ill-matched couple fret and fume,
> And thus, in strife themselves consume
> Or from each other wildly start,
> And with a noise forever part ...

Ideally the nuts representing a young couple should burn together with mutual fondness, stay together, and finally gradually subside into ashes. In order to discover the name of the future spouse, or, if already married, that of their first child, each person used a knife to cut a long spiral of peel from their apple. This was then thrown backwards over their shoulder, and its shape then studied to determine the vital names' initial letter.[32]

This was also the night when the timid were best advised to stay close to the fire, for anywhere else, indoors or out, they could be startled by the hideous glowing eyes and jagged teeth of a candle-lit turnip-lantern. No-one then made its bastardised American offspring, the pumpkin lantern.

SOULING DAY, November 2nd

The feast of All Souls was celebrated with prayers for all the faithful departed throughout medieval Christendom. After the Reformation it was maintained by the Church of England, while many local communities continued to make 'Soul-cakes' to give away on this day. The following recipe was used by Mrs Gill of Hodnet up to 1884.

SOUL CAKES[33]

1lb 8oz/675g strong white flour *¾pt/450ml tepid milk*
4oz/100g butter *4oz/100g sugar*
1 tbs dried yeast *½ tsp ground allspice*
1 egg, beaten

Rub the butter into the flour in a bowl. If using an 'instant' yeast, it should be mixed in, but if ordinary dried yeast, beat it into the milk with a pinch of sugar, and leave for 15 min. in a warm place until frothy.

Make a well in the flour, pour in the egg and milk, stir it in, knead until it leaves the side of the bowl, then turn onto a floured board and knead thoroughly for 10 min. Form it into a ball, cover, and leave in a warm place to rise until doubled in size.

Return to the floured board, knead in the sugar and allspice for 2 min., then form in about 12 round or oval balls, rolling them flat before arranging them on greased baking sheets, allowing 1ins./2·5cm all round for them to expand. Cover with a light cloth, and return to the warm to prove until doubled in size.

Bake in a pre-heated oven at 230°C, 450°F, Gas mark 8 for 12–15 min., then remove and place on a wire rack until cool.

The same recipe was used by 'a member of a family who have made them in Shropshire for many generations past' at the request of Herbert R.H. Southam, Mayor of Shrewsbury, in 1903. He then sent them on to F.A. Milne of 11, Old Square, Lincoln's Inn in London, so that he could exhibit them to members of the Folk Lore Society, to help their investigations of regional varieties.

Back in the county, the bakers and confectioners' shops piled them in vertical stacks on their counters, just like the pictures of 'shew-bread' in early bibles, shew-bread being the twelve loaves placed on a table beside the altar of incense in Solomon's Temple.[34] When taken home, or home baked, quantities, even clothes baskets full, were kept by housewives who continued the custom up to the mid-late Victorian period. Every visitor on this day might take one, saying;[35]

> God have your soul, bones and all

or;

> A soul cake, a soul-cake,
> Have mercy on Christian soules
> For a soul-cake.

The main recipients, however, were the children who toured the houses in their towns and villages 'a-souling' with their local traditional rhymes. The Market Drayton version went;[36]

> Soul! Soul! For a soul-cake!
> I pray, good missis, a soul-cake.
> An apple, a pear, a plum or a cherry,
> Any good thing to make us merry.
> One for Peter, two for Paul,
> Three for Him who made us all.
> Up with the kettle, and down with the pan,
> Give us good alms, and we'll be gone.

while that from Welshampton was;

> Soul, Soul! A lump of coal!
> An apple, a pear, a plum or a cherry,
> Is a very good thing to make us merry
> I pray you, good missus, a soul-cake!

Then, on peering through the keyhole;

> Soul, soul! A lump of coal!
> I am peeping through the keyhole!
> Up with the kettle and down with the pan,
> *Give us an answer* and we'll be gone.

Soul-cakes could still be bought in Welshampton around 1870, but their use was then in rapid decline as they were being replaced by gifts of apples or money.

MOCK CORPORATIONS

As in a number of English suburbs and villages, the inhabitants of Meole Brace on the outskirts of Shrewsbury set up their own 'Ancient Incorporation', in imitation of those of major boroughs. Claiming to have been set up in 1617, they held an annual mayoral election, that of 4th November 1884 being held at the Red Lion. Here about forty sat down to a supper presided by the 'Mayor', such a good time being had that 'The company did not separate until an early hour.'[37]

ST THOMAS' DAY, December 21st

As in most parts of England, every farmer put a sack of wheat by his back door, so that they could measure out perhaps a pint or a quart to poor cottagers who called, depending on each one's personal circumstances. This was certainly sufficient for baking a good batch of bread for Christmas. In Clun, the cottagers usually carried two sacks from farm to farm, getting one dole of wheat for themselves, and another of barley for their pigs. This stopped in 1870, when the farmers decided that it would be much fairer and less troublesome for all if they amalgamated their contributions of corn at the Town

Hall to be properly distributed to the *deserving* poor. The custom was already in general decline however, the corn being replaced by either left-over food or money even where old-fashioned housekeepers still made St. Thomas' Day gifts.[38]

WASSAIL – CUP SINGERS

By the nineteenth century the practice of singing carols outside houses and halls in order to obtain the contents for a festive wassail-cup had already been almost forgotten. The original verses with which the traditional carols were commenced and terminated were still continued, year after year, wishing those in each home good fortune and good food and drink over the next twelve months;[39]

> I wish you a merry Christmas
> And a happy New Year,
> A pocket full of money,
> And a cellar full of beer
> And a good fat pig in the sty
> To last you all the year.
>
> God Bless the ruler of this house,
> And send him long to reign
> Among your friends and kindred
> And those you love so dear,
> I wish you a joyfull and a happy New Year.

CHRISTMAS EVE, December 24th

For centuries, Christmas Eve in virtually every home, whether great or small, was a time of vigorous activity, as everything had to be prepared for the following day. All the necessary food and drink had to be carefully planned, either by checking out the larders, or by buying in from the local markets or tradesmen. In less well off families this might mean buying their meat etc. late in the evening, when the butchers dropped their prices in order to sell all their stock, for it might not keep over Christmas in days before refrigeration. Over the past few days their shopfronts had been festooned with neat rows of every available item of fresh meat, poultry, and game, while the shelves inside held large stocks of pies, black puddings, white puddings, sausages, hams, brawns etc. Now the orders placed weeks ago had to be fulfilled, and every personal customer supplied before finally closing the doors.

It was usual for housewives all over the country to make sure that their homes were spick and span for Christmas, but in Shropshire the cleaning operations were particularly thorough. The following scene, observed at Preston Hospital around 1850, would have been re-enacted in many cottages, farms and manor houses;[40]

> The tessellated marble floor of the hall underwent entire purgation; its quaint stools and forms were piled together in a huge heap on the lawn, the agent's room, the matron's rooms, the dormitories, the fine old kitchen (with its service of pewter plates and dishes) ... were all besieged by six or seven little housemaids, in mob caps and checked bed-gowns ... The cleaning of the pewter, which takes place only once a year, is the most important affair of all. It has to be boiled, scoured, and rubbed, making, altogether an elaborate process. But the reward comes when it is set on its oak dresser, with holly between, and it shines like silver. Beautiful it looked as it scintillated in the blaze of the great Christmas fire.

When as much as possible had been completed, most families began their Christmas festivities with this evening's supper. Among other things, this usually included wigs and ale. Originating in the 15th century, wigs were light, yeast-raised and spiced bread-buns. They were usually round in shape, and their top slashed in a cross-shape, so that they could be easily broken into quarters.

WIGS[41]

12oz/340g plain flour *4oz/125g sugar*
1 tbs dried yeast *1 tbs caraway seed*
6fl.oz/170ml tepid milk *½ tsp ground ginger*
4oz/100g butter *½ tsp mixed spice*

Sift the flour into a bowl, make a well in the centre, pour in the yeast beaten into the warm milk, and mix in to form a light dough. Using the hands, beat in the softened butter,

Fig 28 Dating from around 1760-1800, this 'Minsterley' Shropshire dresser named after the Shropshire village around which they were made, bears its load of pewter plates, each burnished to silver-like brilliance after their annual pre-Christmas polishing.

then the sugar and spices. Cover, and leave to rise in a warm place for 2 hours.

Knead the dough, using sufficient additional flour to make it easy to handle, then form into four oblong cakes. Space these apart on a floured baking sheet, cover with a light cloth, and return to the warm for some 20 min.

Bake at 190°C, 375°F, Gas mark 5 for about 15 min.

CHRISTMAS DAY, December 25th

Every effort was made to ensure that the Christmas dinner was as rich and plentiful as possible, but its size, quality and content depended entirely on the circumstances of each particular family. For poorer folk it would probably be little different to a basic everyday dinner, perhaps aided by a few luxuries. Others might enjoy a rare taste of butchers-meat in the form of a joint, or even the luxury of a fowl. For most farming and middle class families there would be a prime joint of locally-bred and fed beef, roasted before the fire, and served with all the 'trimmings'.[42] Up to the mid nineteenth century its usual accompaniment was a boiled sweet pudding, lightly fruited, its open texture enabling it to absorb the rich gravy, and eat well with the beef and vegetables. It only went out of use when its role was replaced by potatoes. In a similar way, a 'gritty pudding' made of coarse oatmeal groats was traditionally served with roast goose in Shropshire, to counteract the richness of the bird.

GRITTY PUDDING[43]

8oz/225g pinhead oatmeal   *¼ tsp salt*
6 tbs chicken or vegetable stock   *3 tbs soft brown sugar*
1 tbs currants (optional)

Tie the oatmeal in a piece of muslin, allowing room for it to swell, and boil for 2 hours. Remove it from the pan, squeeze them dry, mix in the remaining ingredients, tie tightly in the muslin once more, and boil for about an hour before turning out and serving.

Up to the eighteenth century the Christmas dinner often started with a rich pottage called plumb-broth, the following Shropshire recipe dating from around 1720;

PLUMB BROTH[44]

2pts/1·2l strong beef stock
10oz/275g currants
2oz/50g raisins
2 tsp mixed ground cinnamon, clove and mace
6oz/175g prunes
6 tbs/90ml sherry
¼pt/150ml claret
4oz/100g sugar

Put all the ingredients except the sherry and claret into a covered saucepan and stew gently for 15 minutes, then pour in the sherry and claret, and serve in a large bowl.

From the early nineteenth century those suet puddings which had been eaten with the meat moved on to become Christmas puddings, ever-increasingly richer, and now served separately at the end of the meal. This Shropshire country house version dates from the 1830s – 40s, when they were still relatively plain;

PLUM PUDDING[45.]

4oz/100g fresh white breadcrumbs
4oz/100g currants
4oz/100g chopped apples
grated rind of 1 lemon
4oz/100g suet
4oz/100g sugar
3 eggs, beaten
½ a nutmeg, grated

Mix all the ingredients. Rinse an 18ins/45cm square muslin, squeeze it dry, dust one side with flour, and place it over a basin. Put the pudding mixture inside, gather the muslin over it, tie it with string, lift out of the basin, and plunge into boiling water. Cover, and boil for 3 hours.

Afterwards there might be light cakes, or pikelets, mince pies and Christmas cakes. Today's mince pies contain no meat, but, as their name suggests, they originated as pies of minced mutton with a seasoning of dried fruit and spices. This early eighteenth century Shropshire recipe uses tongue, a typical ingredient for this period;

FESTIVE FOODS

MINCE MEAT[46]

1 200g tin of tongue
1lb/450g currants
2oz/50g candied lemon peel
10oz/275g sugar
3 fl.oz/90ml sherry

$\frac{1}{2}$ tsp ground cinnamon
$\frac{1}{4}$ tsp ground clove
$\frac{1}{4}$ tsp ground mace
$\frac{1}{4}$ tsp salt

Finely chop the tongue, mix with the remaining ingredients, refrigerate overnight, then use to fill mince pies in the usual way.

Fruit cakes began to be made in England in the late sixteenth and early seventeenth centuries. They were basic bread doughs enriched with dried fruits, butter, sugar and spices, ideal for serving with a glass of wine or ale at festive occasions.

By the nineteenth century Christmas cakes were made to richer recipes, now relying on eggs rather than yeast to raise them.

CHRISTMAS CAKE[47]

12oz/325g butter
8oz/225g sugar
4 medium eggs, separated
12oz/325g plain flour
2oz/50g ground almonds

12oz/325g currants
12oz/325g sultanas
8oz/225g candied peel
2 tbs brandy

Grease, line and tie paper around either an 8in/20cm square or a 9inch/23cm round cake tin, and pre-heat the oven to 150°C, 300°F, Gas mark 2. Mix the almonds, peel and dried fruit.

Cream the butter with the sugar, then add the beaten yolks and flour little by little, beating continuously to form a smooth, stiff mixture. Mix in the almonds, fruit and peel, along with the brandy, finally folding in the egg whites previously beaten to stiffness. Pack into the prepared tin, and bake for about 4 hours.

For supper, there would be a variety of cold meats, including the remains of the roast beef, pigs' or white-puddings, pork pies, and goose pies.[48] The latter might contain up to three geese, all boned and folded together within a deep hot-water crust.[49]

GOOSE PIE

Filling	**Pastry**
1 goose, boned out	4lb/1·8kg plain flour
1 onion, finely chopped	1lb/450g lard
2 apples, peeled and chopped	1pt/600ml milk and water mixed
1 tsp salt	2 tsp salt
4oz/100g butter	

Sift the flour into a bowl, make a well in the centre, and pour in the boiling milk and water, lard and 1 tsp salt. Stir this together and then knead to form a ball of dough. Cut off one-third, and use the remainder to raise a pie-crust, or to line a tin mould, large enough to receive the goose.

Season the goose with salt and spices, pierce the skin in a few places with a sharp knife, and arrange breast uppermost in the crust, layered with the onion and apple.

Roll out the remaining pastry to form a lid, wet the edges with a little of the egg, place on top, seal and trim the edges and press between the fingers to form a neat wavy border.

There might also be a large joint, perhaps a round, of pickled beef, ideal for providing a constant source of tender and flavoursome cold cooked meat throughout the Christmas period.

PICKLED BEEF[50]

about 5lb/2·4kg silverside	12 cloves
8pt/4l water	12 black peppercorns
6oz/175g muscovado sugar	1 tbs saltpetre
1lb/450g salt	3 bay leaves

Bring the water, sugar and salts to the boil, skimming if necessary, and strain into a large lidded container of pottery or plastic. When cold, add the remaining ingredients, placing a plate and a weight on top of the meat to ensure it is always completely submerged. Turn the meat from time to time as it pickles, keeping it somewhere cold over the next ten days. When required, remove, rinse and wipe the joint dry, place in a large pan, cover it with water, bring to the boil, skim, and then add;

1 carrot *10 black peppercorns*
1 onion *10 cloves*
3 bay leaves

Simmer gently for 3 hours, testing its tenderness with a skewer, then allow to cool in its own liquor. Finally drain it, and press finely-chopped parsley into it for decoration. (N.B. The beef will lose about half its weight while being salted and boiled).

A large ham, home-cured earlier in the year, made a similarly welcome addition to the sidetable in prosperous farmhouses and halls.

DRY-CURED HAM[51]

A 20lb/9kg leg of pork *1½lb/625g black treacle*
1lb/450g cooking salt *2oz/50g powdered saltpetre*
1lb/450g coarse sea salt *2oz/50g ground black pepper*

Lay the pork in a large deep dish or tray which is impervious to salt, mix the salts and the pepper, and rub this vigorously into the meat. Lay the pork in the centre of the dish, and heap all the loose salts on top, before leaving it in a cold place for 4 days. Next, spread the treacle over it, leave it a day, then baste and rub it with the collected sweet brine over the next month, turning it regularly. Finally soak it in water for a day, rinse it, wipe it, and hang it up in a well-ventilated location to dry out. Hooks on the ceiling high above the kitchen fireplace were usually provided for this purpose.

To cook the ham, place it in either a large pot or pan (in many homes the best utensil was the washing boiler) on a bed of sweet hay. The following are now added;

1 carrot, 1 onion, 1 head of celery, 1 turnip, 1 parsnip,
2 bottles strong brown ale

Cover the ham with cold water, bring it slowly to the boil, then simmer very gently for 20 minutes per pound/450g. When tender, take off the heat, and leave in its own liquor in a cool place for 24 hours.

Drain the ham, wipe it dry, and then coat with a glaze made of:

2 tbs/10ml gelatin   *1 beef stock cube*
½ pt/300ml water   *a little salt and pepper*

Beat the dry ingredients into the water, allow to stand for 5 minutes, then heat until hot, but not boiling, stirring continuously. Allow to cool until tepid, but not set, before brushing it over the ham.

The third form of cold meat for the Christmas season was that major regional speciality, Shrewsbury brawn. Records show that this formed one of the main dishes at the Shrewsbury Corporation's Christmas day 'breakfasts', served in the Guildhall after its attendance at church during the 16th century.[52]

Today the word brawn tends to have two quite separate meanings, referring either to a jellied mass of pig's head-meat, or to the muscular upper body of a really fit man. A third meaning was the wild boar, more particularly its thick shoulders and the hard, horny 'shield' which developed across them after about two years of age. In nature, it protected the boar from the razor-sharp tusks of its adversaries, but in culinary use it provided the raw material for one of the most prestigious of all medieval, Tudor and Stuart winter feasts, soused brawn. After wild boars became firstly rare, and then extinct, tame boars continued to make a convenient substitute until boar-brawn fell out of fashion in the late Georgian period – except in Shrewsbury.

'The Shrewsbury brawn is unrivalled and has lately been patronised by His Majesty William the Fourth. Brawn is a Christmas dish of great antiquity, and may be found in most of the ancient bills of fare for coronations and other great feasts . . . It is prepared from the flesh of boars fattened for the purpose.'[53] This was H. Pidgeon's opinion in 1837. Thirty years later an American visitor to the town failed to find any of this famous delicacy, which he believed to be 'a sort of sausage of beef'. The butchers soon corrected him however, informing him that they only produced it over the cold winter months. By 1875 there were only two or three making it, cutting and rolling the shield into a drum- or collar-shape, packing it into a cylindrical mould, filling the middle up with prepared meat and fat, and finally boiling it for hours.[54] The following is the usual Victorian method;

BRAWN FOR CHRISTMAS[55]

1 boned side of pork, excluding the shoulder and the ham
salt

Lay the pork skin-side down in a large tray, sprinkle and rub with the salt, and leave in a cool place for at least three hours, then drain it, and wipe it dry with a clean cloth. Sprinkle the flesh-side with a little more salt, and then roll up, skin on the outside, to form a collar, tying it in place with close-spaced bands of broad cotton tape. If necessary pack in additional pieces of pork to give a neat cylindrical shape.

[If having the necessary skills, it is advisable to make a deep hoop of tinplate to enclose the brawn. With open, overlapping ends, this can be tied tighter and tighter around the meat as it shrinks while being cooked. This reduces the risk of scalded fingers, and produces a much neater result].

Put the brawn into a large, deep pan of boiling water, placing a trivet or a few stainless forks beneath it, to stop it touching the bottom. Cover, and simmer very slowly for some 6 hours until very soft and tender. As it shrinks, it should be periodically removed and its tapes tightened in order to keep it in shape, and ensure that it retains all its own juices and flavour.

Meanwhile boil the following brine for 30 min, strain, and leave until cold;

8pt/5l water
2oz/50g salt
½pt/300ml bran [or a handful of sweet hay]

10 bayleaves
large sprig of rosemary

When the brawn is tender, leave it in its cooking liquor until cold, then rinse it, let it soak in the brine in a cool place for three days, after which it is ready for serving.

The mince pies made in Shropshire were virtually the same as those made elsewhere. They had originated as pies containing minced beef, mutton, veal or lamb, flavoured with spices and dried fruit. By the nineteenth century the meat content had virtually disappeared, leaving an often over-rich and sickly-sweet compound in its place. To be offered a mince pie was considered to bring good luck. For every house in which you ate a mince pie during the twelve days of Christmas, you would enjoy a happy month in the coming year.[56] Although made at other times, a distinctly local form of mince pie was the chitterling puff. This had cooked chitterlings as its most economical of fatty meat content, and used puff pastry, as in Georgian recipes, rather than the shortcrust we are used to today. Since chitterlings are not generally available today, the following recipe uses suet as a practical substitute. It then follows the Shropshire instruction to 'Ack 'em as small as small, an' get some corrans an' rais'ns an' candied peel an' spice, an 'ack some apples, an' blend 'em all together, an' mak puffs on it'.[57]

CHITTERLING PUFFS

6oz/175g suet (for chitterlings)
6oz/175g baking apples, chopped
4oz/100g candied peel, chopped
2oz/50g raisins, chopped
1 egg, beaten

8oz/225g currants
½ tsp mixed ground cinnamon, clove, mace & nutmeg
1½lb/675g puff pastry

Thoroughly mix all the ingredients except the pastry and the egg.

Roll out the pastry ⅛inch/·3cm thick, and cut out 12 3inch/10cm rounds for the lids. Knead together the remaining scraps of pastry, roll out, and either use to line a dozen large tart-tins, or arrange them on a dampened baking sheet. Put a large spoonful of mincemeat in their centres, dampen their edges with a little of the egg, set the lids in place, and press their edges lightly together. Brush the tops with beaten egg, making sure it does not trickle down the cut edges. For a more ornamental effect, 8 vertical cuts may be made around their perimeters, which gives an authentic puffed rim.

Bake at 230°C, 450°F, Gas mark 8 for about 20 minutes.

Later on in the evening there would be games such as 'sousing for apples', for which apples were floated in a large tub or bowl. Those participating had their hands tied behind their backs, as they bowed down to try and grasp an apple in their teeth, someone being sure to duck their heads underwater at the critical moment.[58] The traditional supper of toasted cheese eaten with toast and bread might also be served:[59]

SWIG

1pt/ 600ml strong brown ale
4 large slices of bread
1 tbs sugar
¼ tsp mixed ground nutmeg
& ginger
Cheshire cheese

Place the cheese in a fireproof dish, and melt it either before an open fire, beneath a grill, or in a hot oven. Toast the bread, put one slice in a deep bowl, sprinkle the sugar and spices on top, and pour on the cold ale. Serve the bowl of 'swig', the dish of melted cheese and a plate with the remaining toast cut in broad fingers all at the same time. These were then passed around the table, each person taking some of the cheese with the toast, and a 'swig', or drink, from the communal bowl.

NEW YEAR & TWELFTH NIGHT

Up to the mid-19th century, the celebration of Christmas extended from Christmas Eve through to Twelfth Night on January 6th. This was the feast of the Epiphany, commemorating the visit of the Three Kings to Bethlehem. As Britain became industrialised, this long break proved commercially impossible, and so the holiday was condensed to Christmas Day and Boxing Day in most towns and cities. In rural Shropshire, however, the traditional long Christmas was still celebrated in the 1850s, as described in the following observations by Miss Meteyard. Finding that she had to cater for an unexpected visitor, she had to make a moonlight tour of the local farms to gather her essential supplies. At these she found;

> Such pleasant warm homes, such pretty rustic festivals; such pigs and home-brewed ale; such crab-apples dancing on the top, such steaming puddings, and pies, and roasts ... In most cases we were hospitably asked in – in some to taste the cheer. At last, after wandering through the deep snow of a primitive orchard, on we came to a small farmhouse and were admitted to a kitchen where a wood fire roared up the chimney centuries old. [Here we enjoyed] a hot jug of spiced elder-berry wine, against the tasting of which no negative would be taken.[60]

Hot home-brewed ale with crab-apples on top was a popular beverage either on Twelfth Night, or the previous Twelfth-Night Eve, in many parts of England. Being soft, warm and comforting, it was known as 'Lambswool', the following recipe being typical;[61]

LAMBSWOOL

about a dozen crab-apples *5oz/150g brown sugar*
2pt/1·2l strong brown ale *4 tsp ground ginger*
8 tbs rum or brandy

Place the crab-apples on a baking sheet, and cook at 190°C, 375°F, Gas mark 5 for about 20 minutes until tender (this will vary according to their degree of hardness). When the apples are almost ready, bring the brown ale, sugar and ginger up to the boil, pour into a deep bowl, drop in the hot apples, and finally stir in the rum or brandy.

The tradition was for each person in turn to use their spoon to scoop up an apple as the bowl passed around the company, everyone then drinking from the bowl as it circulated once more. This marked a fitting end to the cycle of events, these recommencing shortly afterwards with the onset of Lent.

In the great houses, two other special Christmas dishes were made to both ornament and provision the sideboard in the dining room, being available for slicing cold whenever required. Katherine Kenyon described them in her account of the festivities in her Shropshire home;[62]

Christmas was a busy time ... The clothes to be given away, the packets distributed to the old people, besides the family to think of and all the household arrangements. A bullock would be killed for the tenants. The larders and store-rooms filled with good things, and the kitchen a hive of industry for weeks beforehand. A porker would have been chosen for its head to be cooked and dressed in *boar's head* fashion and there was a *pie* made every Christmas whose fame lasted long after it ceased to be made in Edwardian days. A goose was partially cooked and boned and into its skin was returned the best parts of itself together with the boned flesh of two chickens, a hare, a pheasant, a brace of partridges, two ducks, a small neat's [calf's] tongue ready boiled, two rabbits, the whole seasoned with salt, white pepper, mace, nutmeg, cloves, and a little cinnamon. Besides all the household provisions, the sick were not forgotten and special soups and jellies went out to them.

These great goose and game pies appear to have originated in Yorkshire, and eighteenth century recipes for them are entitled either Yorkshire Christmas, or Yorkshire Goose Pies. From at least the mid nineteenth century they had become a standard dish in most country houses, even Queen Victoria having a huge one baked every year for her Christmas sideboard. Being large and impressive versions of the ordinary goose pies previously described, they appear to have been served by cutting around the perimeter of the lid, so that it could be replaced after each slice had been removed from the interior. This ensured that it always retained its pristine appearance, and did not encumber diners with unwieldy lumps of tough pastry.

As for the boar's head, these enjoyed a great revival in the Victorian period, growing ever larger and more impressive as breeds such as Large Whites grew bigger and bigger. Television series on Edwardian country house life have shown boars' heads being simply cleaned, shoved into the oven, brought out, dished, and served onto the table. This is totally inaccurate, and produces a largely inedible mess which cannot be neatly carved. The true boar's head recipes are much more sophisticated, involving boning, curing, stuffing, cooking, glazing and decorating, as in this recipe from Jules Gouffé's *Royal Cookery Book* of 1869;[63]

THE BOAR'S HEAD

Stage I. Boning and pickling, 2 to 3 weeks before required

1 pig's head, about 12–14lb/5·5 – 6kg.
3lb/1·5kg pork shoulder with skin
12oz/350g dark brown/muscovado sugar
12oz/350g salt
1oz/25g saltpetre
8oz/225g large-crystal sea salt

Boil a kettle of water, and pour a little boiling water over each part of the head in turn, scraping it with the edge of a knife to remove all dirt and hair. Do not immerse the head, for this will raise the temperature of the meat. Today, a disposable razor may effectively remove the bristles. Finally pour boiling water into the ears, nostrils, and use a stiff paintbrush to remove every trace of dirt.

Rinse the head in cold water, dry with a cloth, and lay face down on a board. Using a sharp knife, make a deep cut from beneath the tip of the chin back to the neck, then cut the gums from the lower jaw, to leave it completely exposed. Now remove the tongue.

Turn the head face upwards, probe for the top of the skull with the point of the knife, then gradually cut the flesh free from the forehead and cheek, linking up with the cuts made along the gums so that it may be peeled back. Be careful not to pierce the skin.

Continue working down to the snout, finally cutting through its tough sinews to remove the face completely.

Cut the rind from the pork shoulder and cut the meat into long strips some 1ins/2·5cm square, along the grain of the meat. Place the rind, strips and face in a shallow ceramic container.

Mix the salts, sugar and spices, tip onto the meat, and rub them into all the pieces for a total of 10 minutes.

Place the container in a cool but frost-free place, and rub the meats in their own brine for 5–10 minutes each day, until required.

FESTIVE FOODS

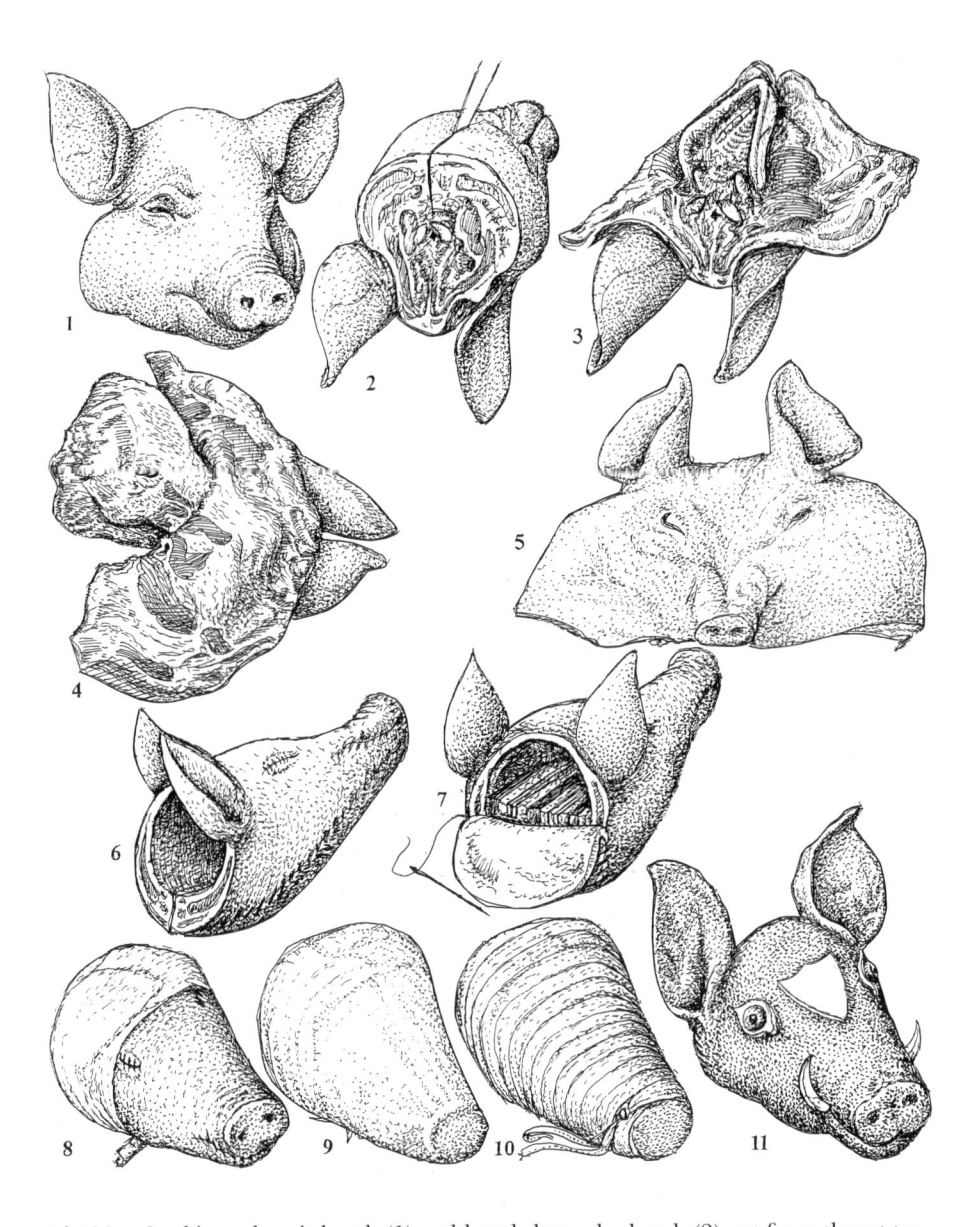

Fig 29 Cooking a boar's head: (1) scald and shave the head: (2) cut from throat to chin: (3) expose the bottom jaw: (4) turn over and expose the skull: (5) remove the face and cure with salt etc.: (6) sew up the throat and other orifices: (7) pack with pork forcemeat and strips of cured pork, sewing up the neck with a piece of cured belly pork: (8) bandage the ears down: (9) tie in a piece of linen cloth: (10) truss with bandage, boil, cool, and (11) rub with wood-soot and lard, erect the ears, and garnish with tusks, and the eyes etc. in lard.

145

Stage 2. Boiling, the day before serving

Drain and rinse the meat, dry with a cloth, and, using a strong trussing needle and strong twine, sew up the eyes and mouth. Cut the cured rind to fit the open back of the head, and sew the bottom half in place.

Prepare a forcemeat by finely mincing and grinding the following;

3lb/1·5kg pork shoulder meat	*2oz/50g salt*
3lb/1·5kg rindless streaky bacon	*2 tsp mixed spice*
meat of 4 rabbits	*half a nutmeg, grated*
8oz/225g English onions	*2 tsp ground black pepper*

Cut a further 1lb/450g streaky bacon into long strips about $\frac{3}{4}$ in/2cm square.

Line the bottom of the head with some forcemeat, lay on a few strips of the cured pork shoulder alternating with those of the streaky bacon, covering these with more forcemeat, continuing this process until the head is completely stuffed.

Sew up the loose flap of rind to completely enclose the stuffing. Lay the head face upwards on a board, fold the ears down across the forehead, and bind in place with a broad strip of muslin. This prevents the ears from dissolving during boiling.

Lay the head face down on a 2ft/60cm-square of muslin, and tie diagonal corners tightly together to cover the head.

Using some 20-foot by 3-inch (6m by 8cm) strips of muslin, tightly bind the head, to give it the required shape.

Place the head either on a trivet or on a bed of carrot, parsnip and onions in a large pan, cover with water, bring slowly to the boil, skim, and simmer gently with the lid on for 5 hours. (Victorian recipes boil the head in rich stocks with Madeira.)

Remove from the heat and allow to cool. When tepid, drain, turn onto a large dish, remove the binding, and carefully unfold the ears to their erect position, holding them in place with skewers stuck into the ear-holes. Leave in a cool place overnight to set.

FESTIVE FOODS

Stage 3. Garnishing, the day of serving

8oz/225g lard
1 pair boar tusks (or celery curled to represent them)
black food-colouring paste (replacing chimney soot)
1 glacé cherry (formerly, artificial glass eyes were used)
sprays of fresh bayleaves and rosemary

Chill half the lard. The remainder is beaten or warmed a little until soft and beaten with the black food colouring to form a black paste. Rub this over the head to give it the colour of a black wild boar.

Set the head on a bed of bay and rosemary on its serving dish, and prepare the skewers in the ears with sprigs of rosemary. (Those who put herbs in their ears and nostrils to prevent catching the Plague were said to resemble boar's heads.)

Fig 30 A selection of Victorian boar's heads, showing how they were garnished with piped lard, piped and cubed aspic, wreaths of bay and long ornamental skewers.

Cut open a little of each side of the mouth and insert the tusks.

Cut out a flat shield-shape from the chilled lard, decorate with an appropriate coat of arms or badge, and set in the centre of the forehead.

Cut eye shapes from the thin slices of the chilled lard, place over the eyes, securing a half-round of glacé cherry over each one with a clove.

Having been brought in with the appropriate ceremonial, the head may be sliced across, working from the neck end, and trimming off the skin around the area to be sliced. It has a very good flavour, resembling that of a very superior pork pie.

As Kathleen Kenyon described, 'The boar's head used to stand on a little table by itself, the dish resting on a raised carved platter. It was thickly glazed all over, held an orange in its mouth and had glass marbles with twisty insides for eyes. I used to feel incredulous that anyone could eat it, but I clearly remember Mr—- cutting himself slices from the back of the head and saying how good it was.'[64] He was obviously a man of taste who appreciated the good things in life, for it is a truly delicious dish, well worth the effort of its preparation. Those I have cooked for Christmas and the New Year's parties always create great interest, and rapidly disappear, down to the very snout.

CHAPTER 5

FROM THE CRADLE TO THE GRAVE

In all communities and families, the arrival of a new baby, the joining of a couple in marriage, and the departure of friends and relatives at death have always brought people together to share their respective emotions. Even though England is quite a small country, and one which had a single main religion for centuries, the traditions associated with births, weddings and funerals varied considerably from one area to another. Beyond the formal church services, there might be all manner of celebrations, from processions on horseback to races, removing garters, singing, drinking games etc. Compared to many of these, the culinary aspects of Shropshire's folk traditions tended to be relatively conservative, exhibiting all the norms, but little that was exceptional.

To start at birth, it was considered important that the first food ever given to the new-born baby should be of the richest and best. It was therefore given butter and sugar, perhaps unsuitable, but at least unlikely to be harmful.[1]

For weddings, it was usual to follow the service with a substantial wedding breakfast. If at a large farm or hall, there would be insufficient space for everyone to sit down inside, and so two separate meals were served, one for the chosen few in the dining room, and another for the rest somewhere outside. Mary Webb described such an event at *The House in Dormer Forest*.[2] In the formality of its dining room the table was laid with the best that could be provided, including 'the wold big cloth with the farmyard border.' Linen manufacturers made these in large sizes just for such occasions, especially during the great prosperity of agriculture during the mid 19th century. At Dormer, the table had seventeen place-settings around the perimeter, while its centre apparently held 'The tremendous wedding breakfast, with its mountains of flesh, its rows of little corpses of various sizes – turkey, goose, duck, chicken, pheasant – all tastefully laid out by Mrs Gosling' (who, incidentally, laid out most of the local humans too!). The wedding cake would also have been displayed in the dining room, ready for cutting by the bride and bridegroom. At this date it would no longer be the relatively plain 'Bride-cake' of earlier times, but an elaborate multi-tiered confection encrusted with piped and moulded icing sugar. The rich fruit cake beneath would be little different from the usual kind, except for having far more candied peel in it, in common with other Shropshire bakery.

WEDDING CAKE (half recipe)[3]

8oz/225g butter *12oz/325g currants*
8oz/225g sugar *8oz/225g raisins*
8oz/225g eggs, beaten *1 nutmeg, grated*
10oz/275g flour *2oz/50g cherries*
1lb/450g candied peel *2oz/50g flaked almonds*

Prepare either a 8inch, 20cm square or a 9inch, 23cm round tin by lining it with greased greaseproof paper, and tying a double layer of paper around the exterior. Pre-heat the oven to 150°C, 300°F, Gas mark 2.

Beat the butter to a cream, cream in the sugar, then beat in the eggs and flour little by little to form a smooth mixture. Thoroughly mix in the remaining ingredients, pack into the tin, and bake for some 4 hours.

While the most important enjoyed their lavish meal inside, the villagers were entertained to a 'knife and fork tea' at long tables set up in the barn. Here again food and drink would be just as substantial, if rather plainer, than that in the dining room.

As at weddings, there might be similar social divisions at funerals. For the nobility, gentry and merchants, professional undertakers would make all the necessary arrangements, as detailed in the following trade-card of the 1760s;[4]

Richard Chandler, Armes-painter and Undertaker, at St. Luke's Head, in Hill Lane in SHREWSBURY. Compleately Furnishes Funeralls with Coffin, burying suit, Pall, Hangings, Silver'd Sconces

& Candlesticks, Cloakes, Hatbands, Scarves, Favours, Funeral Escocheons, Coaches, Hearse, Wax Lights, Flambeaux Links, Torches, Ticketts &c. and performed after ye same manner, as by ye Undertakers at LONDON, at reasonable rates.

At fashionable nocturnal funerals such as these, a suitably impressive meal would be provided for the upper class mourners, and a more basic one for all others. The form of polite funerals in Shrewsbury in the early 1660s was noted by Monsieur Jorevin, who was then visiting the town,[5]

> The relations and friends being assembled in the house of the defunct, the minister advanced into the middle of the chamber where, before the company, he made a funeral oration. It is to be remarked that during the oration there stood upon the coffin a large pot of wine, out of which everyone drank the health of the deceased. This being finished, six men took up the corpse and carried it on their shoulders to the church.

There are few details regarding the catering at later funerals, but in 1873 the Rev. G.L. Wasey of Bridgnorth recorded that among the guests at the funerals of high class and farming families, it was the custom for all but the nearest mourners to sit down for a '*Déjeuner à la Fourchette*' at 11a.m. Literally a 'breakfast with a fork', this was in effect a luncheon provided with cooked meats etc, and served with wines and spirits.[6]

Further down the social scale, the arrangements would usually be much simpler, the laying out being carried out by a neighbour who had a reputation for doing such things decently. A local joiner would then act as undertaker, and the funeral refreshments provided by the family, at their own home. One particular Shropshire custom among the poor was to place a pewter plate of salt on the breast of the deceased until the coffin was about to be closed, in order 'to keep it from swelling.'[7]

From the 17th century, it had become fashionable to serve crisp sponge cakes with wine as part of the funeral entertainment. At the funeral of John Hardinge, gentleman, on 26th March, 1669, the mourners were provided with large quantities of claret, sack, white wine, 'one pound of mackaroons and four dozen of sugar cakes', for example. At this date the latter might have been either Shrewsbury Cakes, or else the sponge fingers used for this purpose in later centuries.[8] Such biscuits then began to take on rather different roles.

In some areas they were sent out beforehand as an invitation to the funeral, while in Shropshire they were distributed at the funeral itself. Descriptions include; 'long sponge biscuits, something in the shape of a Coffin, neatly folded in black-edged paper used to be given to each guest to take away', or, from north and east Shropshire 'oblong sponge biscuits somewhat smaller than ordinary penny sponge cakes, one of which, wrapped in black-edged writing paper, and sealed with black wax, were sent to every relative or friend not present.'[9] These represent a continuation of the usual practices during the Georgian period, but by the mid 19th century they were being substituted by other forms of cake, as this custom gradually fell out of use.

Around Wem, ordinary sweet biscuits or cut pieces of cake, accompanied by sprigs of rosemary for remembrance, were distributed in the 1870s. Beyond Oswestry, on the borders with Denbigh and Montgomery, the Welsh form of funeral cakes was followed up to around 1850.[10] Here the less well off still served funeral biscuits, but they had grown to the size of a large saucer, and were accompanied by a pewter tankard of hot spiced ale. The better off, meanwhile, abandoned biscuits entirely, having one large rich plum cake, and one large seed-cake, a piece of each being sliced off, folded in paper, sealed down, and given to each mourner. At Hopton Castle in west Shropshire, even the poorest families preferred to provide a single funeral cake, rather than the sponge biscuits. One Newport confectioner was still receiving orders for funeral cakes in 1879, but only from the old-fashioned families. As in other parts of the country, such old customs were being rapidly replaced by a much more standardised approach to every rite of passage, so that, whichever part of England we should visit today, there is little or nothing to differentiate between one region and another.

Fig 31 The great kitchen at Ludlow Castle was used to prepare food for the courts of Prince Arthur and Mary I, and later for the Council of the Marches. Their fare was distinctly royal and noble however, and appears to have contributed little to the traditional diet in Shropshire.

CHAPTER 6

HAVING A DO

Throughout the centuries feasting in one form or another has formed one of the most important ways in which special events have been celebrated. In general, it took two distinct forms, the most exclusive being the provision of lavish entertainments for both visiting dignitaries and corporate bodies, while the most democratic provided plainer but still substantial fare for the population at large.

When Henry VII, Queen Elizabeth of York and their son Prince Arthur stayed at Shrewsbury Castle at the end of the fifteenth century, the Corporation's hospitality included four oxen, twenty four castrated rams, and a large quantity of bread. All this was washed down with 3,520 pints of ale and around 2,900 pints of wine, in addition to sweet wine, spices and sugar used to make hipocras for her majesty.[1] In the sixteenth century, the arrival of the King's Commissioners for the dissolution of religious houses in 1535 saw the corporation providing them with four lambs, twelve capons and some 590 pints of wine, in the clear hope that this would help to promote the town's interests.[2] The 1581 visit of Sir Henry Sidney, the Lord President of the Council of the Marches, took place in far happier and more certain times, and so featured that most popular of Elizabethan upper class pleasures, the sweetmeat banquet. This involved setting out tables with every conceivable variety of fresh fruit, dried fruit, jellies, creams, and elaborate sugar confectionery. And spices, on which the guests would browse, buffet-style, while enjoying music, conversation, and sweet spiced wines.[3] On May Day, the four masters of Shrewsbury School made such a banquet for Sir Henry in front of their original building in Castle Gates, each one providing ten dishes carried by the boys, each group being headed by a 'shewer' (i.e. 'head waiter') who exclaimed the name of his master within an appropriate couplet;[4]

These are all of Larrence Lore,
Accompt hys hart above hys store.

These ten are all of Barker's bande
Good wyll, not welthe now be scande.

These ten are all in Atkys chardge,
Hys gifts are small, hys good wyll lardge.

These ten coom last and are the least
Yet Kent's good will ys with the beast (i.e. best).

Over the succeeding reigns royalty and other infrequent distinguished guests were received with similar hospitality, but the Corporation also provided far more regular entertainments for itself. In towns and cities in all parts of England, civic banquets formed one of the few material benefits provided for their unpaid councillors. They therefore took great pains to ensure that there was no stinting when it came to the provision of the very best food and drink. In Ludlow, for example, the Bailiffs Feast held every 28th October up to 1835 was a particularly jovial and sumptuous affair, followed next day by a buck-hunt and an evening ball.[5] In Wem, meanwhile, there were originally four feasts each year, featuring roast beef and ale.[6] A fuller impression of the contents of top-quality municipal gastronomy comes from the records of Shrewsbury corporation, the following examples coming from the Commonwealth and the Restoration periods;[7]

Feby. 2[Nd] 1653
Four henns & a bantam				8s	
A legge of mutton & sauce				2s	8d
A piece of boiled beefe and turnips				5s	2d
A rib of beefe				11s	6d
A turkey				3s	6d
A couple of capons				3s	6d
A couple of cocks				1s	
A brace of partridge				1s	4d
A tarte				3s	
A neats [calf's] tongue				1s	
A dish of butter					4d
A joint of gamon				2s	6d
Frute and cheese					6d
Bread and beare				3s	8d
Wine 12s	Strong beare	5s	Fire	10d	
Sum Total is £4 3s 4d.					

HAVING A DO

Mayor's Feast, 1661

3 Leggs of mutton	7s	6d
2 Leggs of pork	3s	4d
1 Head of Pork	1s	4d
3 Boyling pieces of beefe	11s	8d
3 Geese	7s	
2 Ribs of beefe	18s	
3 pigs	4s	6d
3 Turkies	6s	
3 couple of ducks	4s	6d
5 Partridges	2s	6d
1 couple of woodcock		7d
1 Duzen & half of pedgions	3s	
3 Tartes	7s	
3 Quince pies	9s	
2 dishes of ling	4s	
Pd. the cooke	5s	
beere & ale	11s	
[Sum Total	£5 8s 2d]	

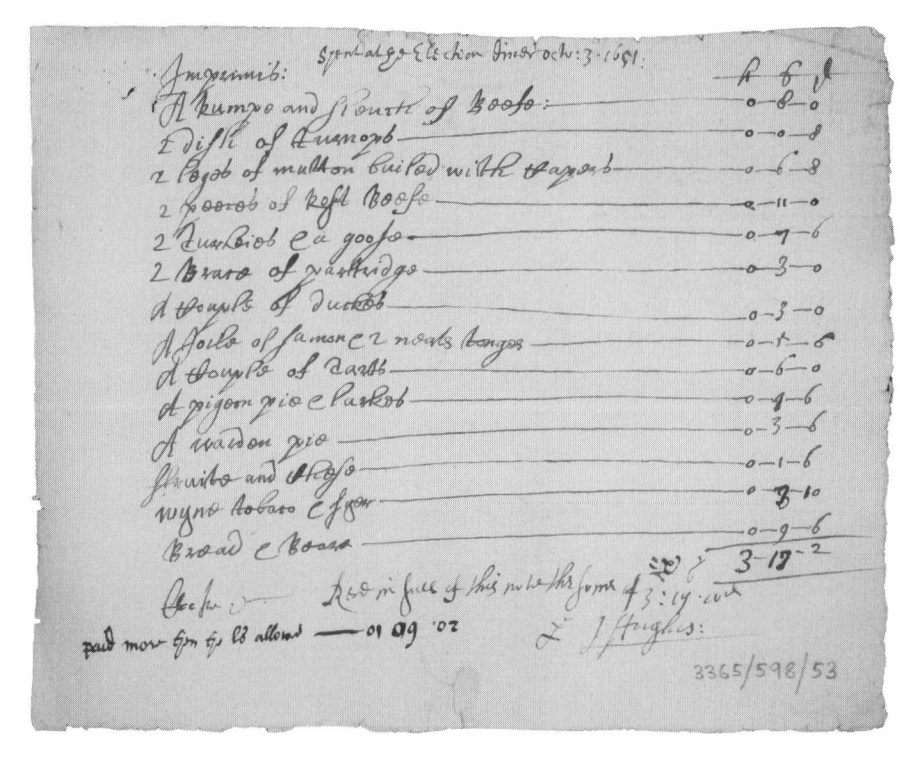

Fig 32   The accounts for the Shrewsbury Elections Dinner, 3rd October 1631.

157

Such dinners, with their boar's head, sucking pigs, boiled and roast joints, tarts, fruit and cheese served up in around thirty dishes was certainly good food for the period, but would have appeared very down-market to the critical and well-experienced stomach of a Victorian alderman. His expectations, groomed on decades of such extravagance was for something far more rich and elegant. To illustrate this we can follow the menu of a dinner given for Cllr. G.J. Holt, the newly-elected Mayor of Shrewsbury, in 1890. It was prepared by Mr T. Plimmer, confectioner, of Castle Street, and served to a party of thirty one in the reading room of the Music Hall in the Square.[8]

SOUPS
Clear Turtle   Julienne

FISH
Crimped Cod Fish   Oyster Sauce   Fried Filleted Soles
with Shrimp Sauce

ENTREÉS
Sweetbreads and Mushrooms   Mutton Cutlets with Tomatoes
Lobster Cutlets   Cardinal Sauce   Chicken Rissoles

JOINTS
Sirloin of Beef   Horse Radish Sauce   Roast Turkey
York Ham   Boiled Chicken with Tongue
Roast Ducks

GAME
Haunch of Venison with Beans   Leverets   Pheasants
Partridges

SWEETS
Sir Watkin   Cabinet   Fig and Snowden Puddings
Maraschino   Macedoine Jellies   Genoese Pastry, Italian
Cream   Swiss Cream   Ice Pudding

DESSERT
Hothouse Grapes etc.

The wines are not listed, but these too would have been of the very best to accompany each course, and for the numerous toasts and responses which concluded the evening.

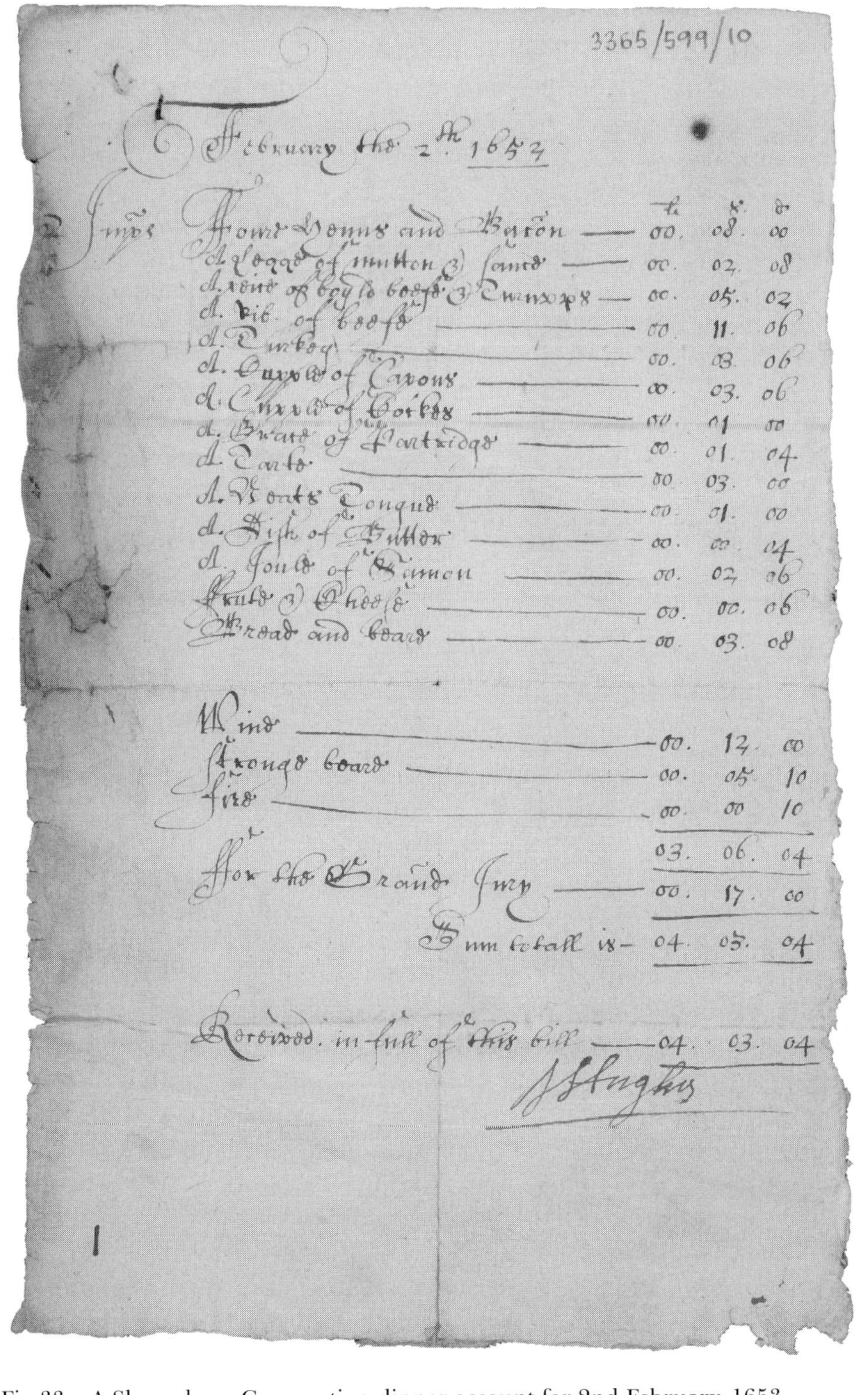

3365/599/10

February the 2th 1653

		li	s	d
Imps	Foure Henns and Bacon	00.	08.	00
	A Legge of mutton & sauce	00.	02.	08
	A rine of boyld beefe & Turnops	00.	05.	02
	A Rib of beefe	00.	11.	06
	A Turkey	00.	03.	06
	A Couple of Capons	00.	03.	06
	A Couple of Cockes	00.	01	00
	A Brace of Partridge	00.	01.	04
	A Tarte	00	03.	00
	A Neats Tongue	00.	01.	00
	A Dish of Butter	00.	00.	04
	A Joule of Samon	00.	02.	06
	Fruite & Cheese	00.	00.	06
	Bread and beare	00	03.	08
	Wine	00.	12.	00
	Stronge beare	00.	05.	10
	Fire	00.	00	10
		03.	06.	04
	For the Grand Jury	00.	17.	00
	Sum totall is	04.	03.	04
	Receaved in full of this bill	04.	03.	04

J Hughes

Fig 33 A Shrewsbury Corporation dinner account for 2nd February, 1653.

Not all public dinners were on quite so grand a scale however, as may be seen in the following menus for those served after H.R. Corbet had unveiled the Jubilee Fountain at Market Drayton in 1898;[9]

FISH

Salmon   Soles

[JOINTS]

Roast Beef   Lamb   Spring Chicken

Guinea Fowls

Boiled Chickens   Ham   Tongues

SWEETS

Jellies   Blancmanges   Lemon Creams

Stewed Fruit   Cream and Pastry

WINES

Champagne   Port   Sherry

or the Jubilee old Folks' Dinner served by the Mayor, ladies and gentlemen of Shrewsbury to all who had achieved Her Majesty's age of 68;[10]

Roast Beef   Veal   Ham

Potatoes

Plum Pudding etc.

Such celebrations were not confined to public bodies, but could be organised by individual families or communities to suit any number of different events. These 'Do's' were usually intended to include as full a representation of the local population as possible, not just the great and the good in whose honour they were held. To show their form we can follow the return of Mr & Mrs Frank Bibby to Hardwick Grange after yachting off Scotland in 1890.[11] In preparation, ceremonial arches had been erected, and the band of the Shropshire Artillery engaged to provide the music. After the actual ceremonies had been completed 'Upwards of 500 persons sat down to a substantial meat tea in a large marquee erected in close proximity to the hall, the tea being supplied by Mr F. Latter, whose catering gave every satisfaction, afterwards the marquee was cleared for dancing, and a very enjoyable evening was spent . . .' In the same year, when

Mr & Mrs Rowland Hunt returned home from their honeymoon to Boreaton Hall, they were presented with the portraits which had been commissioned by their tenants. Following the usual Victorian custom of segregated public dinners, two tents had been put up in the park, the tenants being served a 'capital dinner' in one, while their wives and children took tea (i.e. the meal, not the drink alone) in the other.[12]

Every major family celebrated the 21st birthday of its rising heir with similar large-scale events. For the coming-of-age of Mr Evelyn Milnes Gaskell in October, 1898, his father hosted a dinner to all the tenants of his Much Wenlock estate, each working his way through;[13]

SOUP
Clear

FISH
Mayonnaise of Salmon   Soles in Aspic

ENTREÉS
Cutlets   Sirloin of Beef   Targets of Lamb
Chaudfroid of Chicken and Tongues
Roast Chicken   and   York Ham

GAME
Pheasants   Partridges

SWEETS
Champagne Jellies   Maraschino Jellies
Creams   French Pastries

DESSERT

with numerous wines, and seven toasts and responses.

For really impressive public events, including comings-of-age, special open-air hearths were built and large spits obtained in order to roast entire animals. In the Georgian period sheep were the animals of choice, one actually being roasted on the River Severn when it froze solid in the winter of 1739. Others were roasted to celebrate Lord Hill's visit to Shrewsbury on June 30th, 1814, after the Peace of Paris has seemingly ended the Napoleonic Wars, in

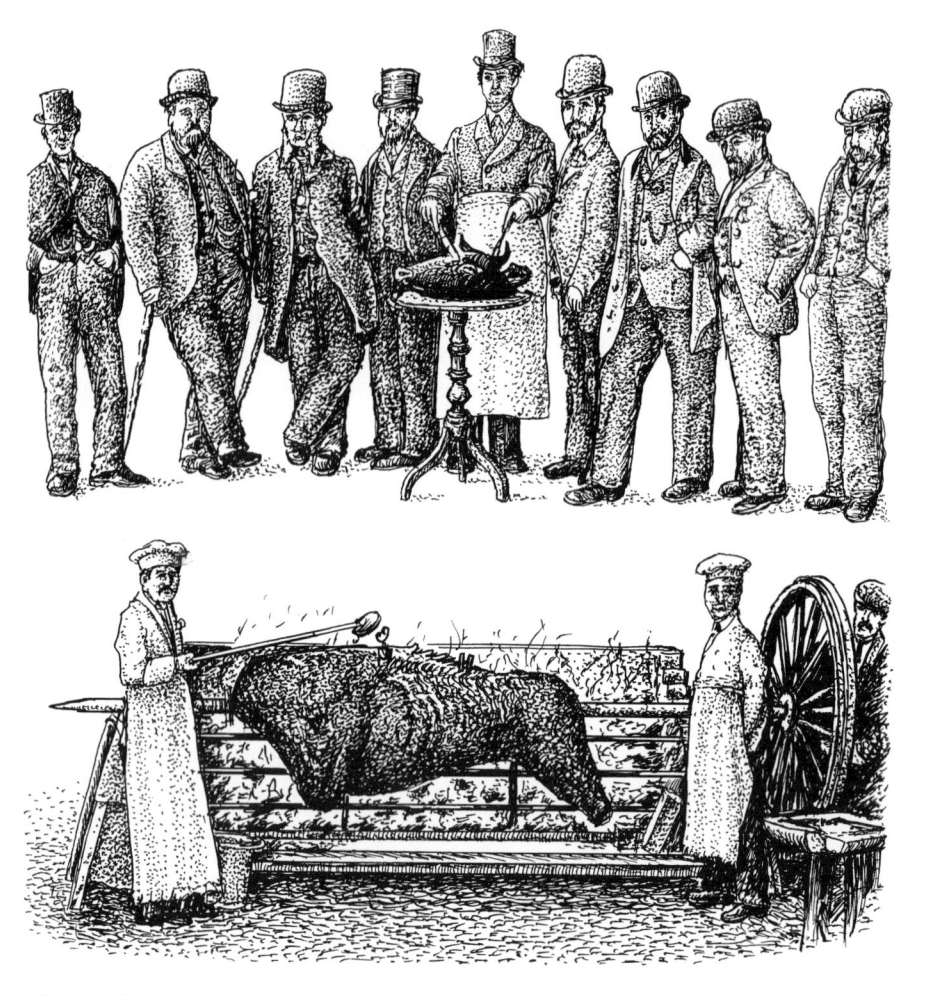

Fig 34   Ox-roasts were particularly associated with the comings-of-age of the heirs to the great land-owning families. Resplendent in frock coat and top hat, and broad apron, Sir Reginald Corbet (above) poses with his ox-head for his 21st birthday photograph of 1878. The ox being roasted whole in Newport market place in August 1909 (below) was for the coming-of-age of the Marquis of Stafford, heir to the magnificent Duchy of Sutherland.

which he had proved to be 'the man Wellington could depend on.'[14] The Victorians preferred the ox-roast, with its associated ceremonies. One which took place in Market Drayton about 1878 saw the roasting operation completed in the market square, where three men dressed in black and yellow liveries carefully basted the slow-rotating beast. It was then placed in a waggon in as lifelike a posture as possible and decorated with over-arching greenery. Such roast oxen might then be decorated by gilding the horns or hanging garlands of flowers around the neck. With a blue-smocked butcher standing just in front, knife in hand, they could set off for a two or three mile journey to their destination at a particular house, there to be carved and served to the assembled crowds.[15]

Much further down the social scale even more informal, but probably just as enjoyable meals also took place from time to time. The 'poor folk' around Baschurch used to carry food on their seven-mile journey back from Shrewsbury Market, for example, so that they could enjoy a communal picnic and dance in some farmer's field.[16] In the Pulverbatch district the autumn evenings were enlivened by other gatherings of farm servants etc. called 'cakings'. Having made a number of small identical cakes from the wheat gleaned after harvest, the hostess sold them at a penny each to allcomers, who then either lost or gained them by playing cards. By buying in the 'lost' cakes at three for tuppence, she was able to build up quite a profit, as much as eight or ten shillings on a good night, plus the enjoyment of the whole affair. It was events such as these that ensured a good social life for the whole community.

CHAPTER 7

IN HALLS & MANOR HOUSES

We have already seen how the scale and quality of the kitchens and utensils used in great Shropshire houses was always far superior to those of ordinary homes, but these are only some of the differences. One of the others was the employment of professional cooks, men and women who were trained up in their craft from an early age. Working under highly experienced masters or cook/housekeepers, they absorbed the true, long-established traditions of the finest English cookery, following a repertoire of dishes which had proved favourites for generations of their employers. Such cooks are usually among the most anonymous of historical figures, recorded, if at all, simply by the appearance of their names in household accounts or census returns. We are therefore very fortunate to find a number of Shropshire cooks who rose to considerable importance, and of whom there is still good written evidence.

In the seventeenth century, when the profession was still an entirely male preserve, some provided services just to their own local communities. Bartholomew Mansell not only worked for Mr Chambre of Petton, but was also 'very serviceable to his neighbours in dressing meate att feasts, and in slaughtering beeves and swine, all of which hee did att a very reasonable rate.'[1] Others moved away to take up some of the country's top culinary positions.

One of these was Richard Hayward, a younger son of Thomas Hayward of Balderton. Thanks to Richard Gough, we know more about him than virtually any other cook of this period, even that he stood up straight, was slim, rather tall, had crisp sandy brown hair, and small legs. From being a boy he wanted to become a cook, and so his father apprenticed him to Richard Hunt, a native of Myddle, cook to Sir Humphrey Lea of Langley. After serving seven years as a scullion boy, he worked there for a further seven years as master cook. During this time he gained the friendship of Walter Bromley, cook to King Charles I, who brought him to London, and found him the position of cook to Sir Robert Hitcham. Over the next nine months he cooked for this great lawyer, travelling with him as he followed the circuits of the courts. He then received a message from Bromley, instructing him to hand in his week's notice, collect his £10 wages, and return to London as fast as possible. This he did, travelling so quickly that his trunks and luggage had to be sent on later. The need for this urgency was that the Bishop of London's cook had just died, and Hayward stood a good chance of replacing him.

In the early 1630s William Juxom had been a private chaplain to the King, but due to royal and church influence he had enjoyed a meteoric rise, becoming Bishop of London and Lord Treasurer by 1636. This made him third in precedence in the country's administration, just below the Archbishop and the Great Seal. Due to Bromley's influence, Hayward got the job, and so became responsible for providing all the regular meals and feasts served within the Bishop's properties. All this came to an end some years later, when Parliament abolished all bishoprics, causing their households to be dispersed. Having discussed his future with the Bishop, Hayward now applied for the post of master cook to William Pierrepont, a son of the Earl of Kingston, and a leading Parliamentarian. At the interview, Pierrepont graciously stated that he would willingly accept a servant of so noble a person, and the best of Bishops, and set out his terms of employment. Hayward was now to purchase the ingredients and cook sufficient food to supply eight dishes for dinner every day, for £8 per week. However, if Oliver Cromwell or other important guests had to be entertained, each dish had to be more substantial and richer, the list and prices of the additional materials to be noted on his bill. For all this he was to receive £12 a year, plus tips from guests. It was also agreed that if Bishop Juxon should be restored to his office, Hayward would be free to return to him, as happened a full twelve years later.

The Bishop had been one Charles I's most loyal subjects, sharing his last imprisonment, and accompanying him at his execution in Whitehall on 30th January 1649. After the Restoration in 1660 Charles II rewarded Juxon by making him Archbishop of Canterbury, Hayward now being re-appointed to supervise the kitchens of Lambeth Palace etc. Given the scale and quality of the meals required by such an establishment, he must have been one of the most able cooks of his generation After a few years, when he found himself growing old, he was able to buy up his eldest brother's interest in the old family home at Balderton and retire back into the Shropshire countryside. Here he lived out the rest of his life, wealthy enough to set up a charity to give a monthly dole of bread to the poor, until he died, and was buried in the north aisle of his parish church at Myddle.[2]

Thomas Barker was a contemporary of Hayward, being born at Meole Brace where, he claimed, there was not 'a girle of ten yeares of age, but can make a pie.' Although a freeman and burgess of Shrewsbury, he worked in London, where he was able to absorb all the new recipes and techniques of continental Europe by cooking for various ambassadors from around the 1610s to the 1650s 'Though I have been no traveller, I may speake it,' he wrote, 'for I have been admitted into the most Ambassador's Kitchins that have come into England this forty years, and do wait on them still at the Lord Protector's charge, and I am paid duly for it.' In addition, he appears to have enjoyed aristocratic patronage, for it was to Edward, 2nd Baron Montagu of Boughton, General of Cromwell's navy and a Lord Commissioner of the Treasury that he dedicated his book *The Art of Angling* of 1651, and *Barker's Delight, or the Art of Angling* in 1657. Although not so famous as Isaac Walton's *The Compleat Angler* of 1653, it was an exceptionally fine work, giving every detail of not only how to catch fish, but also how to cook them by the most advanced and approved methods;

> Restorative broth of Trouts learne to make;
> Some fry & some stew, and some also bake.
> First broyl and then bake, is a rule of good skill,
> And when thou dost fortune a good trout to kill,
> Then rost him, and bast first with good claret wine,
> But calver'd boyl'd trout will make thee to dine
> With dainty contentment, both the hot and the cold,
> And the Marrienate Trout I dare to be bold
> For a quarter of a year will keep to thy mind,
> If covered close & preserved from wind.
> But mark well good brother, what now I doe say,
> Sauce made of Anchoves is an excellent way,
> With oysters and lemmon, clove, nutmeg and mace,
> When the brave spotted trout hath been boyled apace ...
> The French and Italian no better can doe,
> Oberve well my rules; and you'l say so too.

Fig 35   The 17th century joiners of Shrewsbury were able to produce some of the best oak furniture of the period. Some pieces still remain in use in the Draper's Hall, including the draw-leaf table and chair made by Richard Ellis in 1662, and forms made by Francis Bowyer in either 1632 or 1635.

The roles of cook and angler are usually quite separate, but Barker's masters expected him to perform both almost simultaneously. Late one evening his lord asked him to provide a dish of trout by six next morning. This he did, using a combination of 'lob-worms' and artificial flies, after which he was commanded 'to turn Cook and dress them for dinner', cooking trout in broth, two dishes of calvered trout hot (one with anchovy sauce, one with oyster sauce), two dishes of calvered trout cold, one of broiled trouts, one of fried trout, and perhaps others too. The term 'calver' indicates a method of cookery employed particularly for freshly-killed fish. By cutting them a few times across the back and plunging them into a scalding vinegar or salt and wine pickle, their flesh became 'calvered', apparently holding its shape so as to be neatly carved for the table. It was a skilful operation, first recorded in England by Barker, who noted that 'Every scullion dresseth that dish against his will, because he cannot calver them.' For any period, he was a cookery writer of the very finest quality, adopting an almost conversational, instructive style, pointing out every useful detail as he follows each dish from its raw materials through to completion. Some of his recipes will be given later.[3]

The best known Shropshire writer on culinary affairs and recipes was not a professional cook, but the daughter and wife of prosperous upper middle class families. Maria Ketelby was born in Ludlow in 1745, her family having been successful lawyers there for several generations and owning houses in both Castle Square and Castle Street. In 1766, at the age of twenty-one, she married Thomas Rundell, a surgeon with a good practice in Bath, where they set up their home and raised two sons and three daughters. After Thomas' death in 1795 she removed to Swansea and began to occupy her time in organising the collection of housekeeping information and recipes she had gathered over the years, so that it could be passed on to her daughters. There was no intention of converting it into book form at this time, but in 1806 she submitted it to an old family friend, John Murray, the major London publisher. He immediately recognised its potential, and issued it as *Domestic Cookery* by 'A Lady'. An immediate success, a second larger edition soon followed, sixty-five editions appearing over the next thirty-five years, with annual sales of between five and ten thousand copies. It was the best-selling cookery book of its period, even enabling Murray to use its copyright as security for a four thousand pound mortgage to buy a central London property.

As this commercial success was completely unexpected, no royalty agreement had been drawn up, Mrs Rundell being initially surprised to receive a gift of £150 from Murray in 1808. By 1814 however, she had changed her mind, accusing him of neglecting her book and hindering sales, so both were forced to go to law to settle their differences. Eventually she accepted the enormous sum of two thousand pounds to discharge her claims.[4] As the first manual of household management with any real claims to completeness, it set out clear directions for her intended readers, the young mistresses, not the servants;

'The Mistress of a family should always remember that the welfare and good management of the house depends on the eye of the superior and consequently that nothing is too trifling for her notice, whereby waste may be avoided; and this attention is of more importance now that the price of every necessary of life is increased to an enormous degree.' [just as true in 2009 as in 1806] 'Happy the man who calls her his wife, Blessed are the children who call her mother.

Anticipating Mrs Beeton by fifty years, her ideal gentlewoman/housewife was not to be a creature entirely committed to status, fashion and polite accomplishments, but also to be an active, engaged and prudent manager of her entire household. This is clearly demonstrated in the selection of recipes, for although aimed at a national, rather than a local readership, they include many with sound vernacular origins. Her 'Forced Hog's Ears', might not be known as a Shropshire dish, but would certainly fit very comfortably into the county's traditional habit of making something appetising out of what others might think of as inedible waste.

To anyone with an interest in food history, the name of Mrs Rundell is still extremely well-known. Similarly, anyone interested in the most magnificent English gold, silver and ormolu tableware of the late Georgian period knows the name Rundell, Bridge and Rundell, gold and silversmiths to the royal family, the government, the church, the army and the nobility. However, few realise that both were members of the same family. Mrs Rundell's husband was a close relation, probably a brother, of Philip Rundell, the millionaire head of the company based at 32 Ludgate Hill to the west of St Pauls in the City of London. After her husband's death her two younger daughters went to live with their London relations, as did her son, who was taken into the partnership in 1804–5. In 1814 his company was commissioned by the government to provide a full set of diplomatic tableware for William Hill, ambassador to the court of Sardinia. It was huge, 5,833 ounces of solid silver, 1,066 ounces of gold plate, plus table plateaux, candelabra and dress-stands by Pierre-Phillipe Thomire, the finest maker of ormolu in Paris, and an 136-piece porcelain dessert service by Pierre-Louis Dagoty of Paris, manufacturer to the Empress Josephine.[5] Napoleon was a prisoner on Elba, and the courts of Europe were now to experience the wealth and power of victorious Britain at every diplomatic function. Such services were intended to remain government property. However, Prime Minister William Pitt appears to have used it as an inducement to persuade William Hill to retire so that a Pitt nephew might take his place. As a result, Hill brought it all back to England, where he inherited his family estate of Attingham Park, together with the title of Lord Berwick, in 1832. After several generations, the Berwick family generously presented it, together with their house and its most significant contents, to the National Trust. In 2008 it was completely re-displayed in the Attingham dining room, resplendent with replicas of all the sugarwork, wax flowers, hot-house fruits and colourful confectionery it was originally intended to complement. Almost two hundred years after it was created, the service still retains its power to impress, stopping visitors in their tracks as they first catch sight of its gleaming magnificence.

This was a great contrast to Mrs Rundell's early life in Ludlow, but such commissions to her in-laws brought material benefits even greater than those of her book. When the head of the firm died he left her a considerable sum, which enabled her to maintain a prosperous lifestyle. At her death in Lausanne, Switzerland, in 1828, she had a fortune of almost nine thousand pounds, a huge sum for that time. It is interesting to consider that a better living was to be had from writing about cookery and providing tableware than was ever possible by slaving away in the kitchen. Although country house cooks and cook/housekeepers were among the best-paid of household servants, their lives were hard and their responsibilities considerable. They would be lucky to save sufficient to keep themselves in old age, without the support of their employing families.

We currently know little of their lives, since, as elsewhere, theirs was a closed world, even within the confines of a country house. Their duties, and the deliberate planning of domestic quarters to keep each sex and department quite separate from one another, coupled with having to work through family and servants mealtimes, could leave them in great isolation. For the head of the kitchens, this was a life-long experience, but for many of the kitchen and scullery maids it provided a few years of excellent training between adolescence and marriage. Years afterwards, when probably operating their own cottage or farmhouse kitchens, they would still retain the standards of culinary cleanliness, order and quality, if not the great expense, of the country house.

Another of the great differences between upper and lower-class life in Shropshire was the range and quantities of foods cooked and served each day. This is immediately obvious when we look through kitchen account books, such as those of the Talbots of Longford Hall

Fig 36 A selection of the ormolu centrepieces, candelabra and dress stands made by Pierre-Phillipe Thomire of Paris and supplied to William Hill when ambassador to the court of Sardinia in 1814. They are still to be seen at his family home, Attingham Park.

in the mid-Elizabethan period. Each day a list was made of what was in the larders, and how much was consumed, together with purchase prices from which the weekly expenses could be calculated. The sheer range of what was eaten is quite amazing;[6]

MEAT		FISH	
Beef		Beckett sea-bream	
Steer, cut into 26 pieces		Carp	
Veal, " " " "		Cod	3s 4d
Mutton (ewe)		Eels	
Wether (castrated ram)		Haberdine (large dried cod)	
Porkett (young porker)		Lamprey	100 for 1s
Pig (sucking)	8d.	Ling & Newling	
Coney (rabbit)		Moddfish (loach)	
Doe (venison)		Mussels	100 for 3d
POULTRY		Oysters	300 for 4d
Capon		Perch	
Chicken		Plaice 3d	
Goose 8d		Roche	
Peacock		Salmon	
Turkey		Tench	
WILD BIRDS		Thornback	1s 6d
Bittern		Whiting	2d
Blackbird	3 for 2d	GROCERIES	
Crane		Butter	1 quart for 8½d
Curlew		Mustard seed	4oz for 3d
Heath Hen (female black grouse)		Nutmeg	4oz for 1s 8d
Heron		Salt	1 bushel for 2s
Lark		Vinegar	1 pint for 6d
Mallard		GRAIN (per bushel)	
Moorcock (male red grouse)		Wheat;	
Pheasant		(for manchet bread)	4s 6d
Plover	2s 6d	(for cheat bread)	4s
Snipe	1d	(for pastry)	4s
Swan		Muncorn (wheat & rye)	
Teal	4d	(for household bread)	3s 4d
Woodcock	3d	Malt	2s 2d
EGGS		Peas	3s 3d
Hens	5 for 1d		

and so are the quantities. Here are the lists of what was eaten on a Monday, a normal meat-day, and a Friday, one of the weekdays on which meat was banned by law to encourage the consumption of fish and the development of English naval power.

Monday 23rd December 1577

    7 pieces of beef   12 pieces of mutton
    1 sucking pig   5 rabbits   1 goose   1 teal

Friday 27th December 1577

    7 pieces of newling fish   12 pieces of mud fish
    12 eels   1 carp

In addition, great quantities of bread were consumed, the weekly accounts suggesting a daily use of about ten manchet loaves of fine white bread, each weighing about 2lb., ten cheat loaves of whole wheat with only the coarsest bran extracted, each weighing about 4lbs., and perhaps forty muncorn loaves of coarse wheat and rye. Malt was also purchased for brewing into beer, of which a hogshead, 420 pints, was used each day. The fact that neither fruit nor vegetables appear in the accounts should not be taken as evidence that they were never eaten. It only shows that they were not included because they were home-grown, and had therefore cost nothing to produce.

    The same applied to pigeons, for they largely fed themselves from the surrounding countryside. Many of the county's larger houses have fine dovecotes, either square in plan, round or polygonal, their insides lined with hundreds of nesting boxes. Since each pair of birds could produce a pair of chicks eight to ten times each year for about seven years, their unfledged 'squabs' were constantly available for the table, regardless of the season.[7]

    In houses such as Longford Hall the family's meals were served as a complete tableful of different foods, some sweet, some some savoury, so that all those seated around could help either themselves or each other to whatever they chose. It was almost like a buffet table, but was surrounded by place-settings. Gradually this arrangement became formalised into what became known as *Service à la Francaise*,[8] despite its at least equal English ancestry. It continued virtually unchanged from the Elizabethan through to the mid Victorian periods, differing in its detailed contents rather than its formalities over the years. The following mid eighteenth century table plans are typical;[9]

FIRST COURSE
Gravy Soup
Fricasey of Rabbits   Scotch Collops
Stewed Oysters
Boiled Chicken   Calf Foot Pie
A Ham

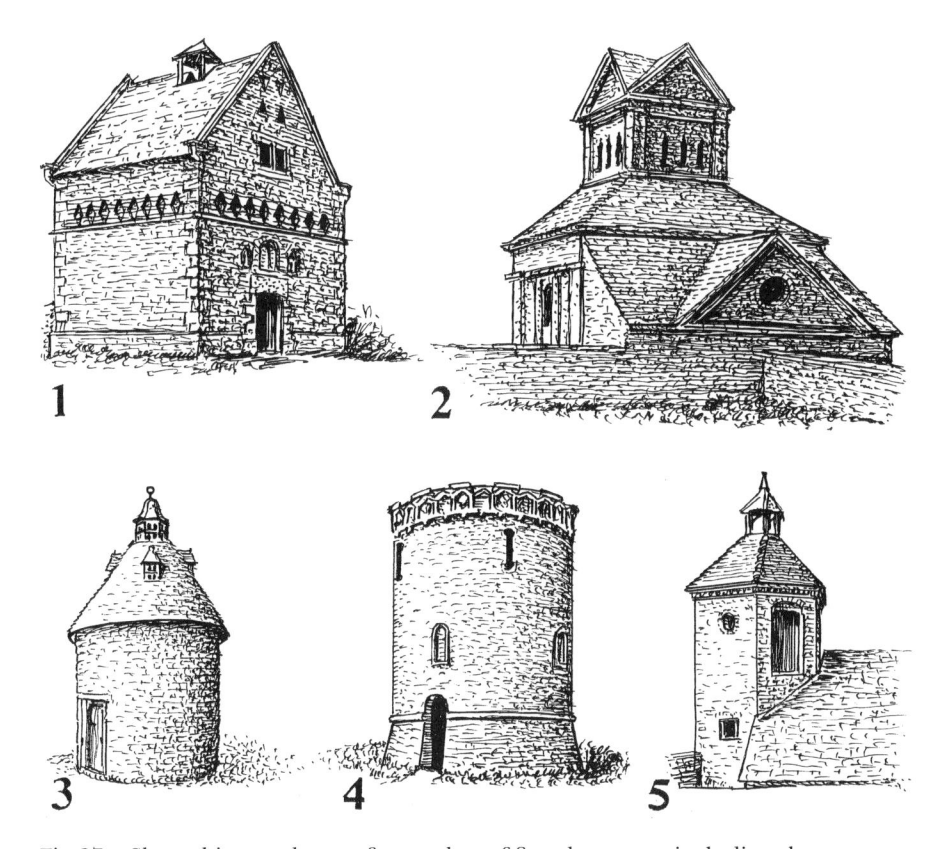

Fig 37 Shropshire can boast of a number of fine dovecotes, including these at;

1. Hodnet Hall, *c.* 1650
2. Millichope Park
3. Walcot Hall
4. Davenport House
5. Golding Farm, Pitchford

(after the mistress had helped everyone to soup, it was removed, and replaced by a dish of fish, which she then served to anyone who wanted it, everyone then eating any of the other dishes, having a clean plate for each one. Meanwhile the master would carve and serve the ham)

SECOND COURSE

Wild Ducks

Lobster   Tarts

Jellies or Lemon Possets

Cream Curds   Stewed Pears or Preserved Quinces

A Turkey

Such a table would be sufficient for perhaps ten people, but the number of dishes could be simply increased or decreased according to the numbers invited.

The following recipes, all from original Shropshire sources, would have been served in this way, the soups being offered first, then the fish, and then a variety of different dishes for the first course, with another selection for the second.[10]

Some of the soups were quite substantial, as may be seen from the following version of mulligatawny which was adopted in India in the mid eighteenth century. Taking its name from the Tamil *milagu-tannir*, meaning 'pepper-water', it has a rich, creamy curry flavour.

MULLIGATAWNY SOUP, *c.* 1840

1 free-range chicken
2½lb/1·1kg English onions, sliced
8oz/225g butter
3 light stock cubes
4oz/100g flour
1 tbs curry powder
2oz/50g macaroni
juice of 1 lemon
¼pt/150ml single cream

Remove the breasts and legs from the chicken.

Using a large pan, fry the onions, breasts and legs in half the butter until golden brown. Add 3pt/1·8l water, bring to the simmer, continue for 10 min. then remove the breasts and legs, add the chicken skin and carcase, and simmer for a further 2 hours.

Boil the macaroni until just tender, drain, plunge into cold water, and set aside, meanwhile dividing the breasts and legs into spoon-sized pieces.

To finish the soup, fry the flour in the remaining butter until a pale straw colour, then use a wooden spoon to beat in the curry powder and ½pt/300ml cold water. Remove the chicken carcase from the pan, add the butter and flour mixture, and stir continuously as it thickens and returns to the boil. Finally stir in the chicken meat, drained macaroni, lemon juice and cream and allow to heat through without boiling, just before serving.

TOMATO SOUP, c. 1840

1lb/450g ripe, well-flavoured tomatoes
3 or 4 chicken, lamb or vegetable stock cubes
1oz/25g butter rubbed into 1oz/25g flour
salt & pepper to taste

Simmer the tomatoes and stock cubes in 2pt/1·2l water for some 10–15min. until completely tender, then rub them through a wire sieve, together with all the stock.

Return to a clean pan, add the kneaded butter in small lumps, beating them in with a whisk as the soup is returned to the boil. Season to taste, and serve hot.

GRILLED TROUTS, 1659

For each prepared trout take 3–4tbs finely-chopped mixed fresh
thyme, marjoram and parsley and 2oz/50g butter.
For the sauce for 2 trout take 1oz/25g butter, 3tbs/45ml white wine
vinegar, and 1 raw egg yolk.

Make a number of deep cuts across each side of the trout, pack them with the herbs, and set aside in a cool place for an hour or two to enable the flavours to be absorbed.

Place the fish on a lightly-greased or oiled grill-rack and grill for about 4 min. on each side under a medium heat, meanwhile basting with the butter, until the flesh is tender but firm, and the skin brown and speckled.

For the sauce, beat all the ingredients over a gentle heat until thickened and creamy, but not boiled until curdled, and serve separately in a small sauceboat.

STEWED TROUT, ITALIAN STYLE, 1659

To every 3 prepared trout take ½ bottle/375ml white wine, pinch ground clove, ½ tsp ground mace, pinch ground ginger, a quarter of a nutmeg, grated.

For their sauce take 2oz/50g butter and the juice of 1 lemon.

The stock is best prepared about an hour or two before cooking, by bringing the wine and spices to the boil, leaving them to go cold, and passing them through a coffee filter-paper.

Place the trout in a shallow pan, pour the stock over them, cover, and poach for some 15–20min. over a gentle heat, until tender.

Remove the trout on to a hot dish, beat the butter and lemon juice into the stock, and serve separately in a sauceboat.

The French used the same method, but added one or two rashers of dry-cured bacon to give a more piquant taste.

STEWED SALMON STEAKS, 1659

4 thick salmon steaks or cutlets   ½ tsp salt
½ pt/300ml white wine vinegar
a few sprigs of rosemary, thyme and marjoram.

Place the salmon steaks in a dish, bring the vinegar to the boil, pour this over the salmon, and leave it to go cold.

Bring 2pt/1·2l water to the boil in a broad pan, add the salmon, vinegar, salt and herbs, cover and simmer for 5–10 minutes until found tender when tried with a skewer.

To serve cold, leave the steaks to cool in their own liquor. To serve hot, beat 2oz/50g butter, 5tbs/75ml white wine vinegar, ½ a lemon very finely chopped, and 1 raw egg yolk together over a gentle heat until curdled. Serve the drained steaks with a separate sauceboat of this sauce.

FISH RECHAUFFÉ, 1845

1lb/450g cooked fish, with all bones removed
½pt/300ml single cream
2 tsp mustard
1 tbs mushroom ketchup
2 tbs flour
2oz/50g butter
2 tbs tarragon or garlic vinegar
1 tbs anchovy sauce

To cover, ½pt/300ml fresh white breadcrumbs mixed with 2oz/50g melted butter

Place all but the covering into a saucepan and stir while heating almost to boiling point, then turn into a shallow fireproof dish.

Spread the breadcrumbs over the top, place under a pre-heated grill until browned, and serve immediately.

Much of the meat served in the country houses was simply roasted before the fire or plain-boiled, relying on its own excellent flavour and texture to demonstrate its quality. Sometimes these basic methods were combined;

LEG OF PORK À LA BRAIRIE, c. 1840

1 leg of pork
4oz/100g salt
4oz/100g dripping
browned breadcrumbs
1 onion, peeled & chopped

One or two days before required, place the pork in a cool place and rub with the salt for 10 min. each day.

Rinse the joint, remove the skin, sprinkle it with the breadcrumbs, weigh it, and place on a rack over a dripping pan holding the dripping and onions. Roast in an oven pre-heated to 180°C, 350°F, Gas mark 4 for some 25 min. per lb./450g until tender. This was served with sage and onion stuffing boiled with additional stock to give the consistency of a sauce.

There was also a considerable demand for meat to be prepared to increasingly complex recipes, each of which provided more interesting flavours.

SCOTCH COLLOPS, c. 1719

Leg of veal or lamb, cut across the grain as thinly as possible.
Plain flour seasoned with salt, pepper and mixed spice.
Suet [or other fat] for frying.

Dip the collops in the seasoned flour, to cover both sides, then stir-fry in the hot fat until just tender, before turning on to a hot dish and serving immediately.

A CHICKEN FRIGACIE, 1719

1 free-range chicken, skinned and divided into joints
3 shallots, finely chopped
1tsp mixed marjoram, parsley & thyme
1 nutmeg, sliced
pared zest of 1 lemon, the remainder sliced
½ bottle of white wine
1 beef stock cube
4 anchovy fillets
1 blade mace
1oz/25g butter
pepper & salt

Place the chicken, skin side up, the shallots, spices, salt and pepper into a shallow pan with the white wine, stock cube and sufficient water to cover, and simmer for about 1 hour until the meat is tender Add the anchovies, butter and lemon slices, continue cooking for a further 10 min., then turn out into a hot dish The sides may then be garnished with sliced lemons, forcemeat balls, and sprigs of parsley.

CUTLETS À LA DOMINIE, c. 1840

4 best end of neck large lamb chops
6 shallots, finely chopped
2 small mushrooms, finely chopped
2 tbs parsley, finely chopped
2oz/50g butter
juice of 1 lemon
½pt/300ml Espagnole sauce
2 raw egg yolks
¼pt/150ml single cream
1 egg, beaten
brown breadcrumbs
fat for deep frying
Pinch of salt & cayenne pepper

Scrape the ends of the chops very neatly, and fry in the butter with the shallots, mushrooms, parsley, lemon juice, salt and cayenne for 20 min., turning frequently. Transfer these (but not the chops) into a dish, and mix with the Espagnole, yolks and cream. Use this to coat each chop, then dipping them in the beaten egg, then the breadcrumbs, before deep-frying for 5 min. and serving immediately.

A HARE PIE FOR A COLD TREAT, 1732

1lb/450g hare [or any other game or red meat]
6 eggs, beaten
2 rashers dry-cured bacon

$\frac{1}{4}$ tsp mixed ground clove & mace
1 tsp marjoram
1oz/25g butter

Pastry
1lb/450g flour
2 tsp salt

8oz/225g lard
9fl.oz/250ml water

Coarsely chop and then grind/process the meat to a smooth paste.

Stir the eggs and butter over a gentle heat until they have solidified, ensuring they do not stick to the pan, and mix into the meat along with the very finely chopped bacon, the marjoram and the spices.

Sift the flour into a bowl, make a well in the centre, and pour in the melted lard, salt and water at boiling point. Rapidly stir together, knead in all the flour, and allow to cool.

Either hand raise, or raise within a 6 ins/15cm hoop or loose-bottomed cake tin, two-thirds of the pastry, pack with the filling, dampen the edges, and add a lid made with the remaining pastry. Trim the join, and pinch between the fingers to produce a zig-zag rim to the crust.

Bake at 200°C, 400°F, Gas mark 6 for 20 min. then reduce to 180°C, 350°F gas mark 4 for a further 1 hr. 40 min. Check the internal temperature is at least 90°C, remove from the oven and leave until cold.

CHICKEN PIE, 1719

Make as above, but filled with 2lb/900g of raw chicken pieces, ½ tsp mixed ground pepper, mace and nutmeg, 2oz/50g butter, and the grated zest of a lemon. Make the pie some 7½ ins/18·5cm diameter, bake as above, then pour in ¼pt/150ml white wine in which 1oz/25g butter and an anchovy fillet have dissolved at boiling point, and serve hot.

LORD ROBERT GROSVENOR'S MACARONI, 1845

2oz/50g macaroni *⅓pt/200ml single cream*
1oz/25g butter *2 tsp made mustard*
2 tbs flour *2oz/50g grated Parmesan*
1 light stock cube dissolved in 4 tbs boiling water

Plunge the macaroni into a large pan of boiling salted water, and boil for some 10 min. until tender, then drain. Melt the butter in a clean pan, stir in the flour and cook for a few minutes, then mix in the remaining ingredients. Stir together over a gentle heat until boiling, then add the macaroni, cook for a few minutes more until all is hot, then serve.

The sweeter foods required for the second course, to accompany the fresh fruits etc. for the following dessert, or to be enjoyed in the summerhouse during fine afternoons and evenings, were usually prepared in a separate housekeepers' kitchen. Since this had been where the ladies of the sixteenth, seventeenth and eighteenth century had distilled their own cosmetics, medicines and liqueurs, it had become known as the stillroom, continuing with this title long after its stills had fallen out of use. Here all the fruit grown in the gardens and hot-houses was prepared for use throughout the year, or made into jams, jellies and syrups, and all the teas, coffees, cold drinks, cakes and biscuits required for teas and other meals. The following recipes demonstrate just a few of the dishes made in Shropshire country-house stillrooms.

TO MAKE SYRUP OF MULBERRIES, RASPBERRIES, [RED, BLACK OR WHITE] CURRANTS, 1736

1lb/450g fruit   *about 8oz/225g sugar*

Place the fruit in a large square of muslin placed across a bowl, then squeeze them with the fingers to form a soft pulp. Lift up the corners of the muslin, twist them together to enclose the pulp, and continue to knead and squeeze it to extract all the juice.

Weigh a large heatproof jar, pour in the juice, weigh it again, and add the weight of the juice in sugar. Originally the jar was then placed in a pan of boiling water for 2 hours, but a modern alternative is to heat it in a microwave, carefully stopping when it suddenly rises to the boil, then stirring to ensure that all the sugar has dissolved, before bringing it to the boil once more, and leaving it for a few minutes to cool.

Finally skim off all the pale scum, pour into sterilised bottles, and seal down for storage in a cool place. Today these syrups are excellent for making soft or alcoholic drinks, for pouring over ice creams etc.

RASPBERRY TART, 1736

¼pt/150ml syrup, made to the recipe above   *8oz/200g flour*
1pt/600ml single cream   *4oz/100g butter*
2 tbs flour   *4 eggs, beaten*
4oz/100g trifle sponges or boudoir biscuits   *3–4 tbs cold water*

Rub the butter into the 8oz/200g flour, stir in the water with a round bladed knife to make pastry, roll this out, and use to line a large 2pt/1l pie dish.

Crush the biscuits into very fine crumbs, and beat into the cream to make a smooth paste. Beat in the eggs, sugar and remaining flour, and finally the syrup.

Pour this into the lined dish and bake at 140°C, 275°F, Gas mark 1 for about an hour, until completely set. [Although not in the original recipe, better results are obtained by blind-baking the pastry at 200°C, 400°F, Gas mark 6 for 15 min. and allowing it to cool before adding the filling.]

The following recipe is unlike anything made today, being an apple jam boiled until it holds its shape when left to set in a mould, but is still not caramelised and tough. To make it successfully requires a good deal of skill.

GATEAU DE POMMES, c. 1840

1lb/450g well-flavoured eating apples
grated zest of 1 lemon
12oz/350g sugar

Peel, core and finely chop the apples, and place in a pan with the lemon zest and a few tablespoons of water, then stir and simmer until they are reduced to a smooth, soft pulp. Stir in the sugar, and continue stirring over a high heat until the pulp has darkened in colour and begins to leave the bottom of the pan. Vigorous continuous stirring is essential at this stage, otherwise it quickly burns, spoiling both the colour and the flavour.

Turn into a lightly-greased mould or small basin, pack down solid, and leave until cold. Finally turn it out on to a plate, and serve with double or whipped cream.

HARTSHORN JELLY, c. 1719–20

¼pt/150ml dry sherry
juice of 1 orange
juice & zest of 1 lemon
½ tsp mixed ground cinnamon, ginger, clove & mace
1 sprig rosemary
½ a nutmeg, crushed
3 tbs sugar
5 tsp gelatin
whites of 2 eggs, lightly beaten with a little water

Put the sherry, juices, zest and spices into a pan with ¾pt/450ml water, cover, bring to the boil, remove from the heat, wrap in a cloth, and leave to cool.

Beat in the egg whites, and return the pan to the heat, slowly stirring, until the eggs have set, formed a thick scum, and clarified the liquid. Leave to stand for 5–10 min., then pour through a coffee filter paper containing the rosemary sprig, into a clean pan, pouring through a second time if necessary, to obtain perfect clarity.

Sprinkle and stir the gelatin into ¼pt/150ml cold water, and set aside for 10 min. to soak.

Add the gelatin and the sugar to the liquid, and stir over a gentle heat until dissolved, but do not allow it to boil.

Finally pour into metal moulds, leave in a cold (not frozen) place to set overnight, then unmould on to a dish, and serve with cream.

LEMON SYLLABUBS, 1840s

½pt/300ml double cream *4oz/100g sugar*
⅓pt/200ml dry white wine *grated rind & juice of 1 lemon*

Whisk all together for 10–15min., pour into six wine glasses, and leave overnight in a cool place to set.

Today we do not make creamy fruit butters such as the following, but they are extremely rich and delicious. They are good in profiteroles, with scones, or, for the truly decadent, scooped up on boudoir biscuits.

LEMON BUTTER

1pt/600ml single cream *5 tbs fresh lemon juice*
3 eggs, beaten *2oz/50g sugar*

Place the eggs in a jug and beat in a little of the single cream. Bring the remaining cream to the boil, and as it rises rapidly pour it from a height into the eggs to thoroughly mix them together.

Return to the pan, stir, then stir in the lemon juice and set it aside for 10–15min.

Line a sieve with a double layer of freshly-rinsed muslin, pour in the mixture, gather up the edges of the muslin, and hang it over a bowl to drain overnight in a cool place.

Scrape the lemon butter into a bowl, add the sugar, beat until smooth, then leave in a cool place until required within the next 24 hours.

Ice cream was first made in England during the later seventeenth century, but its popularity ensured that the facilities for making it were soon being provided in every major country house. The most important requirement was ice. As there were no mechanical means of refrigeration, this had to be gathered from ponds and lakes in the depths of winter, and then stored in ice-houses, well-insulated and well-drained underground chambers where it could remain frozen throughout the coming year. About forty ice-houses have been recorded in Shropshire, but only two are open to the public, one at Attingham Park, and another originally from Tong Castle now removed to the Avoncroft Museum at Bromsgrove. At Badger Hall near Bridgnorth the ice house was of typical egg-shaped form 13ft 6 ins in diameter by 25ft deep, its upper part being entered by a passage insulated with three consecutive doorways.[11] The whole outdoor staff of fifteen were needed to break the ice on the ponds and load it into a punt, transfer it to the landing-stage, break it into small pieces, transfer it into a cart, carry it to the ice house, and there pack it down into a single compact mass. Blocks were then cut out at least once a week, being wrapped in sacks and barrowed up to the cellar beneath the Hall, ready for use by the cook, housekeeper and butler.

This Shropshire recipe dates from around 1719, being a particularly early example.[12]

TO MAKE ICE CREAM, c. 1719–20

Take some cream and sweeten it to your tast, put it into a tin pot that it lys at the bottom [with a] lid that will scrue on. get some Ice and brake it in lumps and put it into an earthen pot with some bay salt and salt peter under it and over it, then set the tin pot of cream on it. put bay salt and salt peter and Ice upon it. set it in a seller and tow hours it will be frozen, then turn it out with raw cream and serve it.

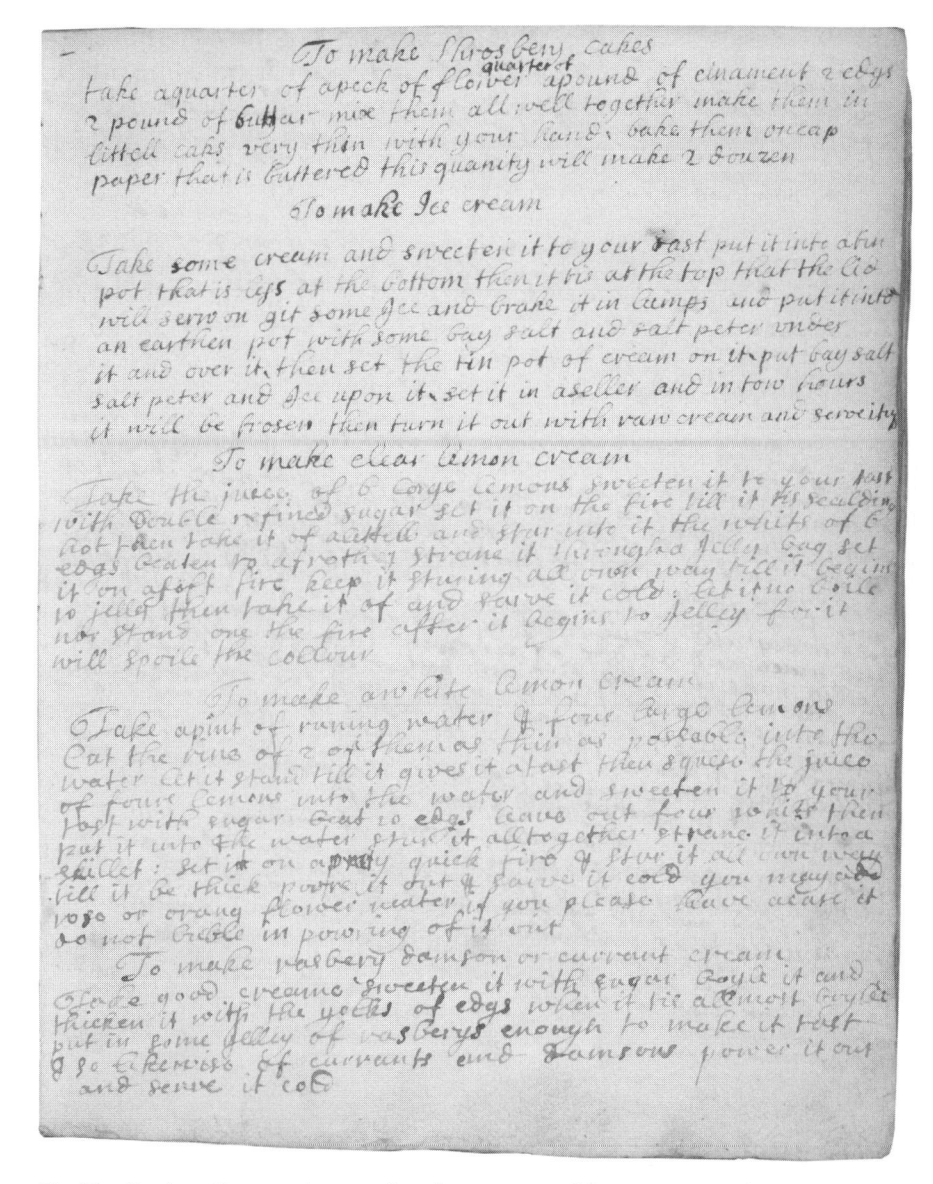

Fig 38 Recipes for strawberry cakes, ice cream and lemon creams from a Shropshire cookery manuscript of around 1719.

It will be seen that there was no attempt to stir the cream as it froze, so the result would have been a single block of frozen cream, rather than the soft, smooth, minute-crystalled ice cream we should expect by the eighteenth century.

Chocolate was another seventeenth century introduction, first being prepared solely as a hot drink, but then as a flavouring for creams etc. Even in the eighteenth century it might still be necessary for it to be processed from the raw beans which had been purchased from the grocer;[13]

'TO SWEETEN COCOLET WHEN IN THE NUTTE, *c.* 1719–20

Take your nut and shave it very thin, then put a brass morter over the fire and let it be very hot, then take 2 ounces of your chocolet and 2 ounces of white sugar and put it in your morter and keep it suring all the while till your morter is very hot, then take it of and beat it till it comes to an oyley past, then put it upon a plate and make it into cakes.'

'TO MAKE A CHOCOLET CREAME'

1pt/600 ml milk   *4 egg yolks, beaten*
1oz/25g 85% dark chocolate   *3 tbs sugar*

Beat a little of the milk into the yolks in a jug.

Stir the remaining milk, sugar and grated chocolate together over the heat until it rises to the boil, then rapidly pour it from a height onto the egg yolks. Return all to the pan, and stir for few minutes over a gentle heat until it has thickened, but not boiled to a curd. Pour into a dish, and allow to cool before serving.

TO MAKE RASPBERRY, DAMSON & [BLACK, RED OR WHITE] CURRANT CREAM, *c.* 1719–20

Follow the above recipe, but substitute a few tablespoons of the jelly or cheese of these fruits for the chocolate.

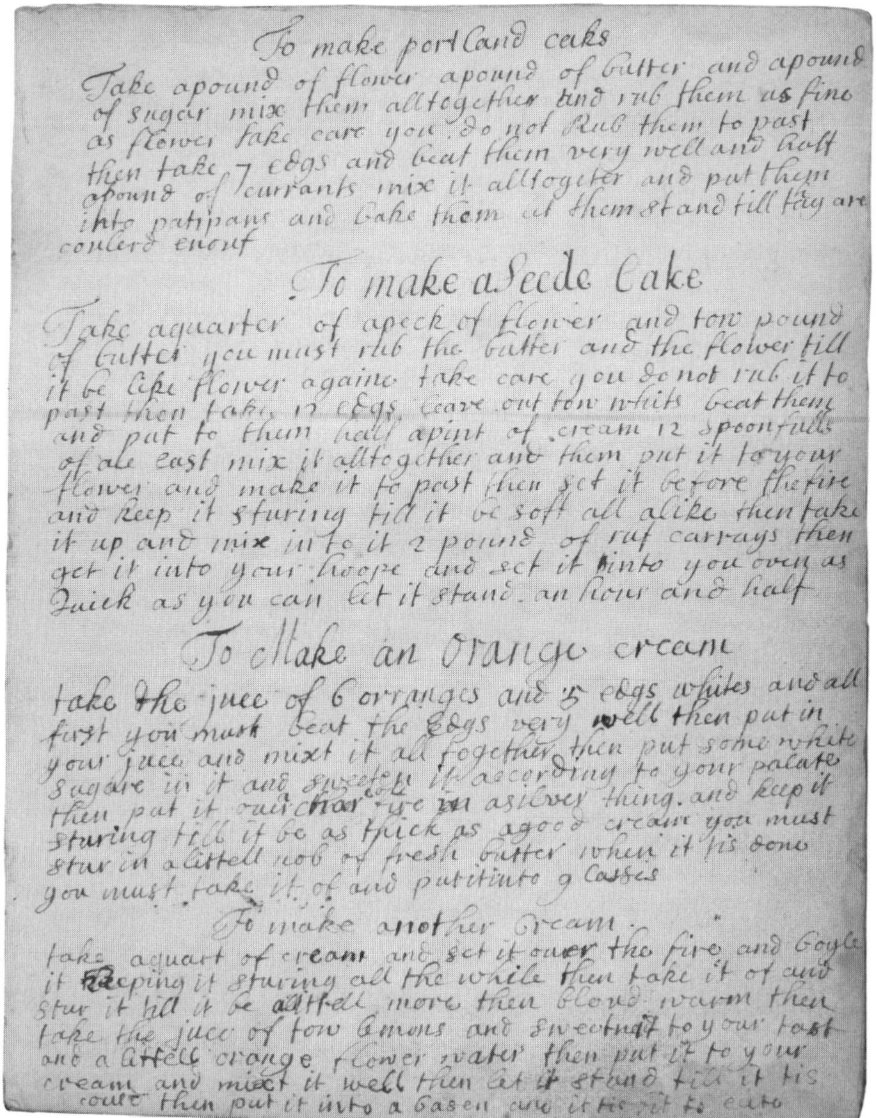

To make portland caks

Take apound of flower apound of butter and apound of sugar mix them alltogether and rub them as fine as flower take care you do not Rub them to past then take 7 egs and beat them very well and half apound of currants mix it alltogether and put them into patipans and bake them at them stand till they are coulerd enouf

To make a Seede Cake

Take aquarter of apeck of flower and tow pound of butter you must rub the butter and the flower till it be like flower againe take care you do not rub it to past then take 12 egs, leave out tow whits beat them and put to them half apint of cream 12 spoonfulls of ale east mix it alltogether and them put it to your flower and make it to past then set it before the fire and keep it sturing till it be soft all alike then take it up and mix into it 2 pound of ruf carrays then get it into your hoope and set it into you oven as quick as you can let it stand an hour and half

To Make an Orange cream

take the juce of 6 orranges and 5 egs whites and all first you must beat the egs very well then put in your juce and mixt it all together then put some white sugare in it and sweeten it according to your palate then put it our char tye in a silver thing and keep it sturing till it be as thick as agood cream you must stur in a littell nob of fresh butter when it is done you must take it of and put it into glasses

To make another Cream

take aquart of cream and set it over the fire and boyle it keeping it sturing all the while then take it of and stur it till it be altted more then blood warm then take the juce of tow lemons and sweetnit to your tast and a littell orange flower water then put it to your cream and mixt it well then let it stand till it is coule then put it into a basen and it is fit to eate

Fig 39 The Portland Cakes, Seed Cakes and Orange Creams of this Shropshire recipe book of around 1719 demonstrate the high quality of cookery practised in the households of the country's gentry.

CURDS, c. 1840

1pt/600ml single cream *1oz/25g sugar*
3 eggs, beaten *¼oz/5g butter*

Beat the eggs and cream together in a pan, and bring to the boil while working a flat-ended spatula across the bottom of the pan to prevent it from burning. As it rises to the boil pour it into a sieve lined with a double layer of freshly-rinsed muslin, then leave to cool and drain for a few hours.

Work the butter until soft, then pound it into the curds, along with the sugar, to form a smooth paste. Heap on to a dish, and serve cold.

PETITES CHOSES [Profiteroles], c. 1840

1oz/25g butter *3oz/75g flour, sifted*
2 bayleaves *3 eggs*
pared zest of 1 lemon

Pre-heat the oven to 200°C, 400°F, Gas mark 6.

Simmer the butter, bayleaves and zest in just over ¼pt/150ml water in a covered pan for 5–10 min. then remove the leaves and zest, and rapidly beat in the flour to form a smooth, elastic soft dough, cover, and leave to cool.

Break one egg on to the dough, and work in (using a fork) completely before beating in the other eggs one by one. Grease a baking sheet, and use a spoon to drop walnut-sized balls of dough onto it, allowing some 2–3 ins. (c. 5–8cm) between them, at allow for expansion. Bake for 20 min., and cool on a wire rack. If they should lose their crispness when cold, dry off in the oven for a few minutes more.

To serve, they might be split and filled with thick jam, or dusted with icing sugar, placed on a baking sheet, and either returned to a hot oven or placed under a grill for a brief period until the sugar has melted into a glaze.

MUFFIN & BRANDY PUDDING, 1840s

about 16 trifle sponges
½pt/300 ml single cream
2 whole eggs plus 2 yolks
1–2 tbs brandy

2 tbs sugar
pinch grated nutmeg
a few glacé cherries
angelica and raisins

Butter a 1½pt/900ml charlotte mould, line the bottom and sides very neatly with greaseproof paper, and butter again.

Decorate the base of the mould with a pattern made up of the sliced cherries and angelica, and the raisins.

Trim some of the sponges to fit the base precisely, and other to line the sides, leaving no gaps, but very tight joints. Pack the centre with the remaining sponges and the pieces trimmed off the rest. At this stage the pudding may be layered with jams, grated lemon rind, or ground almonds to provide additional flavours.

Beat the remaining ingredients together and pour over the sponges, topping up as it is absorbed, then leave the pudding for two hours to enable the custard batter to soak into all parts of the sponges.

Cover the top of the pudding with a piece of cooking foil extending well down the sides to prevent the access of any steam etc., then steam the pudding for 1 hour, and allow to cool a little.

Remove the foil, turn the pudding out onto a dish, and remove the buttered papers to reveal the patterned top etc., then serve hot.

AN EXCELLENT [APPLE] PUDDING, 1840s

8oz/225g puff pastry
8oz/225g sharp-flavoured
   apples
juice & grated zest of 2 lemons

8oz/225g sugar
6oz/150g butter
2 whole eggs plus three yolks

Roll out the pastry and use to line a large shallow baking dish.

Peel, core and finely chop the apples, and mix with the lemons, eggs, sugar and melted butter. Spread these over the pastry, and bake at 170°C, 325°F, Gas mark 3 for some 30 min.

If the menus and recipes for the long-established dinners *à la Française* seem lavish by today's standards, they were decidedly plain when compared to the predominant fashions of the later nineteenth and early twentieth centuries, when *service à la Russe* was at its most popular. Instead of having numerous dishes placed on the table for each of two or three courses, individual portions of each dish were now placed before each diner for up to ten or twelve courses. This meant that the centre of the table was now left free for the display of the dessert or grand floral arrangements, and that everyone had their food served when in its prime condition, rather than having stood on the table long enough to go cold. No better example of sheer scale and quality of the dinners served in Shropshire's country houses at this period than the following menu served at the home of Mrs Rebecca Darby;[14]

DINNER AND FETE AT ADCOTE HALL, SHREWSBURY, NOV 11, 1890.

POTAGE	Consommé à la Royale
ENTRÉE	Cotelettes de Mouton, Sauce au Gratin
PIÉCES FROIDS	Chapons farcis, garniture de Gelée d'Aspic

        Galantines de Veau   Poulets rôtis
        Jambon de York braisés   Galantines de Dindon Truffée
        Patés de Gibier en Plumâge   Poulets boullis à la Béchamel
        Faisans au naturel aux Cressons
        Langues de Boeuf garnies à la Macédoine
        Oeufs aux Anchois   Aspic de Foie Gras
        Mauvieteés farcies en Aspic   Cailles en Aspic
                Salade à la Russe

ENTREMETS	Gelées au Citron	Crèmes aux Ananas
	Macedoine des Fruits	
	Crèmes aux Fraises	Gelées au Marasquin
	Gateaux à la Suisse	
	Gelées au Madere	Crèmes au Café
	Bagatelles	
	Crèmes a la Vanille	Gelées aux Cerises
	Petit Demoiselles d'Honneur	
	Eventails Française	

DESSERT

GLACES (served at the Refreshment Table)
    Crème aux Framboises   Crème aux Ananas
    Sorbets au Citron

The families who provided such high-quality fare for themselves and for their guests were also careful to ensure that every other aspect of their dining experience was of the very best. This went far beyond the decoration and furnishing of their dining rooms, to include dress, personal appearance, exemplary good manners and politeness, and an eagerness to make the occasion as comfortable and as enjoyable as possible to all concerned.

On New Year's day, 1852 Miss Anna Maria Fay and her family, visitors from America, enjoyed the traditional bell-ringing and carollers, but then set out in the early evening to dine at Oakley Park, home of Clive of India's family since 1771. On entering the hall, they were received by the groom of the chambers in his black suit, and some of the six or more footmen clad in silver-buttoned blue coats and red silk plush breeches. From here they were ushered into the library to join their hostess, Lady Harriet Clive, with her family and guests. There were twenty in all, including the Earl of Powis and his close family. Following the usual practice, Mr Clive and the Countess of Powis, as the senior lady present, led the procession of couples into the dining room and up to the head of the table, Lady Harriet as hostess, and the Earl of Powis, bringing up the rear and taking the foot of the table. The room it self was hung with family portraits, with a long and broad damask-clothed table in the middle. At its centre stood a mirror-topped gilt plateau bearing two immense candelabra on smaller plateau-like stands being set towards each end.

When everyone had taken their place, the butler, wearing his white waistcoat and cravat, supervised the footmen as they handed

Fig 40   Coalbrookdale's later stoves were ideal for country house use. Here a kitchen maid bastes a rib of beef as a bottle-jack turns it before the fire of their 'KB' range introduced around 1900.

each course in their turn. First came a choice of soups, then of fishes, including a turbot, entrées of patés, mutton chops etc., and a choice of roasts, or of cold meats such as turkeys and chickens displayed on the sideboard. Next came the game course, with its roast birds etc., and the remaining courses, all served on solid silver dishes. After clearing the table, dessert was set in place, with oranges, pears, grapes, every kind of fruit, ice creams and jellies. A large two-handled loving cup filled with toasted ale was now brought in by a footman, who took it to each gentleman in turn, each taking a long draught, before he passed it on to the next.

After a short period, Lady Harriet gave a signal and the ladies got up from each side of the table and processed out, across the hall, and into the drawing room, a magnificently furnished apartment hung with paintings by artists such as Claude and Velasquez. As coffee was served, some ladies sat down to their worsted embroidery, while, on request, Miss Clive knelt on the floor, holding a candle in one hand, as she showed the fine watercolours she had painted in Italy, and prints of her brother Robert's paintings of the ancient sculptures of Ninevah. On being joined by the men, the English hosts played piano pieces by Blumenthal and a selection of German songs, the American guests then responding to requests for 'Negro Melodies!!!', *The Blue-Tail Fly* being received 'with acclamations of delight'. The dinner party ended at 11p.m., when the coaches were called to carry the guests back to their temporary home.

It is doubtful if any meals had ever been served with such a wonderful combination of the very best of home-grown and imported ingredients, cooked in the finest culinary tradition, and served with the most elegant tableware and most polished of manners. Everything was purposely designed and planned to impress, but more particularly to provide enjoyment and a wealth of pleasant memories for both the family and their guests. Such meals were served in most halls up to the outbreak of the first World War, but then slowly began to enter a period of permanent decline.

The economic difficulties of the 1920s and '30s, crippling death-duties and higher taxes made it impossible for families to retain the large numbers of gardeners, kitchen staff and house-servants on which such hospitality depended. This had an enormous but still largely unrecognisable effect on the domestic comfort of society as a whole. The country houses had been one of the most effective training-schools for working-class families, the girls and young men employed in them learning culinary and other civilised life-skills which provided a unique body of practical knowledge and personal standards of excellence which they carried with them for the rest of their lives. State education offered no effective alternative, with the result that in the country as a whole the traditional standards and practices of home cooking went through a period of great decline, and an unhealthy reliance on ready-made, processed and take-away foods. This explains why so many of the dishes described in this book are relatively unknown today.

However, we can take great pleasure in knowing that the inhabitants of Shropshire, probably more than those of most other counties, have tried to resist these trends, and now enjoy access to some of the best foodstuffs available anywhere in England. They have an enviable range of independent food producers and shops, as well as of restaurateurs, hoteliers and landlords, all devoted to serving the best of foods at the best of values. All of these facilities have not only survived, but actually developed, because of strong local demand. So long as these continue, the traditional foods of Shropshire should enjoy an excellent future.

BIBLIOGRAPHY

1. MANUSCRIPT SOURCES

The following were consulted at Shropshire Archives, Shrewsbury;

3365/598/53 Shrewsbury, election bill of fare, 3/10/1651
3365/599/10 Shrewsbury, mayor's feast, 2/2/1653
1416/36 Shropshire recipe book, 1720s?
2001/1 + 2 Two recipe books, 1830s–40s
2288/1 – 2 Newport notebook of remedies and recipes by John Bullock, *c*. 1847–60

2. PRINTED SOURCES

In the following *Trans*. refers to T*he Transactions of the Shropshire Archaeological and Natural History Society,* which commenced its first series in Shrewsbury in 1878, and HMC to the volumes of the Historic Manuscript Commission.

Aikin, J. *England Described* (1818) 161–169.
Alexander, R.G. (ed), *A Plain Plantain – Country Wines, Dishes and Herbal Cures from a 17th-century MS Recipe Book* (1922)
Anderton, E., *Old Country Recipes, Curious and Interesting Places* (Shrewsbury 1978)
Anon, *A Selection of Antiquities in the County of Salop* (1824).
Anon, *The Book of the Household* (1862–4).
Anon, 'Inventory of the Goods and Chattels of Thomas Owen of Condover'. *Trans.* LIII (1950) 200–6.
Anon, *Whittington Castle Cookbook* (Whittington 1988).
Bailey, L.H., *Cyclopedia of American Agriculture* II Crops. (New York 1967)
Baker, H., '*Ludlow Whitecakes*' *Shropshire Magazine* (Nov. 1983) 23.
Barker, J., 'Kingsland & Shrewsbury Show' *Trans.* VIII (1918–19) 173 2188.
Barker, T., *Barker's Delight: or the Art of Angling* (2nd ed. 1659).
Bradley, R., *The Country Housewife and Lady's Director* (1727, 1732) (1736 ed)
Brears, P.,'Rare Conceites and Strange Delights' in Wilson C.A. ed. *Banquetting Staffe* (Edinburgh 1991) 9–35.
   'a la Francaise . . .' in Wilson, C.A. (ed.) *Luncheon, Nuncheon and Other Meals* (Stroud 1994) 91–116.
   Traditional Food in Yorkshire (Edinburgh 1987);
   A Taste of Leeds (Derby 1998);

All the King's Cooks (1999);

Arvals, Wakes & Months' Minds', in Mason, L., (ed) *Food & Rites of Passage* (Totnes 2002);

Cooking & Dining in Medieval England (Totnes 2008).

'A Second Serving of Regency Splendour' *National Trust Historic Houses & Collections Annual* (2008) 46–52.

Brown, P., *In Praise of Hot Liquors* (York 1995).

Burritt, F., *Walks in the Black Country and its Green Borderland* (1868).

Butler, R, & Green, C., *English Bronze Cooking Vessels and their Founders 1350–1830* (Honiton 2003).

Cassell's Dictionary of Cookery (1877–8).

Chambers, R., *The Book of Days* (1866).

Champion, 'John Ashby and the History and Environs of the Lion Inn, Shrewsbury', *Trans.* LXXV (2000) 49–84.

Chandler, J. (ed.) *Travels through Stuart Britain, The Adventures of John Taylor the Water Poet* (Stroud 1999)

Cobbett, W., *Rural Rides* (1885 ed.).

Cromarty, R., *The Water Supply of Shrewsbury 1550–1835*. *Trans.* LXXV (2000) 15–48.

David, E., *English Bread & Yeast Cookery* (1977).

de Gallienne, R., *Travels in England* (1900).

de Saules, M., *41 Shropshire Recipes* (Shrewsbury 2004).

Douglas, W., *Douglas's Encyclopedia* (n.d.)

Driver, C., (ed) *John Evelyn, Cook* (Totnes 1987).

Fay, A.M. *Victorian Days in England* (Ludlow 2002).

Fiennes, C., *Through England on a Side-Saddle* (1888 ed.).

Fussell, G., *The English Rural Labourer* (1949).

Gardiner, *Profitable Instructions for the Manuring, Sowing and Planting of Kitchen Gardens* (1603) (*Trans.* IV (1892) 241–263.

Garrett, T., *The Enclyclopedia of Practical Cookery* (1894).

Gough, R., *Antiquities & Memoirs of the Parish of Myddle* (Shrewsbury 1875).

H.M.C. *The manuscripts of Shrewsbury & Coventry Corporations*. 15th Report Part X (1899).

Hansell, P & J., *Doves and Dovecotes* (Bath 1988).

Hargreaves, B., (ed) *Farmhouse Fare* (1954).

Harper, C.G., *The Holyhead Road* (1902).

Hartshorne, C.H., *Salopia Antiqua* (1841).

Hawthorne, N., *Passages from the English Notebooks of Nathaniel Hawthorne* (1870).

Hippisley Cox, A. & A., *The Book of the Sausage* (1978).

Hulbert, C., *The History of Shrewsbury* (Shrewsbury 1837); *The History & Description of the County* of Salop *(Shrewsbury 1837)*.

Ionides, J.L., & Howell, P.G., *Old Houses in Shropshire in the 19th Century* (Ludlow 2006).

Jackson, G.F., *Shropshire Word-Book* (London, Shrewsbury & Chester 1879); *Shropshire Folk-Lore; A Sheaf of Gleanings* (Charlotte Byrne, ed) (1883).

Jansson, M., *Two Diaries of the Long Parliament* (Gloucester & New York 1984).

Jarrin, G.A., *The Italian Confectioner* (1827).

Jeanes, W., *Gunter's Modern Confectioner* (1861, 5th ed.).

Kenyon, K., *The House that was Loved* (1941).

BIBLIOGRAPHY

Kitchiner, W., *The Cook's Oracle* (1823).
Leighton, S., 'An Inventory taken at Park Hall in 1761' *Trans.* VII (1895) 101–119.
Litten, J., *The English Way of Death* (1991).
Lloyd, A.J. & L.C., *Shrewsbury Cakes* (Shrewsbury 1957).
Malcolmson, R., & Mastoris, S., *The English Pig, A History* (1998).
Markham, G., *The English Hus-wife*(1615).
Mercer, E., & Stamph, P., 'Plaish Hall and Early Brickwork in Shropshire' *Trans.* LXV1967) 90–91.
Mercer, E., *English Architecture to 1900: The Shropshire Experience* (Almeley 2003).
Milnes Gaskell, C., *Old Shropshire Life* (London & New York 1904).
Moncrieff, E., & Joseph, S. & I., *Farm Animal Portraits* (Woodbridge 1996).
Moran, M., *Vernacular Buildings of Shropshire* (Almeley 2003).
Murrell, J. *A Delightfull Daily exercise for Ladies and Gentlewomen* (1617) (1623 ed.).
Norwak, M., *The Farmhouse Kitchen* (1975).
Nutt, F., *The Compleat Confectioner* (2nd ed. 1820).
Oswestry Society for Bettering the Conditions and Encreasing the Comfort of the Poor
  I. *Reports* (Oswestry 1817).
  II. *The Family Receipt Book, or the Cottagers' Cook, Doctor and Friend* (Oswestry 1817).
Payton, J., Hopton Wafers, *Trans.* IX (1909) 267–286.
Pidgeon, *Memorials of Shrewsbury* (Shrewsbury 1837).
Plymley, J. *A General View of the Agriculture of Shropshire* (1803).
Price, R., *The Compleat Cook* (1974).
Pybus, M., *Under the Buttercross* (Market Drayton 1986).
Raffald, E., *The Experienced English Housekeeper* (Manchester 1769, republished Totnes 1997).
Rogers, T.W., 'Vessels and Armour at Woodhouse, West Felton', *Trans.* LVI (1961) 343–5.
Rundell, M., *A New System of Domestic Cookery* (1806 & later editions).
Salopian Shreds & Patches (Shrewsbury, I 1875; II 1877; III 1879; IV 1881; V-VI 1883; VII 1885; IX 1889–90).
Sambrook, P.A., *The Country House Servant* (Stroud 1999).
Sillar, F.C., & Meyler, R.M., *The Symbolic Pig* (Edinburgh & London 1961).
Skeel, A.J., 'Ludlow Castle in 1631' *Trans.*LXIX (1984) 77–82.
Stamper, J.M.B., 'The Shropshire Salt Industry' *Trans.* LXIX (1984) 77–82.
Stradling, J., *The Stories of the Lower Borowes* . . .(Cardiff 1932).
Trinder, B., *The Industrial Revolution in Shropshire* (London & Chichester 1973); *A History of Shropshire* (London & Chichester 1983).
Trinder, B., & Cox, J., *Yeomen and Colliers in Telford* (London & Chichester 1980).
Vane, G.H.F., 'On Licenses to eat Flesh, found in Parish Registers' *Trans.* XII (1900) 48–56.
Victoria County History, Shropshire IV (ed. G.C. Baugh) (Oxford 1989).
Walcott, M.E.C., 'Household Expences of a Shropshire Manor House in the Days of Queen Bess' *Trans.*I (1878) 9–12.
Wallace, K., *Shropshire Food* (Leominster 1986).
Wanklyn, M.D.G., 'Bridgnorth Food Riots 1693–4' *Trans.* LXVIII (1993) 99–102.

Webb, M., *The Golden Arrow* (1918) (1930 ed.); *The House in Dormer Forest* (1920) (1931 ed.); *Seven for a Secret* (1922) 1932 ed.); *Precious Bane* (1924) (1932 ed.).
White, F., *Good Things in England* (1974 ed.).
W.M., *The Compleat Cook and a Queen's Delight* (1655) (1671 ed.).
Womens Institute, Shropshire Federation, *Shropshire Cookery Book* (3rd ed. Shrewsbury 1933).
Wright, T., *History of Ludlow* (Ludlow 1852).

Picture credits

Luttrell Psalter illustrations by permission of the British Library. Stained glass window from Munslow church reproduced by permission of the Rev. I.E.Gibbs. Photographs of the wimberry pie and Elsie Rowson by Phil Jones of the Stiperstones Inn. Photographs of the Stiperstones and wimberries by Ben Osborne. The Soar Ram and the Shropshire Pig are reproduced by permission of the Museum of Rural Life. Paintings of the English Bridge and the Butchers' Row, Shrewsbury, and the new breed cattle are from the Shrewsbury Archives. The blue Herculaneum jug is reproduced by permission of the Walker Art Gallery, Liverpool. The Shropshire brew jar from the Antiques Centre, Knighton, was photographed by Malcolm Payne. The Ginger Man on the rear cover came from Walton's Bakery, Ludlow, photographed by Pete Mackenzie. The endpaper illustration of wimberry pickers on the Long Mynd is taken from a photograph by the Shropshire geologist Dr E.S.Cobbold, *cc.*1920, in the Shrewsbury Archives.

NOTES

ABBREVIATIONS

EDD.   Wright, J., *The English Dialect Dictionary* (Oxford 1923),
OED.   *The Oxford English Dictionary.*
SS & P.   *Salopian Shreds & Patches* (Shrewsbury 1875–90).
Trans.   *Transactions of the Shropshire Archaeological and Natural History Society* (Shrewsbury 1878+).
V.C.H.   *Victoria County History, Shropshire.*
W.I.   Womens Institute, Shropshire Federation, *Shropshire Cookery Book* (Shrewsbury 1933).

INTRODUCTION

1. Fiennes, 191.
2. Defoe, II, 388.
3. Aikin, 161.
4. Fiennes, 191.
5. Hulbert, 37, 97.
6. *ibid.*, 25; Moncrieff & Joseph, 222–3.
7. *ibid.*, 97; Moncrieff & Joseph, 150–151.
8. Hulbert, 25.
9. *ibid.*, 85.
10. EDD, 'Gaun'.
11. *ibid.*, 'Leaves'.
12. OED, 'Shropshire'.
13. De Gallienne, 284–7.
14. Webb, (1916) 47.
15. Jackson, (1879) 'Skim-dick'.
16. Hulbert, 172–3; Pidgeon, 128; Mercer, 208–9, 214.
17. Hulbert, 25.

CHAPTER 1

OF KITCHENS GREAT AND SMALL

1. Webb (1922) 103.
2. SS & P II (1877) 86–7, Trinder (1973) 321.
3. Anderton, 6.
4. Trinder & Cox, 300, 324.
5. *ibid.*, 15.
6. Plymley, 112.
7. e.g. VCH Shropshire IV (1989) 228.
8. Trinder, (1973) 321–324.
9. Trinder & Cox, 213.
10. *ibid.* 198.
11. Jackson, (1879) 'Dressel'.
12. Hartshorne, 'Dressel'.
13. Knell, 159.
14. Webb, (1922 57, (1916) 18, 44. 7 for a Secret 57, Golden Arrow 18,44.
15. Mercer, 138.

16. Jackson, (1879) 'Ronging Hooks'.
17. Hartshorne & Jackson, (1879) 'Chats', 'Chumps'.
18. Hartshorne, 'Kids', Trinder & Cox, 388.
19. Jackson, (1879) 'Chags'.
20. Jackson, (1879) 'Turf '.
21. Gough, 175.
22. Trinder & Cox, 167.
23. *ibid.*, 182, 184.
24. Jackson, (1879) 'Balk', Hartshorne, 'Gaypole'.
25. Trinder & Cox, 285, EDD 'Swayl-pole'..
26. Trinder & Cox, 293, 343, 252, EDD 'Marmit'.
27. Rogers, 343–5.
28. Butler & Green, 134–5.
29. Oswestry, 12.
30. Jannson, 22–3.
31. Anon., (1950) 200–206.
32. Trinder & Cox, 362.
33. Payton, 284.
34. Plymley, 272.
35. Jackson, (1879) 'Purgy-hole', Trinder & Cox, 332, 191.
36. Leighton, 111.
37. Trinder, (1973) 20, 23, 26.
38. Sambrook, 64
39. Harper, 90, 131.

CHAPTER 2

EVERYDAY FARE

1. Webb, (1924) 91.
2. Gardiner, 260, 244.
3. Wanklyn, 99–101.
4. SS & P., I (1875) 91.
5. Trinder, (1973) 378–9.
6. SS & P., V. 117.
7. VCH., 223–5.
8. Oswestry, I.
9. Trinder, (1973) 381.
10. Oswestry, II 3.
11. *ibid.* 4.
12. *ibid.* 12.
13. *ibid.* 8.
14. Chambers, II 582–3.
15. Jackson, (1879) 'Supping'.
16. Webb, (1922) 50; Oswestry, II 4.
17. Jackson, (1879) 'Piggin'.
18. *ibid.* 578.
19. *ibid.* (1879) 'Brothe'; 'Browis'..
20. *ibid.* (1879) 'Piggin'; 'Pollinger'.
21. Hartshorne, 'Four o' clock'; Jackson, (1879) 'Four o' clock', 'Noonspell'.
22. Hartshorne, 'Backstone'; 'Maid'; Jackson, (1879) 'Lazyback'.
23. Shropshire Archives, 2001/1–2.
24. David, 293.
25. Hartshorne, 'Brown George'.
26. Jackson, (1879) 'Batch Cakes'; 'Coal Cakes'.
27. *ibid.* 'Can-dough'; Baker, 23.
28. Jackson, (1883) 228.
29. Brears, (2008) 114.
30. Jackson, (1879) 'Fire-Fork', 'Grig Besom', 'Malkin'.
31. H.M.C. 15.
32. Gough, 61 – 2.
33. Oswestry, 6.
34. W.I., 40.
35. *ibid.*, 14, 17, 32, 16, 15, 15, 13, 14, 25.
36. anon., (1988).
37. Gardiner, 261.
38. *ibid.*, 244.
39. W.I., 42.
40. Oswestry, 8, 13.
41. Oswestry, 8, 13.
42. Oswestry, 8, 13.
43. Oswestry, 8, 13.
44. Malcolmson & Mastoris, 46.
45. Plymley, 267–8.
46. Sillar & Mayler, 34.
47. *ibid.*, 172, 97, 77.
48. Jackson, (1883) 258.
49. 1879, 'Strucken'.
50. Shropshire Archives, 1416/36.
51. Webb, (1918) 175.
52. Webb, (1920) 91.
53. Jackson, (1883), 'Harslet'.
54. Hippisley Cox, 79.
55. Hargreaves, 244.

56. W.I., 28.
57. Pybus, 74.
58. Bradley, II 119.
59. Hulbert, 26.
60. W.I., 29.
61. *ibid.*, 29.
62. Shropshire Archives, 1416/36.
63. Jackson, (1879) 'Scratchings'.
64. W.I., 34.
65. Hargreaves, 243.
66. EDD., 'Shropshire'.
67. *ibid.*, 'Fitchett'.
68. Hartshorne, 'Fitchett Pie'.
69. White, 345–6.
70. Anderton, 12.
71. Jackson, (1879) 'Blanks & Prizes'.
72. Bradley, II 77–9.
73. Pybus, 89.
74. Norwak, 170.
75. Webb, (1922) 129.
76. Jackson, (1879) 'Figgetty Dumpling'.
77. W.I., 61.
78. Jackson, (1879) 'Apple-Gob'.
79. *ibid.*, 'Figgetty Dumpling'.
80. W.I., 61.
81. Cassell, 871.
82. anon., (1988).
83. Jackson, (1879) 'Beestin', 'Bar- fut'.
84. Anderton, 20.
85. EDD., 'Leaf'.
86. Anderton, 20.
87. Jackson, (1879) 'Sage-cheese', 'Marigold Cheese'.
88. W.I., 49.
89. *ibid., 50.*
90. ibid., *51.*
91. Jackson, (1879).
92. W.I., 52.
93. anon., (1988).
94. Jackson, (1879) Flummery.

CHAPTER 3

SOMETHING FOR TEA

1. Trinder & Cox, 333, 243, 446, 454.
2. Leighton, 110.
3. Brown, 58.
4. Trinder, (1973) 339–40.
5. Brears, (1998) 42 & Norwak 98.
6. Hartshorne, 'Pikelet'.
7. Jackson, (1879) 'Flap'.
8. Webb, (1922) 80.
9. Cassell, 869.
10. 1817 recipe from David 416.
11. Jackson, (1879) 'French Wheat'.
12. *ibid.*, 'Cat'.
13. Webb, (1922) 57.
14. W.I., 111.
15. Webb, (1920) 86.
16. Webb, (1922) 47.
17. Jackson, (1879) 'Apple Feet'.
18. The following account of Shrewsbury Cakes is taken from Lloyd.
19. OED, 'Bake' (a).
20. Brears, (1999) 159.
21. Alexander.
22. W.M., 119.
23. Driver, 144, 174.
24. Price, R. 260.
25. White, 297.
26. Raffald, 157.
27. Kitchiner, 492.
28. Garrett, I 255–6.
29. Hawthorne, I, 310.
30. SS & P., I 221.
31. Pybus, 37–48.
32. Jarrin, 183, Fig. 2. no. 1.
33. Jeanes, 271, 131, & Nutt, 7.
34. Shropshire Archives, 288/1–2.
35. W.I., 93.

CHAPTER 4

FESTIVE FOODS

1. Jackson, (1879) 'Black Quarter'.
2. Vane, 48, 51, 53.
3. Jackson, (1883) 318.
4. SS & P., III 158.
5. Jackson, (1883) 324.
6. Hulbert, 99.
7. Hartshorne, 'Simnel'.
8. Chambers, 336–7.

9. Markham, 77.
10. Kitchiner, 493.
11. Chambers, I, 336.
12. *ibid.*, I, 337.
13. Hulbert, 99.
14. *ibid.*,
15. *W.I., 142, 144.*
16. Webb, (1916) 352.
17. Jackson, (1883) 331.
18. *ibid.*, 341.
19. *ibid.*, 340.
20. SS & P., I, 10 & II 217.
21. Jackson, (1883) 493.
22. Kitchiner, 492.
23. W.I., 93.
24. Shropshire Archives, 1416/36.
25. Jackson, (1883) 446.
26. Barker, 173–188 & Chambers, I, 704–8.
27. Pidgeon, 110.
28. Jackson, (1883) 372, Hulbert, 101, Hartshorne, 'Mare'.
29. Webb, (1916) 228, 231.
30. *ibid.*, 235–6.
31. Hone, I, 1410.
32. Webb, (1916) 271.
33. Jackson (1883) 382.
34. SS & P., I, 91.
35. Webb, (1916) 265, & SS & P, I, 9.
36. Jackson, (1883) 382.
37. SS & P., VIII, 127.
38. Jackson, (1883) 392.
39. SS & P., VIII, 137.
40. SS & P., IX, 333.
41. Jackson, (1879) 'Wig', & David, 486.
42. Jackson, (1883) 407.
43. Hartshorne, 'Grits', & Garrett, I, 721.
44. Shropshire Archives, 2001/1–2.
45. *ibid.*, 2001/1–2.
46. *ibid.*, 1416/36.
47. W.I., 91.
48. Jackson, (1883) 407–8.
49. SS & P., IX, 328.
50. Pybus, 34, & Mrs B. Locke, *Market Drayton Advertiser* Nov, 1984.
51. W.I., 33–4.
52. SS & P., I, 60.
53. Pidgeon, 205.
54. SS & P., III, 221.
55. Anon., (1862–4) 152, & Douglas, 139.
56. Jackson, (1883) 408.
57. OED., 'Chitterlings'.
58. Jackson, (1883) 408.
59. *ibid.*, Hartshorne, 'Swig', & Jackson (1879) 'Swig'.
60. SS & P., VII, 267.
61. Brears, (1987) 181.
62. Anderton, 4.
63. Brears, (2008) 167–171.
64. Anderton, 4.

CHAPTER 5

FROM THE CRADLE TO THE GRAVE

1. Jackson, (1883) 285.
2. Webb, (1920) 120–21.
3. W.I., 103.
4. Litten, 133.
5. Brears, (2002) 91.
6. Jackson, (1883) 308.
7. *ibid.*, 299.
8. Lloyd, 8.
9. Jackson, (1883) 309, 304.
10. *ibid.*, 305.

CHAPTER 6

HAVING A DO

1. Hulbert, 29.
2. *ibid.*, 174.
3. Brears, (1991) 9–35.
4. Hulbert, 30
5. Jackson, (1883) 471.
6. *ibid.*, 470.
7. Shropshire Archives, 3365/599/10.
8. *Shrewsbury Chronicle* 21st Nov. 1890.
9. Pybus, 81.
10. SS & P, VIII 63.
11. *ibid.*, IX 264.

NOTES

12. *ibid.*, IX 254.
13. *Menu,* Private collection.
14. Hulbert, 266.
15. *ibid,* 277.
16. Jackson, (1883) 474.
17. *ibid.*, 474.
18. *ibid.*, 473.

CHAPTER 7

IN HALLS & MANOR HOUSES

1. Gough, 93–4
2. *ibid.*, 122, 127–8, 181–4.
3. *Burker,* 19–20, 23, 42.
4. *Dictionary of National Biography*, 'Rundell, M.', Rundell (see Bibliography) and information provided by Julia L. Ionides.
5. Brears, (2008) 46–52.
6. Walcott, 9–11.
7. Hansell, 25.
8. Brears, (1994) 91–116.
9. Moxon, 212.
10. The dates of the following recipes indicate their sources; 1659 – T. Barker; 1719;Shropshire Archives MS 1416/36; 1732; R. Bradley; 1840–45 Shropshire Archives MS 2001/1–2.
11. Beaumont & Roaf, 383–4.
12. Shropshire Archives MS 14/6/36.
13. *ibid.*
14. *Garrett II 810.*

GENERAL INDEX

Acton Scott 14
Adcote Hall 38, 192
Adney, G. 3
All Halloween 126–7
Alltree, W. 36–7
Arthur, Prince 155
Atcham 38, 62
Attingham Park 3, 23–5, 40–42, 84, 171–2, 186

Badger Hall 186
Bakestones 19, 32–3, 49
Balderton 165, 167
Banbury Cakes 120
Banquets, sweetmeat 155–6
Barham, Rev. R.H. 102
Barker, T. 167–9
Basechurch 163
Bate, W. 12
Batho, Mrs E. 58
Beestings 77
Benthall 16
Berrington 119
Berwick, Lord 3–4, 171
Bibby, Mr & Mrs F. 160
Billington Family 107–9
Births, food at 149
Bishop's Castle 12
Blakemore, Mr 100
Boreaton Hall 161
Boughey, R. 108
Bowen, J. 45
Brawn, Shrewsbury 138–9
Bread 50–51, 174
Bridgnorth 4, 44, 151, 186
Briscoe, W. 12

Bromley,
  H. 94
  W. 165–6
Broseley 16, 45
Brewis 49
Brown, J. 21
Buchas, Mr 94
Buckwheat 88–90
Bullock, J. 107
Burnford, Mrs 99
Buttry, J. 111

Caking 163
Caradoc Wakes 120
Carrots 43, 59
Cats (for dishes) 28, 90
Cattle 3–4
Chambre, Mr 165
Champion, N. 29
Chandler, R.D. 150
Charlton, J. 27
Cheese 5–6, 48, 78–81, 141
Cheesecakes 92
Cherbury 112
Cherry Pie Wake 119
Chesters, W.I. 108–9
Cheswardine 108
Chitterlings 63, 140
Chocolate 188
Christmas, food at 130–41
Churchyard, T. 15
Clive family 193–4
Clod Halls 9
Clun 63, 77, 129
Clungunford 119
Coalbrookdale 11, 17, 19, 29, 31–7, 61, 194

Colliers 44–5
Condover, Cottages 9
Condover Court 21
Corbet,
    H.R. 160–1
    M. 34
Cox, W. 108
Craven Arms 88
Crump, V. 101
Custards 77

Dairying 4
Dagoty, P.-L. 170
Darby, A. 28
Darby, Mrs Rebecca 192
Davenport House 175
Davies, Mr 11, 100
Davis, W. 4
Defoe, D. 2
de Gallienne, R. 5
Divining 126–7
Disbrowe, J. 84
Dos 160–3
Dog Wheels 17, 21
Donnington 83

Easter 118–9
Easthorpe, W. 36–7
Eastrup, J. 10
Eel pie Wakes 119
Edgmond 112
Elizabeth of York 155
Ellesmere 90, 123
Ellis, R. 168
Essex, Earl of 94
Evans, W. 10
Eyton, J. 83
Egton-upon-Severn 95

Fay, Miss A.M. 193
Feasts 156–9
Fiennes, C. 2
Fireplaces, see Grates
Fish & Fishing 4, 167–9
Fish days 111
Food shortages 43–5, 95
Fox, W. 95
Frying Pans 22–3, 31–2, 42, 85

Fuel
    broom 15
    charcoal 26
    coal 16–26
    gorse 15
    turf 15–16
    wood 15, 26, 52
Funerals, food at 150–3

Gardiner, R. 43, 59
Geese 143
Gibson, J.E. 36
Gill, Mrs 127
Gingerbreads 106–10, 120–1
Girdles, see Bakestones
Gomme, Lady 113–4
Good Friday 118
Googe, B. 5
Gooseberries 77
Gough, R. 16, 30, 165
Grates & Ranges 16–7, 26–7, 33–7, 42, 194
Grosvenor, Lord R. 182

Hancock, W. 21
Hare, Lady 93
Haremeare 52
Hardinge, J. 151
Hardwick Grange 160
Harper Family 107
Harris, of Ludlow 51
Harvest, food at 125–6
Hayward,
    B. 120
    T. 165–6
Herbert, Lord 95
Henry VII 155
Higgins, J. 95
Hill, Lord 161
    Mrs 100
    W. 170–2
Hitcham, Sir R. 166
Hodnet 127, 175
Holland, Mrs H. 73
Hopton Castle 153
Hopton Court 23–5
Hopton Wafers 17, 21

GENERAL INDEX

Hughes, S.T. 108
Hunt, Mr & Mrs R. 161, 165

Ice cream 186
Ice houses 186
Ironbridge 4, 34
Jacks 21–2, 30, 194
Jorevin, Mr 151
Juxon, Archbishop 166

Kenyon, K. 142, 148
Ketelby, Mrs 169
Ketley 10, 12
Kinlet Hall 23–5
Kitchens 9–42

Land, Archbishop 119
Langley 163
Latter, F. 160
Lea, Sir H. 165
Leighton,
   Sir B. 10–11
   S & M. 84
Lent 111–2
Lewis, E. 112
Lightmore 86
Lilleshall 11–12, 37
Llanvairwaterdine 62
Llwynymaen 19–20
Longford Hall 171, 174
Long Mynd 77
Loton Park 84
Ludlow 3, 17, 26, 51, 112, 119, 156, 169

Madeley 16, 45, 85
Mansell, B. 165
Market Drayton 5–7, 73, 106–9, 120–1, 128, 160, 162
May Day, food at 155
Menus 58, 158, 160–1, 173–5, 192
Mercer, R. 52
Meole Brace 129, 167
Meteyard, Miss 142
Mid-day meals 49, 85
Millichope Park 175
Milne, F.A. 128
Milnes Gaskell, Mr E. 161

Minsterley 12, 132
Mint cubes 120
Mock Corporations 129
Montagu, Lord. 167
More, Sir G. 95
Morgan, B. 90
Mothering Sunday, food at 112
Much Wenlock 45, 161
Munslow 62
Murray, J. 169
Myddle 16, 165, 167
Myddleton, Sir T. 20

Nash, J. 23–5
Newell, T. 83
Newport 107, 112, 152, 161
New Year, food at 141–8, 193
Niggards 16, 26–7
Norton Hill 120
Oakes, F. 44
Oakley Park 193
Offal 62–4
Osley, Mr 94
Oswestry 10, 18, 20, 38, 46, 53, 85, 152
Ovens 32–3, 52
Owen, T. 21, 103
Ox roasts 162–3

Palin, J. 100–3
Palm Sunday, food at 118
Pancakes 112
Park Hall 27, 83
Parr, T. 47
Pelham, Mr 117
Pellam, Sir W. 94
Petton 165
Phillips, R. 94
   Stores 103–4
Pidduck, Mr 100
Pierrepont, W. 166
Pigeons 174
Pigs 3–4, 10, 71, 173
Pitchford 175
Plaish Hall 13–14
Plimmer, T. 101, 103, 158
Plomer, Col. 99
Poisoning 65
Porridge 48

Potatoes 45
Pots 18–22, 28–9, 31
   chafers 19, 22
   kettles 18, 22, 31–2
   maslin kettles 18
   marmelets 18
   skillets 20
Pots, manufacture of 20–32
Powis, Earl & Countess of 193
Preece, Molly 87
Price, R. 51, 99
Pulverbatch 51, 63, 87, 112, 163
Purgatories 26

Ranges, *see* Grates
Reece, Mr 52
Rice 46–7
Rundell Family 169–71
Bridge & Rundell 170
Ruyton 51

Scratchings 51, 67
Sheep 3
   roast 161
Shifnal 145
Shrewsbury 3–4, 6–7, 36–8, 43, 45, 52,
   59, 65, 67, 77, 111–2, 128, 150–1,
   161, 168
   bakers 52, 123–4
   brawn 138
   butchers 123–4
   cake 93–106, 151
   castle 155
   corporation 123, 138, 155
   feasts 119, 156–60
   school 117, 155
   show 123–5
   simnels 112–117
Shrovetide 112
Smalman, T. 14
Smith,
   B & J. 84
   F. 23–4
Socket, W. 24
Souling Day, food at 127
Southam, H.R.H. 128
St. Thomas' Day 129
Stafford, Lord. 93, 162

Steuart, G. 23–4
Stiperstones 77
Stottesden 112
Stourbridge 45
Stoves 26–7
Suppers 78–81
Sutherland, Duke of 10, 37
Sydney, Sir H. 94, 155

Talbot Family 171
Tantrum, H. 51
Tea, food at 83–93
Thomas, Mr 107
Thomine, P-P. 170, 172
Thorne, E. 59
Thorpe, J. 21
Titterstone Wakes 120
Tong Castle 186
Treflack Hall 14
Tripe 67
Trevithick 37
Turnip Lanterns 127
Twelfth Night, food at 141–8

Upton Magna 11

Wakes, food at 119–23
Walcot Hall 175
Walton, I. 167
Wasey, Rev. G.L. 151
Wassail-cup-singers 130
Webb, M. 5, 9, 77, 91, 118, 149
Weddings, food at 149–50
Wednesbury 45
Weekly chores 45
Wellington 10, 21, 44–5, 83
Welshampton 129
Wem 152, 156
West Felton 18–19
Whitchurch 2, 6
Whittington 58
Wilderhope Manor 14–15
Williams, Mr 100
Wimberries 77
Winnington 47
Wodehouse, P.G. 62.
Wrekin May Sunday 120
Young, A. 61

RECIPE INDEX

Apple
   feet 93
   gateau 184
   gob 74
   pudding 191

Bacon
   Blanks & Prizes 71
   & Eggs 69
   Fitchett Pie 69–70
   & Kidney 64
   & Liver 65
   'Shropshire' 69
   Shropshire & Worcestershire Dish 65

Bakeston Cakes
   Buckwheat Cakes 89
   Flaps 87
   Oatcakes 49
   Pikelets 87

Beef
   Pickled 136
   Pottage 53

Biscuits
   Finger 167
   Ginger, Shrewsbury 96–9, 104, 106

Boar's Head 144

Brawn 139
   Granny Morgan's 68

Bread
   Muncorn 50
   Pudding 76
   Wigs 131

Buckwheat Cakes 89

Cabbage, savoury 61

Cakes
   Banbury 121
   Christmas 135
   Fried 86
   Oat 49
   Shrewsbury 96–9, 104, 106
   Shropshire Buckwheat 89
   Simnel 114
   Soul 127
   Wedding. 150

Carrot Pudding 75
   & Peas 59

Cheese
   & Milk Soup 57
   Scrambled 80
   Shropshire Supper Dish 79
   Toasted 80
   & Tomato Supper Dish 81

Cheesecurds
   orange & lemon 92

Chicken Frigacie 180
   Pie 182

Chitterling Puffs 140

Christmas
   Cake 135
   Chitterling Puffs 140
   Boar's Head Brawn 139
   Goose Pie 136
   Mincemeat 135
   Pudding 134

Chocolate Cream 188

Cranberry Jelly 91

Creams
   chocolate 188
   currant 188
   damson 188
   ice- 186
   raspberry 188

Curds 190
   (see Cheesecurds for the jam variety)

Currants
    cream 188
    syrup of 183

Damsons:
    cream 188
    pickled 173
Dumplings
    fig 74
    onion 74

Faggots
    Shropshire 63
Fig
    Dumpling 74
    Pudding 75
Finger Biscuits 107
Fish
    Rechauffé 179
    Stewed Salmon Steaks 178
    Grilled Trout 177
    Stewed Trout 178
Fitchett Pie 69–70
Flaps 87
Flummery 81
Fried Cakes 86
Furmity 122

Gingerbreads 107, 109, 121
Goose Pie 136
Gritty Pudding 133

Ham, dry cured 137
Hare Pie 181
Hartshorne Jelly 184
Heart & Kidney Pudding 64
Herb Roll, Shropshire 70
Hippocras 94
Hog's Pudding
    Black 62
    White 67
Hot-Stir 123

Ice cream 186

Jelly
    Cranberry 91
    Hartshorne 184

Lambswool 142
Lemon
    Butter 185
    Cheese 92
    Syllabub 185
Liver & Bacon 66
    Roll 66

Macaroni 47, 182
Milk & Cheese Soup 57
Mincemeat (sweet) 135
Monday Pie 58
Muffin & Brandy Pudding 191
Mulberry Syrup 183
Mulligatawny Soup 176
Muncorn Bread 50
Mutton & Lamb
    Cutlets 180
    Head Broth 55
    Scotch Collops 180
    Soup 55

Oatcakes 49
Onion
    Dumpling 61
    Soup 56
Orange Cheese 92

Pea Soup 57
    Peas & Carrots 60
Petites Choses (Profiteroles) 190
Pickled Beef 136
    Damsons 73
Pies
    Chicken 182
    Fitchett 69
    Goose 136
    Hare 181
    Monday 58
    Rook 73
    Shropshire 71–2
    Wimberry 77
Pikelets 87
Plumb Broth 134
Pork
    leg of 179 (*see also* Boar's Head, Bacon, Brawn, Heart & Kidney, Herb Roll, & Hog's Puddings)

RECIPE INDEX

Potato Soup 57
Puddings
  sweet: Apple 191
  Gob 74
  Carrot 75
  Christmas 134
  Carrot 75
  Fig 75
  Muffin & Brandy 191 (*see* Creams & Syllabubs)
  savoury: Gritty 133
  Heart & Kidney 64
  Herb Roll 70
  Hogs, black 62
  white 47
  Potato 47
  Rice 47
Rabbit
  Savoury 56
  Soup 56
Raspberry
  Cream 188
  Syrup 183
  Tart 183
Rice Pudding 47
Rook Pie 73

Salmon, Steaks, Stewed 178
Scotch Collops 180
Sheep's Head Broth 55
Shrewsbury Cakes 96–9, 104, 106
Shropshire
  Buckwheat Cakes 89
  Fried Cakes 86
  Gingerbread 121

Pie 71–2
Pudding 76
Simnel 114
Soul Cakes 127
Supper Dish 179
& Worcestershire Dish 65
Simnel Cakes 114
Soul Cakes 127
Soups
  Baked 53
  Milk & Cheese 157
  Mulligatawny 176
  Mutton 55
  Onion 56
  Pea 157
  Potato 57
  Rabbit 56
  Sheep's Head 55
  Tomato 177
Spring Mixture 118
Swede
  Braised 60
  Mashed 60
Swig 141
Syllabubs, Lemon 185
Syrups, soft fruits 183

Tomato Soup 177
Trout
  Grilled 177
  Stewed 178

Wedding Cake 150
Wigs 131
Wimberry Pie 78

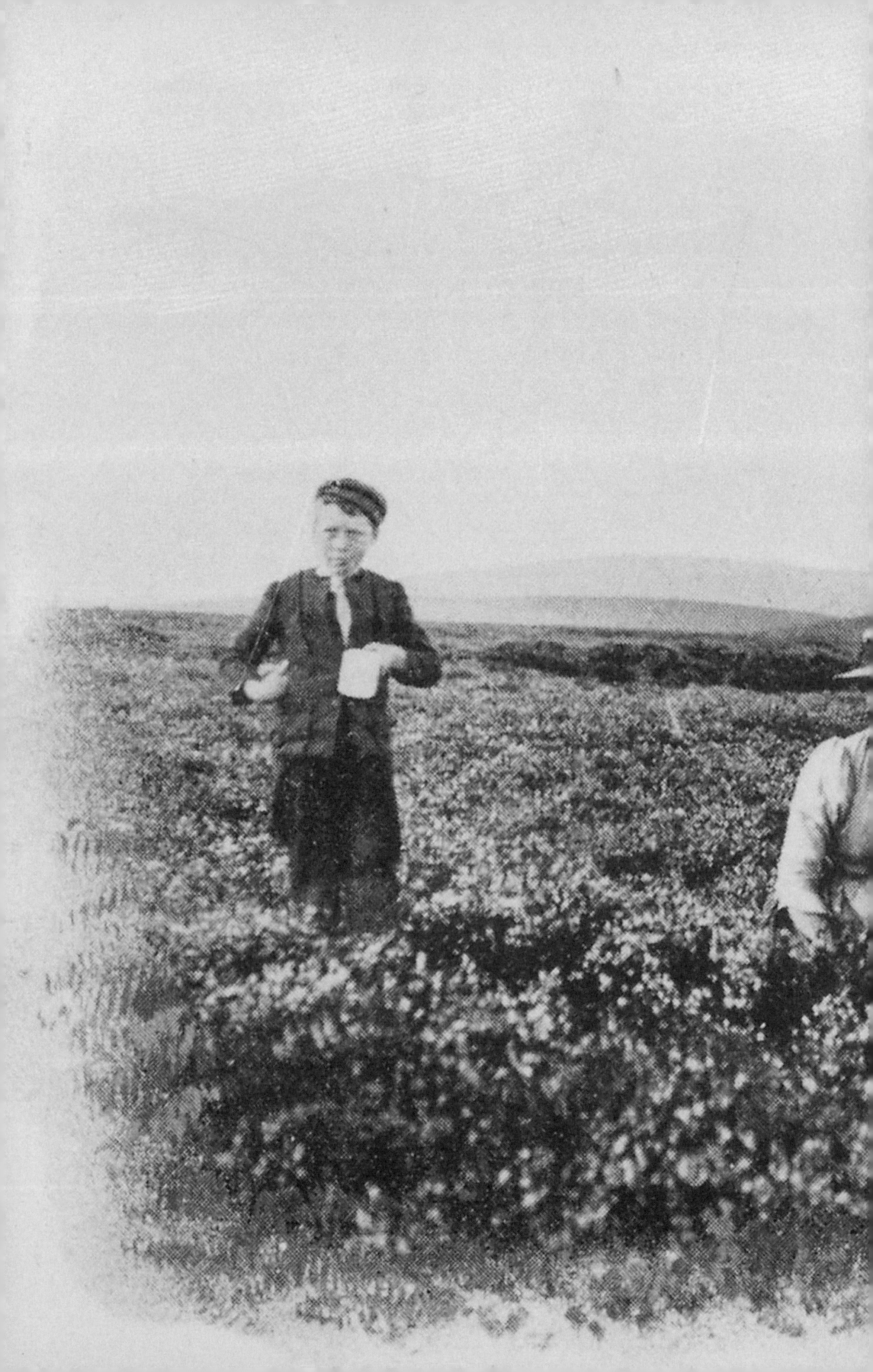